In Search of Eartha White,
Storehouse for the People

Tim Gilmore

ISBN-13: 978-1499611779
ISBN-10: 1499611773

www.jaxpsychogeo.com

Ask, and it shall be given you;

seek, and ye shall find;

knock, and it shall be opened unto you.

For every one that asketh, receiveth;

and he that seeketh, findeth;

and to him that knocketh,

it shall be opened.

—Matthew 7:7-8

vision quest

noun *Anthropology.*

(especially among some North American Indians) the ritual seeking of personal communication with the spirit world through visions that are induced by fasting, prayer, and other measures during a time of isolation: typically undertaken by an adolescent male.

eclogue

noun

a pastoral poem, or poem whose purpose is to celebrate nature or the earth, often in dialogue form.

"If you don't write, everything is lost."

—Raizel to her sister in Arlene Hutton's

Letters to Sala

Preface

By what right do I write this book?

Eartha White was a black woman who shouldered her community's burdens for most of a century until she died in 1974. She lived most of her life prior to the Civil Rights Movement and in the shadow of the South's monstrous Jim Crow laws.

As I write this preface in early 2014, I'm a 40 year-old white man. I was born a few months after Eartha died.

So I admit at the beginning of this book that the burden of proof is too heavy for me to carry through. In fact, it's too heavy for me to lift. I don't know what kind of organized might could shoulder a proof so heavy as to counter the long monumental crime people with my skin color committed against people with darker skin.

Many young white people will say that children shouldn't be burdened with the crimes of their parents, grandparents, or great-grandparents. Sadly (and I love the young people I teach and with whom I work), most of them—whatever their race or background—don't understand the historical forces and movements that built the world in which they find their new lives. Maybe, to differing extents, that's always been a condition of youth, though the extent to which any of us can see these vast tidal forces is humiliatingly miniscule.

Furthermore, if I felt my rhetorical necessity were to prove to the satisfaction of everyone, white and black and otherwise, that I had the right to write, I would find it impossible to begin.

Yet I sympathize much less with the young white person who doesn't understand the question with which I begin this preface than I do with the older black woman who asked, "Why is it that white people feel they need to come and write our history?"

If she'd asked what right I had to presume to understand the long, historic suffering of black people in America, my answer would be that I had no right whatsoever, and that I could never, for one second, presume to know how that particular suffering felt.

Surely that impossibility should not preclude my urgent attempt to empathize. If so, we're all lost.

But the best I can do is not necessarily good enough.

And I say it's not. It's not good enough to write the history of black people in the United States, or in the South, or in Jacksonville, and it's certainly not enough for me to think I've some proprietary right to a history I did not live.

But I attempt something different. This book is not the definitive biography, or the "life and times," or the history of Eartha White. It's the story of *my search* for Eartha White, and it's the story of *my need* to search.

And everything I've learned about Eartha White tells me she would not turn me away.

I'm not a historian, though I hope my book will inspire historians. The story I have to tell you is of my search for Eartha, my need to find her, and our—yours and mine, for the past and the future—need to know her.

Acknowledgements

I refer throughout this book to the people who've helped me along the way, and my inclusion of them in this story is my thanks.

But several people need separate mention, and this is the place for it.

I caught Jim Alderman in his last year before retirement from the University of North Florida library. Without Jim, this book would never have happened. He was always kind, gracious, and helpful. My persistent nagging never seemed to annoy him, and he often followed his own leads when I asked for items from UNF's Special-Collections Eartha White subject index, providing me with what he found. Along the way, Jim became a friend.

Certainly, this book wouldn't have happened without the eminent UNF historian Dan Schafer, who began his own research on Eartha White shortly after she died and was perhaps the key figure in securing the Eartha White Collection's safekeeping at UNF. Whenever I emailed him with questions that kept me awake at two in the morning, his responses always seemed patient and forbearing.

UNF's Eartha White Collection is absolutely invaluable. There, I read innumerable letters to Eartha, listened to 40 year-old interviews from people long dead like Eartha's 27-year secretary Grayce Bateman and Mary Singleton, the first black woman elected to Jacksonville's City Council.

Carmen Godwin's master's thesis, "To Serve God and Humanity: Jacksonville's Eartha Mary Magdalene White (1876-1974)" was wonderfully helpful, as was Peter Dunbaugh Smith's masterful Florida State University dissertation *Ashley Street Blues: Racial Uplift and the Commodification of Vernacular Performance in LaVilla,*

Florida, 1896-1916. I'm also grateful to Abel Bartley for his 2000 book *Keeping the Faith: Race, Politics, and Social Development in Jacksonville, Florida, 1940-1970,* and to Adonnica Toler, museum assistant at LaVilla's Ritz Theatre and Museum, who shared knowledge based on her own research.

There are individuals I've met through my research whose kindness and patience and goodness have staggered me. While I easily imagine a bitterness in black men and women who grew up and lived under segregation, Mary Mungen Jameson invited me out to her house for lunch and discussion before she really even knew I was legitimate. Richard McKissick, the 88 year-old former manager of two LaVilla theaters, who once lived right behind Eartha, toured me through the remnants of this once most vibrant Jacksonville neighborhood and shared his memories with me. Walter Whetstone, the retired insurance salesman who created the Whetstonian in Northern LaVilla, invited me into his downtown home on several occasions and always made me feel welcome. Camilla Thompson, the unofficial Bethel Baptist Church historian, patiently shared memories about West Ashley Street, the Weems Photography Studio, and Christmas at the Mission. These people have reminded me that the world is populated with innumerable Gandhis on smaller stages.

The people who currently make things happen at the Clara White Mission, which Eartha established in 1904, have been nothing but kind and supportive. Meg Fisher shared stories of the revival of the Mission. Kevin Carrico encouraged me throughout the writing of the book and helped me bring it to a public audience. Peggy Ezell toured me through the Mission's culinary gardens and farms and brought me and some friends to lunch at the Mission's "training café," to which I've since returned many times.

Patricia Moman Bell, whose family has long been involved with the Mission, talked to me kindly and patiently when I had questions that only someone who had known Eartha and knew how she worked could have explained and contextualized. Pat has been the leading figure in cataloging the Clara White Mission's Eartha-related materials. Talking with Pat always feels momentous. She speaks with her own particular blend of gravitas and grace, reminding me at times of Maya Angelou or Henry Louis Gates.

Ju'Coby Pittman, the fourth and current president of the Mission, though a person of enormous vision and ambition to help others and carry Eartha's creation forward, was also down-to-earth enough to chat with me in her office and welcome me at the café. With Meg Fisher at her side, Ju'Coby Pittman is one of the most progressive leaders in Jacksonville today. And in my mind, being the third person to run the Clara White Mission since Eartha spent seven decades doing it is a higher position than mere mayor of the city (with whatever apologies are due)

In the Sermon on the Mount, Jesus admonished:

"Take heed that ye do not your alms before men, to be seen of them: otherwise ye have no reward of your Father which is in heaven."

"Lay not up for yourselves treasures upon earth, where moth and rust doth corrupt, and where thieves break through and steal."

"Therefore I say unto you, Take no thought for your life, what ye shall eat, or what ye shall drink; nor yet for your body, what ye shall put on. Is not the life more than meat, and the body than raiment?"

"And why take ye thought for raiment? Consider the lilies of the field, how they grow; they toil not, neither do they spin. And yet I say unto you, That even Solomon in all his glory was not arrayed like one of these."

*

"Death was nothing more than someone handing you a package or crossing the street."

*

The face that smiles through the winter of deciduous trees is as beautiful a face as I'll ever see, and the beauty of this face is embedded in its angelic kindness. The angel's kinky hair stands out from her face like a halo.

"I know you," I say. "I met you once, a long, long time ago."

PART ONE

In the Beginning

In 1992, I graduated from Nathan Bedford Forrest High School in Jacksonville, Florida. The school was named after a Confederate general, as are so many schools in Jacksonville, and this general also happened to be the first "Grand Dragon" of the Ku Klux Klan.

Schools all over the South were once named after Forrest, but most other school jurisdictions found the decency and shame to change the names of those schools. As I write, Jacksonville is one of two locales left with a Nathan Bedford Forrest, though the School Board has finally voted to begin proceedings to change the name.

In 2006, students from the community college where I teach led an effort, of which they should be proud, to change the name of the high school, and one possible new name was Eartha M. M. White.

Eartha Mary Magdalene White was the greatest advocate for poor people, black and white, and for black people as a whole, in Jacksonville's history.

In 2008, the School Board voted 5 to 2 to keep the name. One serious proposal was to misspell the name by removing one "r," so it would seem the school had been named after an anonymous forest.

Campaigns to change the name of the school had failed previously as well. In the late 1990s, School Board Chairwoman Linda Sparks had opposed changing the name four years after she appointed Susan Lamb, co-founder of the Jacksonville-area chapter of the National Association for the Advancement of White People, to a school desegregation task force. The appointment took place almost 40 years after the Supreme Court ordered desegregation, but barely two decades after area schools complied with the Supreme

Court's decision. The NAAWP's newsletters had advocated shooting "hyphenated Americans" and billing their families for the bullets, a scientific basis for "Negro inferiority," and the idea that Jews "divide and conquer thru race war."

In 2013, Nikolai Vitti, on the job for less than a year, became the first Duval County Public Schools Superintendent to support changing the name of the school; 44 percent of the students in the school district are black and 39 percent are white. By the end of the year, the school board finally voted to exorcise the school of Nathan Bedford Forrest.

The city is still spanned by bridges named for racist legislators and former KKK members.

She called them old cronies and asked them what they had come here for when she was so busy.

Clara's father and her ancient cousin came to her as she washed clothes in the wooden tub outside her house.

Father Henry Harrison seemed so old, though he was only 66 and had another half century of living left. By the time of his death, he'll have preached for 89 years. He was tall, lean, and erect, and his white beard fell down over the worn lapels of his jacket. His eyes blazed.

"I am come here to name your baby," Harrison told Clara.

Clara looked at the old prophet in astonishment. She asked how he knew. She said he was always going around meddling in other people's business. Who told them she was going to have a baby?

Harrison said he had come to name Clara's baby Eartha, and never mind how he knew.

Clara looked at him, hard and sad. She didn't need to say what he already knew, but she did. She'd already had 12 babies and all of them had died. Even if she were to have another baby, she asked them, how could they know she was going to have a girl?

Harrison said this baby would live and be a blessing to everyone.

Clara's father had been looking at Harrison with open surprise since the old preacher had spoken the name. What did he want to name her Eartha for? What kind of name was that? Clara's father wanted to name the baby Mary Magdalene. Mary Magdalene had repented of sinful ways. She was there at the Crucifixion and she was there at the Resurrection.

But Harrison said that everything good came from the earth, that this child's name should be Eartha, that she shall be "a storehouse for the people."

And when Clara's father insisted the baby's name should be Mary Magdalene and that, furthermore, he was the child's grandfather, which should carry some weight in the matter, Clara interrupted the escalating argument and said that if her baby was a girl, and if her baby lived, she would give her the whole name.

Here's one story. Hang on to that caveat.

On November 8, 1876, Clara English White gave birth to Eartha Mary Magdalene White, who would become one of the city's most successful philanthropists and humanitarian leaders. She was the first of former slave Clara White's 13 children to live past early childhood.

Eartha M. M. White died in early 1974 at age 97, not three years after the judicial ruling to force Duval County public schools to desegregate.

Her friends included Eleanor Roosevelt, Booker T. Washington, Mary McLeod Bethune, Jacksonville-born A. Philip Randolph, father of the March on Washington, and the poet and novelist James Weldon Johnson, one of the early leaders of the National Association for the Advancement of Colored People and principal in the early 1900s of the Stanton School in Jacksonville's LaVilla area, from which Eartha graduated in 1893.

Eartha Mary Magdalene White was born in a small wooden house, not far from where her mother saw *her* mother sold as a slave. Eartha was the Promised Child. Her most enduring institution in the city would be the non-profit organization serving the poor and disenfranchised and bearing the name of her mother—the Clara White Mission.

But there are other stories about how Eartha White entered the world. Another story concerns the fact that Father Henry Harrison's 1917 obituary contains a glaring contradiction that looks like a mere typographical error.

One sentence reads, "It gave him a great deal of pleasure to refer to Miss Bertha M. M. White, whom he named three months before she was born."

And another sentence: "A short sketch of his life was read by his confidential friend, Miss Eartha M. M. White." The obituary said that anyone who wanted a copy of "this short history may have same by applying to her."

Of his 117 years, so little is known. Including whether or not he was 117 years old. One source says 120. His obituary says he was 114.

His mother was half-Indian, and her name was Maria, but what does it mean that she was half-Indian?

Another source says Harrison was born in 1810, that he "arrived in Jacksonville when it was called Cowford. He played with Native American children and learned their language." Where? When? What tribe? What language? Whom?

His obituary says he played with Indian children and sang their songs. Is this assertion more truthful than the myth of a "grand Timucua city" named Ossachite once thriving where downtown Jacksonville is now? The British later called the site Cow Ford, and Cowford became downtown Jacksonville. According to Wikipedia. But Florida archaeologists say no such Timucua Indian village ever existed, that Timucuans didn't build big villages, much less cities.

But many a brief "history" of Jacksonville repeats the story.

Harrison "saw the first boat that sailed up the St. Johns River, the first house built, and also remembered Tom Flanagan, who delivered the mail in the row boat which came once a week from St. Marys [Georgia, just over the state line]."

His favorite book of the Bible was Revelation. He preached for eight decades. Father Henry Harrison was an Abrahamic-Mosaic prophet born in slavery in the American Confederacy. Or he was John the Baptist, the wild man subsisting on locusts and honey, foretelling the coming Messiah.

Of his 15 children, two were alive when he died. Are any of his descendents alive today?

He spent his final days in his daughter Lizzie Payne's Jacksonville home. "Although he was extremely old, he could go anywhere in the city unaccompanied."

He died from being old and tired and frequently would sing, "I am traveling to my grave, to lay this body down."

"He never touched alcohol. It gave him a great deal of pleasure to refer to Miss Bertha M. M. White, whom he named three months before she was born."

At Harrison's funeral, mourners sang, "Swing Low, Sweet Chariot," "The Old Account Was Settled Long Ago," and "Keep Your Hand on the Gospel Plow."

Eartha knew her father was not the man she said he was.

Her family Bible is kept in the University of North Florida's Eartha M. M. White Collection. In it, in Eartha's handwriting, is the name of her biological father. Upon admission into the collection, the Bible was "protected" under a 25-year seal.

But what did she know of the truth and what part did she believe of the mythos? Or are the two each part of the other?

She named her most lasting institution, the Clara White Mission on West Ashley Street in Jacksonville's LaVilla district, for her adoptive mother.

Sometime in the late 1970s or early 1980s, UNF library staff traced Clara's genealogy. Her parents were Adam English and Jane Green English. Adam's parents had both been born in Africa, and Jane's grandmother was African.

The African lineage points to incomplete but intriguing names like Adam English's maternal great-grandfather, "Plato the African," and it seems criminal that nearly nothing about these fully lived lives can be known.

But Eartha knew her biological father was a white man.

She knew he came from the wealthy Jacksonville Stockton family. Southern aristocracy.

It's less clear whether she ever knew her mother was Mollie Chapman, probably the Stocktons' servant.

Clara had married another former slave, Lafayette White, right before he was "mustered out" of the Union (and then U.S.) Army's "Colored Troops" in 1866. Fifteen years after Lafayette died, when Clara sought a U.S. Army widow's pension in 1896, the army investigated Clara's status because her daughter was suspiciously light-skinned.

The investigator verified twelve of Clara's children, not 13, including one child named Bertha, not Eartha.

Clara said, "I had nine living children and three dead children by Lafayette White. When my husband died, I only had one child living. That child is living yet. Her name is Bertha. I know she was born a month before Christmas. I do not know the date of the month. I do not know the year. I did not have any doctor when she was born."

A physician who saw a baby he called Eartha in November 1875 later looked after a baby whose name he thought was Bertha in 1876 or 1877. He didn't think Bertha could have been Lafayette White's daughter because of "its color."

Did he transpose the names?

Eartha's official birthday in early November matches Clara's statement about Bertha's, about "a month before Christmas." But Eartha's official birthyear is 1876, when the doctor thought he looked after Bertha, not 1875 when the physician said he first examined Eartha.

The army's pension investigation finally concluded that Bertha was born to Lafayette and Clara on November 3, 1875, and that Eartha came to the White home late in either 1875 or 1876.

A century later, Mary Singleton, the first black woman elected to Jacksonville's City Council, would say she thought Eartha was older than the 97 years everyone believed her to be when she died.

The wife of a Union soldier who had fought alongside Lafayette said he and Clara had lost so many children, including a little girl named Bertha.

But Clara informed the investigator that "Bertha has been away from us for years. I wan't able to take care of her. I gave Bertha to Mrs. Callahan. The last I heard from her they were going to Washington. They were white people. They took Bertha a couple of weeks after my husband died."

Clara told the investigator she had never told Eartha she was adopted. "She thinks and everybody thinks she is my child. Only a few know she is not my child. I kept Eartha because I was compelled to. Well! Because I promised to."

More than a century after Eartha came to the home of Clara and Lafayette White, rumors persist that Eartha had some kind of knowledge of Bertha, that late in life, she somehow found and contacted Bertha. If only there were evidence.

If Eartha was a replacement for Bertha, then her whole grand mythology is stood on its head. Not only is she *not* Clara's 13th child and the first to live, but *Bertha* was Clara's 12th child and first to survive early childhood: Eartha becomes a stand-in.

In fact, historian Carolyn Williams points out that Clara most likely named Eartha after her own previous owner, Mary Magdalene Cooper Harrison, from whose family Father Henry Harrison received his last name.

And in 1976, UNF historian Dan Schafer discovered that Clara had made this promise "to white people in the community, several of whom became rather anxiety-ridden during the drawn-out investigation and covertly visited" with the investigating officer.

From the official report: "Several of the most prominent people in the city came to see me relating to the child Eartha and said she was not the child of the soldier [Lafayette] and that claimant [Clara] was sworn never to reveal the child's parentage. The persons referred to refused to be sworn and it does not appear necessary to ventilate an old affair that would cause scandal and inflict on the surviving members of the family."

So many of Clara's babies had died that she was desperately willing to comply with a wealthy white family's lie, and Eartha herself would keep what she later learned secret for life.

After the 25-year UNF library seal lapsed, almost no one would know or remember to ask. But by then, the secret had been widely dispatched, and the stakes of disseminating it no longer seemed so high.

When my wife was teaching *The Narrative of the Life of Frederick Douglass* in a literature course at the University of Florida in 2004, a student walked up to her at the end of class with tears in her eyes.

Douglass's brief autobiography is heartbreaking. He writes about what slavery was like for him as a little boy. His father was most likely his master, and all he remembered of his mother was that, after a full day of work in the fields, she walked for miles just to lie down with him and get him to sleep at night. Then she'd walk back to her cabin to get what sleep she could before waking at the break of dawn to go back to work in the fields. Douglass writes of seeing his aunt stripped to the waist and whipped for hours. He writes of tricking little white boys into teaching him the rudiments of reading. He writes of a slave named Demby shot in the head at close range for trying to get away from being whipped.

But this student's tears were about something else. Douglass records names and dates and locations. He names the people—the Gores, the Aulds, the Hopkinses. He documents what they did and where they did it. It's a brutal and necessary accounting.

This student bore one of those last names. Her family was from the same part of Maryland where Douglass had been a slave. She had called an aunt the night before and asked her about the name. Though her family never discussed it, they knew.

Though Douglass's *Narrative* was published in 1845, the documentation of her forebears' brutality still haunted an 18 year-old student at the University of Florida in 2004. She certainly bore no guilt for what her predecessors had done, but this monstrous cruelty from just before the Civil War broke her good and kind heart in the 21st century.

Such family secrets exist all across the American landscape.

*

Eartha attended a Jacksonville reception for Frederick Douglass in 1889 and kept her 25-cent ticket with her most valuable personal possessions all her life. The ticket survives. It's housed at UNF's Eartha White Collection.

She helped bring Douglass back to Jacksonville a few years later to speak at the Subtropical Exposition, something like a regional swamp-land World's Fair.

James Weldon Johnson remembered being in the crowd. "No one could ever forget a first sight of Frederick Douglass," he writes. "A tall, straight, magnificent man with a lion-like head covered with a glistening white mane."

Johnson sums up Douglass's mythically powerful presence by saying, "As I watched and listened to him, agitator, editor, organizer, counselor, eloquent advocate, co-worker with the great abolitionists, friend and adviser of Lincoln, for a half century the unafraid champion of freedom and equality for his race, I was filled with a feeling of worshipful awe. Douglass spoke, and moved a large audience of white and colored people by his supreme eloquence."

In the 1880 census, when she was four years old, her name appears as "Ida Eartha," and her race as "black." No other mention of the name "Ida" appears anywhere. Ever.

In the 1900 census, "Eartha White" is "black," but in the 1920 census, she is "Mulatto," an official acknowledgement that her father was white. By 1930, "Eartha White" is "Negro."

According to Eartha's private notes, her biological father came from a family after whom streets and parks and schools are now named in wealthy and old parts of town. Eartha knew about him; the public did not. Not officially anyway.

The note in Eartha's Bible says her father was Guy Stockton, one of several children born to William Tennent Stockton, a former Confederate soldier, and Julia Telfair Stockton.

Eartha's uncle, Telfair Stockton, was the real estate tycoon who developed the wealthy historic neighborhoods of Avondale, San Marco, Ponte Vedra, Fairfax Manor, and Oriental Gardens. The (Stock)tons are old stock.

Great leaders often come from grand mythological origins. Or they create them later. It's part of the "cult of personality."

Clara was washing clothes in the tub when the Old Testament-like former-slave prophet-preacher came to her with occult knowledge that her 13th baby would be the first to live, that she should be named for the earth itself and would be "a storehouse for the people."

And. Or.

Clara's 12 babies all died but one, whom Clara yielded to a white family when Lafayette died. Mollie Chapman, likely a maid for the wealthy white Stocktons, became pregnant with a Stockton scion's child. The Stocktons concealed the fact and Mollie adopted out her baby to a former slave who'd lost 12 of her own, 11 to death and one to adoption.

Twelve babies. Number of the ancient tribes of Israel. The story still feels Old Testament, awfully prophetic.

And the number 13 is usually associated with bad luck. But the mythical 13th tribe of Israel is a matter of conspiratorial occult alternate history. And the Beta Israel are Jewish Ethiopians who believe themselves to be descended from the Queen of Sheba, a 13th tribe, and to protect the Ark of the Covenant at the Church of Our Lady Mary of Zion in the ancient city of Axum.

All these vague associations and resonances. In what ways does it matter in what order children are born? Does the seventh son of a seventh son really have special powers? What about Only Child Syndrome?

Eartha Mary Magdalene became the Mother Teresa of Jacksonville. And the secrets of her origins extend from the 19th century into the early 21st.

Meanwhile a knowledgeable writer with a long history of freelance reporting in Jacksonville and other Southern towns tells me, "You need to be careful. You're treading on old social and political and racial tensions that still have power in a town like Jacksonville. I don't care if the mayor's black and city's less than half white. Books on Eartha White have been shut down before. You need to proceed cautiously."

Though the story of Eartha's prophetic naming is apocryphal, it's with respect to that story that I call Eartha "Eartha."

The beginning of this book associates Eartha with the earth and the book will end with the sowing of the earth in Eartha's name 40 years after her death, a sowing infused, inspir(it)ed with Eartha.

If mythology and urban legend suffused Eartha's whole life, the mythos of Eartha is earth-based, chthonic, nurturing and nourishing.

In a 1974 interview, activist and humanitarian Frances Ewell, who first met Eartha in 1909, said the fact of white residents calling Eartha by her first name when she was young, though they gave to her charities and said they respected her, indicated a lack of respect. Her point has to do with Southern codes of personal address.

Ewell says, "She was later known as Miss White, but in early days, she was known as Eartha to all these old families who almost felt that she was like a family retainer, doing something over there that was good for the underdog."

So I have to make clear that I call Eartha "Eartha" against and in the face of this century-old patronizing familiarity, because I find the beauty of the Eartha Mythos far greater than the passive-aggressive insults of Southern aristocracy.

In some renderings of the prophetic naming, Reverend Harrison and Adam English speak in a strange and hokey dialect that sounds like racist depictions of American Indian grammar. In others, their dialogue sounds like minstrelsy.

When Harrison says he's come to "name 'im Eartha," Clara's father says, "I want 'im name Mary Magdalene," and Clara tells the men, "If 'im be a girl, give 'im the whole name." It sounds like Tonto left the Lone Ranger's side just long enough to name Clara's child.

Mythology about this larger-than-life tiny woman always encircled her. Seven decades after the 1901 fire that destroyed downtown Jacksonville, stories still circulated that Eartha had driven a horse and buggy back and forth across the St. Johns River, carrying the belongings of destitute people to safety.

Frances Ewell laughed at this story and said, "I'm sure she was heroic, but I think a deed like that is like saying Eartha walked on water."

Over the decades, Eartha was compared to Mother Teresa, Gandhi, even Haile Salassie. Several stories about Eartha having clandestine romantic and sexual relationships appeared from time to time, but none of them can be substantiated. *Perhaps* there's some truth in a young Eartha using such relationships to get what she wanted, but it seems more likely that suspicions of a young single black woman with so much social and political power might lead to assumptions that a man here and there *must* support her and her enterprises, and that secret sources of white wealth *must* underpin Eartha's organization.

The premise of such rumors could very well be that a *woman*, that a *black* woman, that a *single* black woman, that a *diminutive* single black woman would, by definition, be incapable of having such power in this Southern city.

I'm listening to an interview with Mary Littlejohn Singleton, recorded in February of 1974, conducted by a very polite white woman assisting local historian Dan Schafer. In 1967, Singleton was the first black woman elected to Jacksonville's City Council. By 1974, she'd made her way to the Florida House of Representatives.

MISS MARY E. LITTLEJOHN
Third in balloting for "Miss Jacksonville"
with 307 votes.

Singleton says she doesn't know if it's true, but she's heard several people in the black community say they believe Eartha was even older than everyone thought.

She says an old woman had asked her, when she was on the City Council, when Eartha would be 100 years old. The woman said, "Well, *my* mother and she were good friends, and they, Miss White was older than my *grand*mother. And my grandmother would've been 100 three or four years ago than I'm talkin' about."

Congressman Singleton says, "She seemed to think that somewhere down the line, some years…got by…that nobody could recover."

And Mary Singleton knew Eartha's father was white. Forty years later, I can hear it in the interview. With all the ways segregation cheated the city's black residents, I wonder how heavy the burdens of the city's secrets weighed on the black leaders who knew them.

When asked if Eartha had any other surviving siblings, being the 13th and first living of Clara's children, Singleton says, "I never heard her say anything about sisters, or brothers, nor her father." There's a slight pause. "Nor her father."

Four decades later, having seen what paternal name Eartha wrote in her family Bible, I can hear Mary Singleton preparing to tell her polite white interviewer a secret without telling her the secret. It's a double movement the interviewer doesn't register.

Then Singleton says, "I am afraid that she might have been a victim of, uh, so many people of her era, uh, the mother, probably, now this is my imagination not really running away, but this is the way it was done during that time, uh, perhaps slave, perhaps, and, uh, there were two types of slaves, the kind who worked in the fields and the kind who, sort of, worked in the house, you know, who shared the same things as the mistress did, so to speak, and, because I am told, that her mother was a very, very dark-skinned woman, and she was a very fair-skinned person, and there has been, the question in a lot of people's minds, this is the kind of union she came from."

And then, unbelievably, her interviewer asks about Clara's husband, "And the late Adam English, that was her father?"

I hear Singleton pause. She says, awkwardly, "Uh huh." Then she coughs. Then she clears her throat. Both of them now sound awkward.

Though the interviewer seems to have missed everything Mary Singleton was trying to tell her, in a way it's not her fault.

We're all products of our place and time, and I hear her earnestly working to get at the truth. She wasn't able to hear what Mary Singleton was unable to say explicitly. In contrast, I've the benefit of four decades' distance and my entire lifetime, but the detriment of being that much further removed from Eartha's daily existence in the world.

Eartha learned from Clara that the way to live her life was through helping others. But on the way to becoming the center of her community, Clara worked as maid and cook for wealthy white families in Jacksonville and nearby Amelia Island and as a servant on steamships that cruised from the South to wealthy resorts in Rhode Island and Connecticut.

Sometimes when she had to leave, Clara boarded Eartha with local black families. Sometimes Eartha got to stay with her.

All her life, Eartha remembered living with Clara at Kingsley Plantation.

The plantation house and barn at Kingsley Plantation on Fort George Island, in Duval County's far Northeast corner, where several island keys dot the wetlands along the St. Johns River and the vast marshes into the Atlantic Ocean, date to the late 1700s. The limestone slave quarters date back perhaps to the 1820s.

On the island's one road, the ruins of a never-completed tabby limestone house begun around 1850 for one of slaveholder Zephaniah Kingsley's slave mistresses, Munsilna McGundo, has always called to me.

It's called me with righteous anger against the white residents who preceded my *witness / whiteness* here by two centuries.

It's called me with its Romantic sense of tragedy and demanded retribution, if not its entirely perverse and reprehensible travesty of love.

The tabby house is one of the first places I kissed the woman who would become my wife.

The tabby house is a place I brought my daughters when they were little and told them about Walt Whitman and Jean Toomer's *Cane* and the lyrical-epic-suicidal-tragedy of the South over picnics of sandwiches and peaches. I would talk to them of deeply despicable injustices, and I would talk to them of the lure of the lore, of searching for records of the unrecorded, of the mythical appeal of what happened but can never be known, of what cannot be known but ceaselessly calls for investigation.

I didn't know then that Eartha White, one of the great mythical women of the South, had lived as a child in the house of Anna Madgigine Jai Kingsley, one of the great mythical women of the South.

I call them mythical in the sense of a larger-than-life historical status, though they were as human and individual as my daughters, with so much more to overcome.

Anna Madgigine Jai Kingsley.

Inasmuch as each of us is an entire world, every individual is impossible to fathom.

Dan Schafer's book *Anna Madgigine Jai Kingsley: African Princess, Florida Slave, Plantation Slaveowner* traces her uncanny trajectory in its title alone.

Considering that she was born in the 1790s in Senegal, West Africa, kidnapped and shipped to Cuba where North Florida slave trader Zephaniah Kingsley bought her, later marrying her, you have to wonder, bewildered, even ashamed, who Anna Kingsley ever really was.

The historical evidence hardly concerns her own wondering. Walk through the yellow flies and mosquitos in early autumn by the tabby house, and it seems that wondering who you are is an historical luxury.

For Anna Kingsley, survival meant an almost constant accommodation of new identity that indicated enormous intelligence and unbelievable adaptability.

Walk through Fort George Island swamps and think about the epic transformations that never ceased throughout her life, and you wonder who she was from African girl to slave to petitioner to Spain for land in what's now the Jacksonville suburb of Mandarin, where she was given several acres and purchased her own slaves and livestock.

In the 1820s, one of Zephaniah Kingsley's numerous nieces wrote of Anna what distant relatives might have written of Eartha in the 1890s or even the 1920s.

She was not black. She was not white. She was beautiful. Something about her was iridescent. Something about her light brown skin made her stand out among both whites and blacks.

Her skin was like True Indigo, a color they say doesn't properly fit the prism. Almost no one ever sees it, and if you do, you'll never be able to describe it. You'll probably never see it again. But you'll never forget it.

Her dark eyes and the shapes of her hair made her seem someone new between white and black. Somehow because she was in-between, she seemed above. White and black didn't apply to her. She was both, she was neither, and she was more.

She was quiet. She moved according to her own gravity and orbit. She had a dignity built into her. She was regal but down-to-earth.

Somehow she had come from between worlds and existed between worlds and that made her more than the worlds she moved between.

If anyone denied it, their denial was defense. She wasn't merely this race or that. Being impossible to locate made the whole enterprise of marking her seem silly. Never mind words like mulatto, quadroon, octoroon.

Because she was so much bigger, everyone must be.

That was in the 1820s.

When Eartha was a little girl, Clara was employed to a white family named Rollins. Eartha lived with Clara on Kingsley's plantation in the house built for Anna Kingsley.

Anna's house soon became the kitchen, since kitchens were built away from main houses. Kitchens sometimes caught fire, and if they stood apart from the main house by a yard or a breezeway, they probably wouldn't take the big house down.

A daughter of the wealthy homeowner remembered her pet owl Goggles terrifying the servant's daughter Eartha by lodging itself in her dirty nappy hair.

Eartha knew only as much as any little girl, alone in the moment, in the cold and the dark, distantly small in such great vast distances of trees and swamp, and somewhere nearby was an ocean.

The wealthy white daughter thought the little-servant-Eartha's Fort George Island days both tragic and funny:

"I had a tame great horned owl that I raised from a tiny ball of fuzz. Goggles grew to be six feet from wing to wing and would drop from the sky onto my little arm, clasping claws as big as my hand without ever giving me a scratch."

She writes:

"Goggles greatly disgusted my mother by sitting on his perch near the house with the tail of a rat or snake hanging out of his mouth giving contented squawks."

But then:

"On one occasion Goggles was asleep in the woodshed when Eartha White, then a little girl, went for wood. Goggles woke up in fright and fastened his claws in Eartha's hair. She screamed as she began dragging him out of the shed. I grabbed him but we were obliged to cut Eartha's hair to disentangle Goggles."

Anna Kingsley had no idea a little girl named Eartha White would come to live in her house. Little-girl-Eartha knew little more than her mother and the damp wooden house and the slave cabins that formed a distant crescent moon, and owls and rats, and the stories long lost to us that I would love to have in hand, though I suspect and believe that large parts of old folklore sustain themselves and evolve into our contemporary truths.

Just before Eartha turned 10 years old, a great strange rumbling shook the whole plantation, knocked branches from trees, rattled the plates on the shelves and the lamps on tables.

The little white girl named Asa thought a bear outside the house was trying to shake it apart, but the plantation shook eight more times in the next two months.

Eartha and Clara and Asa and everyone else on Fort George Island had felt the earthquake centered near Charleston, South Carolina that radiated up and down the East Coast. It was felt as far north as Boston and as far south as Cuba.

I wanted to write about Eartha White, "Jacksonville's Angel of Mercy," before I wrote about pseudo-serial-killer Ottis Toole, Jacksonville's "Devil's Child."

I'm embarrassed to say I first imagined one book about them both. *Eartha and Ottis* or *Ottis and Eartha* would be a big decentralized narrative in which the two of them represented the polarities of good and evil on the stage of their North Florida city. Luckily I realized the idea was terrible, not to mention a crime against Eartha White.

So *Stalking Ottis Toole: A Southern Gothic* appeared in August of 2013. The book is disgusting and I'm embarrassed I wrote it. The story is important and I'm proud to have written it. It plays all the different versions of Ottis Toole against each other. His IQ was said to be 75 and he confessed to every horrible crime police put before him like a little boy trying to get as much attention as he could. The book is as much about story and what people do with story as it is about Ottis Toole.

Nevertheless, I feel corrupted by *Stalking Ottis Toole*, and I've looked to Eartha White to cleanse me. How selfish of me! Hopefully it's at least less insensitive than putting them together in one big Southern-Gothic Urban-Omnibus of Good and Evil.

Though seven or eight books had made mention of Ottis Toole, and almost as many had been promised or planned, no one had published a book about Toole before.

Nor has anyone published a book about Eartha White, and that's far more surprising. Her story forms a chapter in several books, like Congressman Charles Bennett's 1989 *Twelve on the River St. Johns.*

Bennett came close to naming the wealthy white man Eartha believed to be her father, but in a footnote, he echoed the army pension investigator's judgment that it was "not necessary to ventilate an old affair" by saying that since publishing the name "may intrude on the privacy of living persons, that information is not included here."

Historian Dan Schafer truncated his manuscript on Eartha shortly after he began it in 1976. Before he helped bring Eartha's papers and materials to UNF, he worked through them in the library and gymnasium once attached to the back of Eartha's cottage at Moncrief Springs. Sometimes when he came out to Moncrief, he'd find that people had broken in and burnt Eartha's effects in metal barrels to keep themselves warm.

Schafer is as gracious a person as he is eminent an historian. He shares his knowledge and his thoughts with me as I sit across a coffee table from him in the high-ceilinged and wide-open living room of the bed-and-breakfast he runs with his wife in Jacksonville's old Riverside Avondale district.

But my project is not his project.

Though racism persists, times are different now than they were in 1976. If I were a young white man writing about Eartha two years after she died, I can't imagine I'd presume I had the necessary sensitivity.

A local newspaper article from 1982, six years after Schafer started his manuscript, still said he was writing Eartha's biography. The article names Eartha's biological mother, but calls her biological father "a prominent white man," perhaps the first mention of that combustible open secret in print.

Do I have the sensitivity and understanding now? I'm not writing an academic history. Clearly there's no way a middle-class white man in 2014 could understand what it was like to be Eartha White. How much more despicable then was my *Eartha and Ottis* conception?

In 1968, the poet Nikki Giovanni wrote:

> and I really hope no white person ever has cause
> to write about me
> because they never understand
> Black love is Black wealth and they'll
> probably talk about my hard childhood
> and never understand that
> all the while I was quite happy

I'm not so much a white man writing about Eartha White as I am a lost man writing about his search. It's of that I continuously remind myself. Though I won't ever understand what it meant to be Eartha, I want to come as close to the true Eartha as I can. At least I'll give her story new life. Maybe I'll influence someone else to do better.

And is it equally selfish of me to hope this city's "Angel of Mercy" wouldn't mind offering me the chance to do what little good I can by writing about her? If writing about Ottis Toole poisoned me, I hope it doesn't sound too fatuous to say that I hope Eartha White might save me, even if she died five months before I was born.

Dan Schafer never published the name of Eartha's biological father. In his manuscript, he wrote, "The judgments of [Investigator] J.A. Davis in 1896 are relevant for 1976 as well, especially since Eartha chose not to reveal the name of her father for 97, or maybe 98 years."

Though the knowledge of this one man's name remained secret, it nevertheless bred its own lines of strange stories throughout Eartha's life and afterward. Several people, black and white, came forward to inform the pension investigator of the man they believed to be Eartha's father. They mentioned the names of several white men from the city's leading families.

Says Schafer, "All informants stressed that this family looked after Clara, gave her money or property, and provided money for Eartha's education, and later, for her humanitarian causes." Several historians, including Schafer, now believe the informants were wrong about all of that.

Story works in mysterious ways. Stories take on lives of their own. They often tell the people attached to them, though people think *they* tell the stories.

So even without the secret knowledge of Eartha's white father, stories about Eartha in newspapers and magazines claimed her humanitarianism hid secret wealth established by occulted machinations of one of the city's leading families.

In a 1971 *St. Petersburg Times* article, Fred Wright says that a relatively small sum given to Clara at Eartha's birth led to "judicious investment in property, much of it in what is now downtown Jacksonville," which provided Clara and Eartha with a great deal of material wealth, some of which they funneled into charity. Wright said that Eartha "is now a millionaire, at least in terms of property owned."

A *Reader's Digest* article that appeared 11 months after Eartha's death in 1974 said she was four and a half feet tall, that she gave up a career singing opera to help the poor and the destitute, that she used portions of the money she received for charity to increase her own personal investments.

Schafer points out that "Miss White's property holdings were extensive at the time of her death, but of relatively little value [...] Properties were deeded to the Eartha M. M. White Nursing Home and to the Clara White Mission, but the essential fact remains: Miss White struggled financially throughout her life; she worked for years without compensation; and most profits earned from private investment were donated to her humanitarian works."

Documents I've recently found in uncatalogued boxes in the Clara White Mission indicate she owned more than two dozen properties close to downtown and in far reaches of Duval County like Bayard and Mandarin, but that the Mission itself, near the time of her death, frequently had little more than $1,000 cash on hand.

Minutes from an August 1974 meeting just months after Eartha died refer to "the gravity of the [financial] situation." The foundation's bank balance was $769.00 and outstanding debts stood "in excess of $3,000." Board Vice President Walter Kramer said there were "lines [sic] against [Eartha's] property" and that about $2,000 was needed immediately "to keep the insurances current."

In Eartha's childhood years, Clara had tried to buy the Clay Street shotgun house she'd been renting in the neighborhood known as Hansontown, which Bethel Baptist

Church historian Camilla Thompson remembers was once colloquially called "Black Bottom," in the northwestern part of downtown near present-day Florida State College at Jacksonville's Downtown Campus. But Clara's lack of funds lost her the Clay Street house.

Still, stories and intrigues that disappeared into anonymity and good-ole-boy-network silences in the 1870s and 1880s worked underground to produce elaborate racial-conspiracy-theory fictions in the 1950s and '60s and '70s.

A handwritten notation in uncatalogued files at the Clara White Mission mentions a March 26, 1980 meeting in which the Eartha M. M. White Foundation Board of Directors agreed to consolidate Eartha's widely dispersed North Florida property wealth and absorb it into the Clara White Mission, Inc., which made it easier for the Mission, under Ju'Coby Pittman's leadership in the 1990s and early-2000s, to sell properties and convert asset poverty into liquid assets.

In 2014, numerous insiders see it clear that Clara took Eartha in from a wealthy white reprobate and his family's servant to make Eartha her own lost daughter, that Eartha fought against financial difficulties for nearly a century to fulfill the commandment Clara had given her:

"Do all the good you can, in all the ways you can, in all the places you can, for all the people you can, while you can."

The Hanstontown Clay Street house hardly kept out the cold in the winter, but the neighborhood kids often didn't notice. The crooked chimney billowed thin blue smoke from the Christmas hearth. The kids bore the brutal heat of humid summers and played in the wet winters of Aunt Clara's Christmas.

The stockings hung everywhere. By the chimney. From the Christmas tree. Up and down the long hall that stretched from the front door to the back door.

The kids believed the gifts came from Santa. They never suspected Aunt Clara. But the adults knew. It wasn't Clara's wealth that made Christmas happen in that wood-frame shack on Clay Street. Maybe some of the kids wondered at Aunt Clara's special connection with Santa Claus.

But Clara's connection was with the community. Since before Eartha could remember. It was a natural relationship. Clara made her own toys for the kids, but the adults brought what little toys, what cheap toys, what broken toys they could, and they couldn't imagine bringing them to anyone but Clara. Clara didn't plan it that way. It's just the way things unfolded.

Eartha's childhood Christmases were Clara's kindness to the poor kids in the neighborhood. She later wrote, "We never knew it was my mother who gave us these little things. I can *see* it now."

The Yellow Fever outbreak of 1888 was the last and the worst of several that frequently rose up from the swamps in which Jacksonville grew. The epidemic hit the city hard and Clara and Eartha got out before armed guards patrolled the perimeters of the city to maintain quarantine.

Her flight from Yellow Fever took Eartha to the beginnings of a career singing opera. She was 12 years old when she began studying "voice culture" in New York City.

By the time she fell in love with James Jordan, she was touring with the Oriental American Opera Company, directed by J. Rosamond Johnson, who later composed "Lift Every Voice and Sing," the "Black National Anthem," with his brother, the poet James Weldon Johnson. James and Rosamond had spent their childhoods playing music on the streets of Jacksonville and visited their father at the magnificent Victorian St. James Hotel on Hemming Park where he was headwaiter.

The opera company was the result of a wealthy Syracusan's belief that "Negroes could learn to sing grand opera as well as folk songs."

James Jordan loved Eartha deeply. Not only was she smart and kind and beautiful, but she was cultured, sophisticated. In fact, it could be a little intimidating that Eartha was traveling the Northeast and the Midwest and Europe, singing opera, while James had moved only as far from his birthplace in South Carolina as Jacksonville, Florida, where he worked every day in a railroad office.

The wedding was planned for June of 1896, when Eartha would be 20.

20

The year after Eartha's death, Grayce Bateman, her secretary for nearly three decades, said Eartha "never needed more than a couple hours sleep a night." She had accomplished so much in her 97 years that she hardly even had time for sleep.

In 1970, when Eartha was 94, she told Angela Taylor of *The New York Times*, "I never married. I was too busy. What man would put up with me running around the way I do?"

Two months earlier, *The Michigan Chronicle* headlined an article, "Attention, Women's Lib: Some Footsteps to Follow." Journalist Rita Griffin asked, "Want to take a lesson in 'feminist movement'? Check the history of Eartha Mary

Magdalene White, a wiry 94-year-old native of Jacksonville, Florida."

In addition to the usual list of Eartha's accomplishments, Griffin says Eartha was possibly the first black woman census enumerator in the country in 1910, and that as the oldest member of the National Business League, formerly the National Negro Business League as formed by Booker T. Washington in 1900, her post as its historian seemed natural. After all, she'd been a member for nearly three-quarters of a century.

In jesting that seems ironic in relation to Jacksonville's many rumors about Eartha's power, Griffin says, "Since Miss White set a precedent by becoming the first woman member, she takes good-natured teasing concerning any ulterior motives."

Then Eartha herself hams it up. She explains her seven decades of NBL membership by saying, "I'm in the process of looking for a husband. The first three qualifications are that he be good looking, highly educated, and have a heap of money."

But that's only half the list. The next three qualifications, Eartha says, "are that he be deaf, dumb and blind."

1-4-95

Dear Friend Eartha,

Your long looked for letter did come at last. I was indeed glad to hear from you for as I said this was the first one I got from you sence I wrote you about my coming and the Photos. Which I was to send you if you wrote dear truth I did not get it. Eartha I trust that this will find you well. And enjoying the cold weather. I am really not well but better than I have been and at work with Mr. Richard. When I get in at night I feel like doing nothing but going to bed. But to night I would not put of any longer. Though I am writtin with led. You don't mind that? I saw your mama to day. She is quite well. My mama is not well at all. She has a very bad cold. And also very horse as for myself I have been very very horse now for near a month. Oh say I need not ask for I know you had a fine xmas. We had a lovely spring day. Even if a freeze is predicted for to morrow same as last Dec. And Jan. 1st was a big day among the people here a big time they did have. The parade was a mile long said to be. We sold the other place three months ago. She got tired of it she said. We have been here at 1119 ½ Ashley Street renting all the while sence.

With much love for your self,

James.

8-31-95

Dear Eartha

Your loving letter of Aug. 16th came safe to hand and I must say found me very well indeed. Also Mama. But sence then Mama has left me and I am keeping house. She has gone to Savannah and from there she shall go to S.C. She will be gone over a month. I got a letter from her this P.m. She is well and having a good time she say. Mr. Mc Morris where here with me to night.

Say how is your Mama. Give my love to her. Mama often speak of you Eartha as her dear sweet girl.

Oh yes tuesday was our great Bycicle day here about three thousand people it is said was out to witness it. And the parade the night before was just lovely. I was out by your house to day I saw Miss Bella. I also was up to Monticello this week with a Base Ball club. We had a very good time in deed.

I returned last night Eartha I did not intend keeping you out of a letter this long but I put it off several time to writ at such a time till I though I would not put of any longer for you might want to think that I am trying to play even. But I am not that way. I am indeed glad to know that you had such a fine time in Cincinnatti and that you are having such a good time in general.

Eartha I must say that I am very much pleased with the Photo. And it looks just like you. What do you think of it. Eartha I haven't got the book as yet but will get it now very soon and read it at your request. The girls and boys are all seeming to have a good time.

Love to all.

Your friend,

J. Lloyd Jordan.

23

11-5-95

Dear friend Eartha.

I wrote you a long while ago and also a long letter and a week later I sent you the photos I did not write you when the pictures where sent as I was looking for a letter from you. Though I now take pleasure in writting you.

I trust Eartha that you are pleased with the Pictures. I think them very good. Also Mama. And Mr. Mc Morris say you might think enough of him to send him one. Of course I would not give any away so I just kept two one for Mama and My self. I trust that this will find you and Mama quite well.

I am feeling very good again. But still have a slight cough. It seems as if no medicine will heal it. For the last five days we have been having some bad weather. It rains a while then gets cool enough for fire turns warm & rain, continues it was raining near all night last night.

Frederick Ward Played here friday and saturday night. He had a large house. Played Damon and Pythias. I had tickets for Mama and I. But Earnest went in her stead as it was so busy a night Saturday night he played Mountebank.

I did not go to that as one night out was enough for me. I havent been out later than 7oclock over four times in two months I dont think.

I hope you did what I asked you to in my last letter, Mama send her best love. Give my love to all the friend and keep a good share for your self.

I am real sorry Eartha. I could not come to New York. But it would be realy detriment to my health to come this winter. Love to Mama.

Yours sincerely

J Lloyd Jordan.

24

12-15-95

Dear Little Eartha

I have realy been looking for a letter from you now for some time. But it seems like my time now to ask if you have ceased cores ponding. Though I can see reason why you should. I really wrote you a long letter before sending you the pictures. Sent them two week later and sence that wrote you. But up to now. I have looked in vain for a reply. It is that you have been moveing. But sure you must be through by now.

I saw your mama a few days ago. She looks very well I think. And Eartha that last Photo taken in Buss of Your Self. I think very good. And I am going to look for one. And that is sure. Send me one will you? How do you like Brooklyn? Better than New York. Say Mama sends her love to you. She speaks of you being her sweet little girl all the time. I trust that this will find you well.

I am not get entirely well. Though lots better than I was when I wrote you last. And am looking better. I shall make an attempt to go to work to morrow in Richardson office. My old employee.

Dont know how long I will hold out. But I hope all ok I will not go to runing as Dr Mitchel says there is two much dust for me. We are having very cool weather here though very changeable. Give my love to all. The town is very lively. And lots going on.

But I dont get out to any thing. As I dont go out at night.

Only in the day. All churches are preparing for xmas, I trust you will have a merry one.

Write soon.

Yours fondly,

Jimmy.

25

Jacksonville, Fla

3-9-96

My Dear Eartha

Your letter of last month was truly received and I enjoyed it ever so much. And have been trying ever sence to ans But But my mind I cant get on writting.

Your mama was here that same night to see me. And your letter of the 7th is also at hand and I am delighted to hear from you. No I am not tired writing.

But dear I keep so poorly and weak that when I get home at night and get a little supper and get through with other little things nothing suits but bed. Now dont think that I delay just so.

And dont write me. But I have other letters in my pocket that I delay I even delay Daughters so you may know now that I dont feel like writting. Often when I can feel good it is all right. I also saw your mama Sunday.

Eartha dear you dont want any Photo now. I have lost 16 lbs. Then I havent the means at present any way. My Dr Bill keeps me to the mark. At present for 21 treatments it is 2.00 a day. The weather is very pleasant at present.

Eartha I must say I am tired

good night

Write to me though

All sends love

I realy can hardly keep up some days

Yours Jimmy

116 Cleveland St.

26

Jacksonville Fla

4/30th 96

Dear Eartha

I Sit With Pen in hand to tell you the Sad News of our friend James Jordan he Pass away this afternoon after four 4-Clock. I did Not get to See him. Witch I Was Very Much disappointed. But I guess he is Better off I do Not No What time the funeral will Take Place I Suppose to morrow afternoon I thought that I Would let you know at once. I have nothing intiristing to tell you in this letter

Your friend

George

PART TWO

To Become the Good Earth

27

The State destroyed the schoolhouse in one quick blow. It took all of Roscoe Avenue with it. I once heard a crime novelist say that when the paint starts to peel on a building in Florida, it's torn down and replaced with a Hooters Restaurant. Certainly very little if anything is sacrosanct here.

The City tried. It applied to the State for preservation, but Eartha White's schoolhouse was an obstacle in the path of a new highway. The City was willing to move the schoolhouse to nearby Genovar Park, but neither the City nor the State would allot an iota of the cost of the new highway to move the 111 year-old one-room schoolhouse.

It stood in tall weeds. The dog fennel with its pungent smell, the ragged palm trees and palmettos, the ligustrum gone mad. Short boxes of buildings had been added to the perimeters of the schoolhouse. Windows had grown dark-green-opaque and old chicken feed signs on exterior walls had become illegible over time.

The schoolhouse had last been part of Two Time Tack and Feed Store. Before that, it was T and J Feeds, "Operated by the Lute Family," as the sign above the front porch addition claimed. At some point the porch was enclosed in jalousie windows. Another sign visible for years identified the store as Jazz Feeds.

Before that, the feed store was a church building. For most of its life, however, it was the schoolhouse for black children who lived anywhere near this remote part of Southeastern Duval County known as Bayard.

Until 2010, when the State demolished it, the original blackboards remained visible beneath broken patches in the newer wall paneling. The ceiling was caving in and the blackboards were breaking through.

And that takes us back to Eartha.

When James died, the story goes, she decided she would never marry. She would give her life to doing good for others, as she had witnessed Clara doing all her life. James's death broke her heart, and the only way she could make it right was by focusing on the needs of others instead of her own suffering.

When Eartha came back to Jacksonville, she enrolled immediately and urgently in Florida Baptist Academy, an outreach of Bethel Baptist Institutional Church. She wasted no time. She graduated and started teaching less than two years after entering "teaching school." James died in 1896 and Eartha was contracted to teach in 1899.

The first thing Eartha had to do after being assigned by the Board of Public Instruction to Duval County Public School No. 126 in Bayard, Florida for a salary of $30 per month was consult with a private landowner for the transfer of property necessary to build the school.

Bartolo Genovar of nearby St. Augustine owned land in several places in Duval County. Eartha talked Genovar into donating land in Bayard, and she made contacts in Jacksonville's business community to secure building materials. She encouraged black people to come together to give their time and labor for free to build the one-room schoolhouse.

She secured the land, she orchestrated the school's construction, and then she taught the Bayard school's first pupils.

Eartha's students were the children of former slaves who embodied poverty when "dirt poor" meant "poor as dirt." Teachers who graduated with expectations of teaching young black students couldn't expect the State to supply them buildings and books.

Even as she took on other enterprises, Eartha taught school for the next 16 years.

28

During the Great Fire of 1901, which destroyed most of what is today downtown Jacksonville, Eartha paid a man in a wagon to help secure and transport policy records and files from the Afro-American Life Insurance Company on Ocean Street between Bay and Forsyth.

After the fire, A.W. Archibald, a white lawyer who'd generously helped raise funds for Afro-American Life, asked company president and founder Abraham Lincoln Lewis to buy all his shares.

A race riot had erupted in the wake of the city's decimation, and Archibald was afraid whites would come after him for his association with black causes.

Lewis accepted.

A black man who drove a dray cart and delivered beer had frequently spent holidays at a house on Forsyth Street where he stabled his horses. One night as the driver was coming in, an irate white man told him to get down from his carriage, said "niggers" had no right to any place a white man found himself, and lost control of his anger when the driver said nothing, just looked at him.

The white man's face grew red in the dark. His hatred boiled over. He screamed and threatened the driver.

The black man still said nothing. From the back of the dray, he grabbed a long stick he used to readjust cargo, smacked the white man in the head with it, went on to his lodgings, and stabled his horses.

When the police came, he told them he'd only just knocked the man in the head. An officer said, "You didn't just knock him, you killed him." Then the riots began. Then

Archibald pulled all his shares from the Afro-American Life Insurance Company.

Eartha did secretarial and janitorial work for the Afro-American. She also cleaned the office and kept the accounts. Every morning she rode to the insurance company on her bicycle.

Her boss at Afro-American, J. Milton Waldron, also pastor at Bethel Baptist, "always praised her for never being late and her records never short."

29

It's not true, according to the usual story, that Eartha never married. As she had been prophesied a "storehouse for the people" and named after the earth itself, Eartha married the people. When James died, Eartha grieved by marrying the community.

Though the Union Benevolent Association had been formed the year before she was born, it wasn't until James died that Eartha herself revived it. Its original purpose was to provide for "indigent persons of color in the city."

After the Great Fire began on a LaVilla street corner, quickly left LaVilla, and burned most of adjacent Jacksonville to the ground, Eartha saw the widespread destitution in the ruins. She saw the crowds of people who'd lost everything, living in tents by the ashes.

So she campaigned for funding and one year later, workers had finished construction on the Colored Old Folks' Home in the black East Jacksonville area of Campbellton or Campbell's Addition. In 1902, it was "a big two story house with a flanking gallery and two or three hound dogs wagging their tails and the smell of hot corn bread and other delicious vittles."

"There is not a one who pays one cent for their keeping," Eartha wrote, "and this institution has no income except what the public gives and this amounts to a very little."

So Eartha wrote letters and paid visits to businesses and well-known city residents who might be able and willing to contribute any little thing.

She drove her horse and buggy around town, negotiating and picking up loads of kindling or leftover chicken or the remnants of a corn harvest to bring back to the old and penniless who lived at the Old Folks' Home.

An old blind man left Eartha the black and white dog that had helped him find his way around Jacksonville for 11 or 12 years. The old man's name is lost. His dog's name was Lilly White. She was all he had to bequeath.

She built the Colored Old Folks' Home in her mid-20s. When Eartha was 89 years old, she would open the 122-bed Eartha M. M. White Nursing Home. After Clara's and Eartha's soup kitchen on Eagle Street, now First Street, the Old Folks' Home was the beginning and early center of what would become the Clara White Mission.

*

Judith Kemps was somewhere between 85 and 100 years old and had "served the white race" for more than 70 years. But Judith could no longer take care of herself, much less serve others, and was therefore "valueless," in the words of a letter a city councilman forwarded to Eartha in 1915. The letter called her "an old negro woman" and "worthy darky," and its anonymous writer wondered what should be done about her, since she now lived as an invalid in a "little hut" in the East Jacksonville neighborhood of Oakland.

So Judith came to live with Eartha at the Old Folks' Home nearby at 1627 Milnor Street, where she was treated with respect and with love at the end of her long and thankless life.

Some of the first inmates of the Old Folks Home, ranging from 60 to 107 years of age

Miss White surrounded by three of the residents of the Old Folks Home

Exterior of the Old Folks Home, one of the chief activities of the Clara White Mission

A bathroom in the Old Folks Home   One of the Corridors in the Old Folks Home

In this comfortable living room at the Old Folks Home many of the inmates spend
their evenings in reverie of bygone days

The first dining room at the Old Folks Home. It has been replaced by a new one that comfortably seats seventy-five, and can accommodate one hundred.

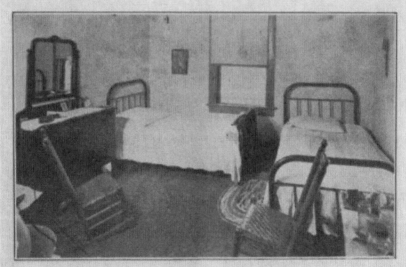

One of the bedrooms at the Old Folks Home

When there were more grapes than they planned to use, Mary or her daughter Marcia called Eartha to bring Old Folks' Home residents out to pick them.

Eartha had charmed Dinsmore Dairy, widely known for supporting civil rights organizations and causes, as she charmed so many others.

In February 1975, Mary Geiger, whose brother Earl Johnson had owned the dairy, wrote UNF historian Dan Schafer, recalling Eartha's visits to her Dunn Avenue farm near Dinsmore Dairy.

"On one of the grape-picking occasions, Miss White had brought with her six or eight old women, some partially crippled, and several young men and boys to help."

Marcia asked the younger people if they knew Rosamond and James Weldon Johnson's "Lift Every Voice and Sing." Of course they did. In fact, they "were anxious to accept when we asked them to come in to the piano."

Then Geiger recalls Eartha's reaction, one that fits so many other remembrances of her.

"But as soon as we were there, Miss White took charge. She knew the song perfectly, of course, but announced that we'd sing only the first and last verses—the last to be sung very softly. Then at once she called for some of the old 'gospel songs' in which the old ladies could join."

Geiger remembers sympathizing with the disappointed young people. Only later did she understand that Eartha "counted the day an outing for her old folks and felt that they should be given first consideration."

The fact that Eartha didn't want or need material possessions the way other people did often confused them.

Sometimes it upset them. They didn't want to see someone make a virtue of turning down the things they wanted. Those same people who envied others' possessions, homes, and status also envied Eartha's rejection of those things.

Often it made people admire her, because it seemed her needs were other than ordinary, higher.

She seemed larger for the lack of the things she rejected. She was bigger for what she did not have.

She was compared, here and there, to St. Francis, who, in rejecting the clothes his wealthy family had afforded him, became a mendicant by stripping naked and leaving the church to go singing in the Italian fields and woods.

Almost seven decades after she first met Eartha, Frances Ewell said, "I remember her telling me after some disaster that she hadn't taken her clothes off for three days."

This powerful little woman, this giant, "used every penny for her people," Ewell recalled. "She dressed so plainly. She had no—why, she had the simplest clothes, and sometimes she just didn't even bother to comb her hair."

The little thought she gave to such things increased her stature. Ewell says she looked like Haile Salassie, "very small and very ascetic."

Ewell combines two depictions of Eartha that at first seem opposites. To understand Eartha, however, these opposites can't cancel each other out: they make her whole.

She speaks of Eartha being the best business*man* in Jacksonville, buying properties and selling them for profits that benefited the Mission and its constantly multiplying enterprises. In the business world, there was nothing it seemed Eartha couldn't do, but while she added constantly to her Mission, she simultaneously deprived herself.

"And she deprived herself in this way. She spent all her waking hours and many when she should have been asleep working for her people. I never saw anybody so single-minded and dedicated. She seemed to feel that she had the weight of the Negro population on her shoulders," and when Ewell first came to Jacksonville in 1909, she says, that depiction of tiny Eartha as Atlas was most accurate.

In 1910, a woman who signed her name Mrs. J.E. Young wrote Eartha a scathing letter, accusing her of "calling for" Young's husband. Eartha replied in kind.

The 1910 exchange shows the kind of suspicion that sometimes erupted toward this single black woman who managed her life independently. Allegations against Eartha lasted her whole life and centered on her uncanny ability to acomplish anything she set about to do. Not only did this single woman connect to black Jacksonville like no one else did, but she connected to white Jacksonville like no black man could and certainly no other black woman on her own.

Whether or not there was truth to allegations of Eartha's romantic relationships with different men in her youth, none of them can be verified.

"Miss White," Mrs. Young writes, "I am very sorry to say but the great charity worker of this city has caused quite a confussion at my home, last nigh when you sent the boys here and the children could not find the key, Frank stopped them, when I came they told me about it, and when I got at him he jumped on me and for me what he nor any other man or woman has ever done. And I blame you. If you and I should live until the trump sounds do n't you ever come nor send any one here with a message to my husband. Get one of your own."

That the letter begins by mocking Eartha's status as "the great charity worker of this city" and ends by telling Eartha to get a husband of her own implies that a single woman who occupies a position of importance is not to be trusted. I wonder how much Eartha's light skin and rumors of secret wealth and a white father could have compounded Mrs. Young's reaction.

Addressing Mrs. Young from her Oakland home at 853 Pippin Street in East Jacksonville, Eartha responded, "I am indeed sorry to hear of your family trouble and my advice would be to you as you and Mr. Young are husband and wife you should keep your private affairs to yourselves. I did not send for Mr. Young. The young men who are in the quartet met at my home and sent for him to practice and as he did not come they went to him. I always credited you of being a woman of high morals and having more common sence. I hope you will think this over and you will see I am not to blame. And as for asking me not to come or send to your home, why, as I have never been into your home, this request will be easily granted. Many thanks for your advice as to getting a husband of my own. That is not a easy matter for husbands are few and far between. When I am ready there is one in store for me without giving you any trouble. As you and I are not our Keepers and as time is fleeting and life is so short, it becomes me as a Christian to tell you that I freely forgive you for the wrong you have done me and I hope you will always observe the Second Commandment. As for casting reflections on my charity work. That is Gods work and he will take care of that. If this is a satisfactory reply please answer."

As I try to read back 104 years, Eartha's response seems convincing. But whom did she mean when she said a husband was "in store" for her when she was ready? Rhetorically, the letter is strongest when Eartha responds on her own terms. When she engages Mrs. Young's terms of the possession and baiting of husbands with an assurance that Eartha too could have a husband if and when she wanted one, she seems to lower her position.

But I know fully well there's no common ground on which I can stand to judge this letter. Perhaps Eartha knew exactly what to say to dissuade her accuser. She asks for a response, but must have known she wouldn't get one, a maneuver that she might have known would end the matter.

And if she was honest about the existence of a husband-to-be-had, gossip and rumors from then until now would accommodate such an assertion. Since those rumors survive, but no proof of their claim does, perhaps they were often, perhaps always, the result of community suspicions of this single black woman's power, and of the common observance that Eartha was so very much lighter-skinned than her mother.

Eartha was not her city's original "Angel of Mercy." Headlines from January 1914 *Florida Metropolis* articles offer prototypes.

Under Sister Mary Ann's influence, numerous women gave their lives and their identities to charity, to helping others, no need of acknowledgement from the public.

These women gave their hours to those suffering from Civil War, from Yellow Fever epidemics of the late 1870s and late 1880s.

Sister Mary Ann was born in Ireland, where she gave herself to God and then to suffering, and upon her death, to the women to whom she bequeathed her caregiving.

Eartha kept clippings of these headlines in her personal effects.

And 60 years before her own death and commemoration as Jacksonville's "angel of mercy," Eartha's clippings of Sister Mary Ann proclaimed, "Passed Quietly Away," and "Will Be Missed by Poor of Jacksonville," and "Entire Life Given to Charity. Many Noble Deeds During War Time and Yellow Fever Epidemic," and "Death of 'Angel of Mercy' Brings Genuine Regret to Residents of City."

I sit diagonally across from Patricia Moman Bell at a long wooden table on the second floor of the Clara White Mission, with several files and an archival catalog Bell compiled five years ago.

Photographs of Eartha with her opera company hang on a nearby wall. An organ donated to Eartha by the Duke Ellington Orchestra stands near her Victrola.

Pat Bell served on the Mission board and helped with the allocation of the surrounding museum pieces after Eartha died. Her father, Lawrence C. Moman, served as chairman of the Eartha M. M. White Nursing Home. Pat's aunt, Ethel Moman Powell, served on the Mission board, but more importantly was Eartha's close personal friend.

Pat's more likely to call Eartha "Jacksonville's Jane Addams," referring to the Nobel Peace Prize-winning social worker, feminist, and co-founder of the famous Hull House in Chicago, than "Jacksonville's Mother Teresa."

Ethel Powell worked four decades as a Florida Home Demonstration Agent, a U.S. Department of Agriculture "Cooperative Extension System" position that required her to visit homes and teach women how to clean, to cook nutritionally, or to make clothes, and this work led her to help Eartha establish a "canning kitchen" at the Mission, preserving locally grown food for those who most needed it.

Pat has a Master's in Museum Science and has curated in San Francisco and New York, where she was the first chief curator of the Studio Museum of Harlem. She grew up on Eighth Street in the black upper-middle-class neighborhood of Sugar Hill, though she says they never called it that then. She speaks with a measured and thoughtful cadence that reminds me of Maya Angelou.

She remembers Eartha from when she herself was a child. "She was very powerful in a very quiet way. She had this self-assurance. And very seldom was she still. To talk with her was to walk with her."

Meg Fisher, vice president of the Mission, tells me, "Eartha did not separate herself from the people she sought to help. She dressed herself from the same piles of donated clothes. She stayed here at the Mission every night, just as they did. And she spoke to them the same way she'd speak to a Mayor or the president of a large company."

Pat Bell tells me it's important to see Eartha's early ventures in the context of the late-19th and early-20th century Negro Women's Club Movement. "Being part of this movement was important," she says, "because this was a network of women all over the country who were trying to do the same kinds of things in their communities."

As Gerda Lerner put it in a 1974 *Journal of Negro History* article, "Contrary to widely held racist myths, black communities have a continuous record of self-help, institution-building and strong organization to which black women have made continuous contributions."

Lerner points to Margaret Murray Washington, who organized and was president of the Tuskegee Women's Club in 1895. The club was prototypical of hundreds of others in the next three decades. Club meetings offered "advice on child care, home economics, vegetable gardening and sewing."

Equally as important, Lerner says, "The welfare activities, as recorded in club records, show strong class prejudices on the part of the club women and reflect a patronizing, missionary attitude in dealing with the poor."

Pat points out to me, "The women who were involved in the Negro Women's Club Movement were the same kind of women who were involved in the Women's Club Movement, their white counterpart," meaning that, yes, they were educated, but as education was the exclusive domain of the wealthy, they were "often women who were married to men who were successful in business, so they had time and means to do their volunteer work and 'community uplift,' the phrase used at the time."

In 1913, Eartha brought Margaret Murray Washington, the wife of Booker T. Washington, to give the primary address at the City Federation of Colored Women's Clubs. One photograph shows Washington in the center of a group of men and women before the Old Folks' Home, with Eartha in front at the side.

The Mission still owns several copies of *The Open Door*, a publication of the Phyllis Wheatley Association, formed in

Cleveland, Ohio in 1911 as the Working Girls' Home Association, renamed that same year for the black American poet of the late 1700s.

Long before I tried to figure out how a black person, how a woman, how a single woman, how a (mostly secretly) "illegitimate" single black woman could possibly have had so much power in Jacksonville, Pat had thought about Eartha's social and historical context and the sequence of events in her life.

"What was it about Miss White? Just because she'd had a soup kitchen, it does not necessarily follow that she'd establish a tuberculosis hospital. Or the Old Folks' Home. Or an adoption agency. Or services to prisoners. Or a home for unwed mothers. It doesn't logically follow just because you have a soup kitchen."

Pat thinks of her Aunt Ethel Moman Powell and her move from Jackson to Jacksonville as indicative of black women's involvement in the Women's Club Movement.

"Ethel came here in the 1920s from Mississippi, where my father's family's from. And her job with the State of Florida offered her security for about 40 years, until she retired. But when she got to Florida, Uncle Powell, we called him Uncle Powell, George W. Powell met her and he fell head over heels and they got married.

"Well, Uncle Powell just happened to be a real estate broker. He owned his own company, and they did land development. People assumed, ah, in the vernacular, that he had money. They were more than financially stable. And that allowed her to do a lot of things she wouldn't have been able to do otherwise."

Though Pat understands Eartha's early institutional organization in the context of the Women's Club Movement, she also believes Eartha stood apart as a single black woman, "though she did have the monetary support of her family, not her black family necessarily."

Even if that support wasn't directly supplied, surely Clara could tell certain people what Eartha needed, as a child, and see that it happened. "I mean, let's face it. Eartha spent time in New York with a wealthy Jewish family as a young girl. She spent time in New York in school and then as part of an opera company. I mean....*hello?* This was not your typical Southern black life. Unless you were part of the black middle class."

The fact that Eartha was not the first of Clara's 13 children to live did not mean Clara wanted any less for her. If Clara did give birth to a dozen children only to watch 11 of them die, only to find she had to adopt out her daughter Bertha, she nevertheless brought Eartha up to think she had a very special purpose on this earth.

She was treated no less as a "chosen child" than if that Old Testament-style myth about her naming were true. In some ways, you might say, the myth is as true as the truth.

38

So the significant role Eartha played in the city's progressive social movements connected her to other centers of power throughout Florida and the rest of the South.

An anonymous conspiratorial letter came to Eartha on November 15, 1927 from Lynchburg, Virginia, which its writer says he is "only passing through." The writer signs off, "Faithfully Yours," but signs no name. The envelope contains no return address.

Mysteriously he writes, "Knowing there is a close watch kept on the mail, I have not attempted to send a line to my people since I left Key West, Nov. 12 last year—"

Who wrote this letter, and from whom was he running?

Was he in legal trouble? Perhaps he was some sort of activist? Or was there some kind of trouble in relation to whomever he meant by "my people"?

He tells Eartha, "It is through you that I am going to take care of all my Unfinished Business at Key West and West Palm Beach."

The writer wishes Eartha to visit Meridian, Mississippi. He gives an address—123 10th Avenue, where she would be able to "stop with my people—Rev. J.J. Overstreet and wife Mary."

Though I've found references to a black Mississippi minister with that name, I've not found anything that would connect him to a conspiratorial or secret cause. Of course, secret causes were kept secret.

And if Eartha should see his wife, he writes, "I want you to tell all that I have told you. Tell her every word just as I told it to you—I mean everything about my business and my headquarters when I am in the South and stopping place when I am in the North—I want to see her and tell her the whole story and how the Lord is taking care of me—"

Though he says he's just passing through Lynchburg, alludes to business in South Florida, and leaves no return address, Eartha evidently knows how to reach him and has recently spoken with him.

"If you ever see any member of my family send word to my wife and tell her to go your home at once and Miss White I want you to ship her to me and I will re-imburse you as it will take a good sum of money to get her from your home to me."

He further states, "I want her to know that you will furnish her the money to come to me after she gets to Jacksonville—Tell her that in going to Jax—to make no display of her trip but get her ticket to Birmingham and then buy another ticket to fund Jax—"

It will take about $20, he says, to get his wife from Meridian to Jacksonville, and from Birmingham she should take the Seminole Limited.

When his wife "gets there," he'll make everything "alright everywhere."

"I want my people to know that you are the only living human that knows anything about my business and I want them to tell you anything and everything that they ought to tell you and I want them to know that they are safe in telling."

Who could this writer have been? Was he as important as he makes himself sound, and if so, how so—religiously, politically, and in what circles? Who were his "people"? Did whatever he meant by his Unfinished Business— capitalizations his—require such clandestine communication?

Furthermore, whatever the answers to these questions may be, what was his relationship with Eartha? Why was she, and how did she become, the one living person who knew the present conditions of his business?

He again expresses regret at not having been in touch with his family and his people, and alludes to a search for him that he's thus far escaped. "I couldn't send any money home by mail—because I know the Drag Net that is spread—"

He speaks vaguely of things news stories have told of him. "I have been accused of some ugly things since I left Key West but I pay no attention to newspaper talk—"

I've been unable to find any newspaper headlines that correspond to this letter.

"If I had had 5 hours notice I could have fixed everything alright but when I saw what was about to happen I walked out and hung up the keys and left that city."

Suddenly I wonder if I'm reading the confidential and urgent appeal of an important man in trouble or the ramblings of a paranoid schizophrenic.

Returning to suspicions of watchers of the mail, he tells Eartha, "Please tell my people to not write to you very much—And if they do write whenever it is convenient to mail their letters from another place."

He closes his letter, "I am relying and depending on you through the power of God."

39

In considering explanations for this mysterious letter, I'm looking for connections between Eartha White and Marcus Garvey's Universal Negro Improvement Association, even though politically, such a connection would make little sense.

The anonymous writer sent his letter to Eartha within two months of Garvey's public dismissal of Florida UNIA division leader Laura Adorkor Kofey. Kofey used Jacksonville as her headquarters and is buried not far from Eartha White in a white concrete mausoleum in Jacksonville's Old City Cemetery.

In 1928, four months after Eartha received this conspiratorial letter, Kofey was assassinated in the pulpit in Miami.

I won't try to force a connection where I don't know that one exists. Garvey was an early Black Nationalist and Pan-Africanist leader who encouraged world-wide black solidarity and the possibility of a "return" to Africa for many black Americans. Eartha's pragmatism and philosophy occupy the opposite end of the spectrum from the romanticism of early Black Nationalism.

Surely Laura Adorkor Kofey and Eartha White were aware of each other, and Eartha was pragmatic enough to partner in select endeavors with people who thought differently, even antithetically, from her.

Pan-Africanists had visited Jacksonville in the past—in the 1880s, the Liberian diplomat and writer Edward Wilmot Blyden stayed at the home of Squire English, the city's wealthiest black merchant—but no leader like Kofey had previously headquartered in Jacksonville.

Her story's extraordinary. She claimed to be an African princess who, while deathly ill in Ghana, heard disembodied voices tell her to go to America. When she decided to do as the voices bid, her people were already preparing her funeral pyre.

So she came to New York, met Garvey, then wandered and preached through Detroit and Chicago. She was destined for Florida, though, where she quickly established her base in Jacksonville.

A Jacksonville reporter for Garvey's newspaper *Negro World* said, "The princess speaks every night in the week and twice on Sunday." *Negro World* articles throughout the summer of 1927 reported Kofey's speaking in Jacksonville, Tampa, Miami, and St. Petersburg, holding each "audience spellbound" and bringing hundreds of new recruits to the UNIA. Three weeks of nightly preaching in Jacksonville added more than 900 new members.

But from Laura Adorkor Kofey's first appearance, people had suspicions. She was also known as Laura Adorka Kofi, Laura Adorker Coffey, and Laura Champion. Rumors spread that she was born in or not far from Atlanta, Georgia. Then came the stories of her embezzling UNIA funds.

In September of 1927, Garvey wrote a UNIA agent stationed at the Richmond Hotel in LaVilla, "I have given Mrs. Kofey no authority to collect funds from members for any kind of African exodus. I know nothing of her proposition for saw mills and ships. I shall not be held responsible for her activities in that direction. If the people have been defrauded they have legal recourse. I authorized no one to give her authority to collect funds for such a purpose."

After her dismissal, Kofey started her own organization based on her considerable Florida following and called it the African Universal Church and Commercial League. Six months later, gunmen entered the Miami church where Kofey was speaking, and one of them put a bullet in her head. The murder was never solved, though authorities suspected UNIA involvement.

After the assassination, a South African named Eli B'usabe Nyombolo and a Sierra Leonean named F. Adineye Ajaye took over the African Universal Church. Sixteen years later, Nyombolo, also known as L'il Brother, headquartered it in a compound he called Adorkaville off New Kings Road on Jacksonville's far rural and mostly black Northside.

When Nyombolo died in 1970, the remains of Kofey's original organization split and a small splinter group still operates as the Tabernacle African Universalist Church in a thousand-square-foot Old Kings Road sanctuary built in 1922. They have an official creed, which includes the lines, "I believe in St. Adorka, / the saintly messenger of God." The creed calls Kofey a martyr.

So does the plaque on Laura Kofey's whitewashed concrete-block mausoleum in the Old City Cemetery. It reads, "1893 1928 Princess Laura Adorkor Kofi 'Affectionately known as Mother Kofi' The Martyred African Princess of Asofa, Ghana (Gold Coast West Africa). Assassinated in the pulpit on March 8, 1928, Miami, Florida. Founder of the African Universal Churches."

After the assassination, the followers of "Mother Kofi" brought her body back to Jacksonville, after enormous funerals in Miami and West Palm Beach. At Pearl and State Streets, Huff's Funeral Home charged a quarter to see her body.

The funeral director sent word to Ghana, but said he didn't hear back for five months. It's unclear to whom he sent word or how he knew whom to contact. He varnished Kofey's dead body daily and more than 10,000 people came to see her corpse in the summer in the humid Jacksonville heat.

When I walk the dirt road through the 11 acres of Adorkaville, all I see is three indistinct ramshackle wooden buildings collapsing into the earth. The other houses, built by the original members, have already been demolished. Cicadas scream in the thick trees. The place is more woods than "ville," and I'm trying to imagine the Africans who supposedly came here to teach Adorkaville residents their native languages.

And at the moment, I seem to have come a long way from Eartha, but I suspect I'm not so far after all. Though Eartha's philosophy and priorities were vastly different from those of Garveyites or Mother Kofi's African Universal Churches, in the 1920s and '30s, all the roads of black Jacksonville somehow led through Eartha. Would Eartha have partnered some random Tuesday with L'il Brother Nyombolo to get some fresh fruit to some needy people? I have no doubt.

I did find a brief notation in Dan Schafer's research notes for his manuscript that says, "Laura Adawkey Koffee, 1928 to Jax, Garveyite church has paper. Soutel Drive on L going to Picketville," and refers to "Koffeeville."

Deacon Kubi Keyes of Tabernacle African Universal Church tells me that church elders recall Schafer's visit, that Schafer had interviewed them about Kofey, but that in searching their archives, they could find no reference to any connection between Mother Kofey and Eartha White.

Schafer tells me his visit was based on a false lead. Someone had given him a tip that the church contained various pertinent memoirs in its archive. Schafer found no connection between Eartha and Mother Kofey. His church interview became part of an historical film series televised across the state, though the only copies were kept in film canisters apparently destroyed or lost years ago.

So I find myself in a strange echo of what, previously unbeknownst to me, Dan Schafer had investigated almost 40 years ago. Maybe it's the postmodernist in me that's likewise intrigued by false leads and dead ends that hyperlink in surprising directions. Sometimes I like to sit outside at night and imagine a map of all these connections and disconnections. It would look like a map of the synapses in our brains.

But what brought me out to this dirt road that cuts through these Adorkaville longleaf pines was that paranoid conspiratorial letter sent anonymously to Eartha White. Even if I never find out who wrote it, all around me I feel the long-ago hum, as of cicadas in the encompassing green, of so many lost and invisible cultural, religious, and political circuit boards operating *sub rosa* in Jim Crow Florida.

Desperate people wrote to Eartha from all around Florida, from around the South, from as far away as Illinois, to ask her if they might be eligible to adopt a child from Eartha's "Orphan Home." Some letters responded to ads Eartha had placed in the important black newspaper *The Chicago Defender*. One letter addressed a "Mr. Ertha White" as "Dear Sir."

On September 8, 1919, a Reverend C.W. White of Plant City, Florida, wrote, "I wrote you some times ago for a lady friend who wanted to Get Infermation concerning as to how to get a GA girl from The Home I havent any answer yet. As her name arpear at the Top will ask you in Gods name Will you pleas write her soon as posible as she is very anctious To hear from you will you pleas write her."

A Ms. W. L. Jones wrote from Tampa in 1929, "I am writing you in Regards to a child That we would like one if you have one under 2 or 3 years old. We prefer a girl if you have one So will you kindly give us a description of the child please let me hear from you by return mail."

And on September 27, 1929, a woman named Ada Hayward at 1507 West Union Street in Jacksonville pleaded, "Mrs Eartha White Just a few line to you my nurse to me to se you about a little Baby. I lost mine in Hospitile and cant get no more since my orpration and I realy. wants one can you help me any. Ans at once Please."

In August, 1929, a woman named Emily Norton Stuart wrote Eartha from Kingston, Jamaica, asking about her mother who had died at the Old Folks' Home.

Before writing Eartha, Stuart had written her mother in Eartha's care. "I wrote her once or twice, poor dear, begging her to come home, the children so much wanted to see her but her excuse was she didn't want to come to be a burden, she was content to remain."

Stuart says her mother wrote to her of Eartha's and Clara's kindness, and implores Eartha to write as soon as possible. "I know you would explain all my mother's circumstances to me as she has been away for such a long period, all of forty years."

Stuart says she's recently lost her home, having fallen on hard times, and that Eartha should reply to her at her daughter's address at 666 East Bay Street, Nassau, Bahamas.

She feels forever grateful for the care Eartha took of her mother, and wonders likewise if Eartha has any advice she could offer her daughter. "Taking you as a friend, do you think Amy, my eldest daughter, would get on with beauty culture or music in Jacksonville?"

Almost a decade after Clara's death, to which I'll soon return, Eartha's Aunt Mirriah McTain wrote her just before Christmas, 1929. "I am unable to come to see you and I want you send me somthing—my clothes is geting thin and I want you to send me some more. I want you to send me some under clothes and some shoes," she demanded.

She reminds Eartha that "xmas" is right around the corner and says, "I am looking for a Box from you like Sister uster send me. I aint hardly got no dishes near all my plates is gone you know that Auntie is looking for somthing from your little hands."

After signing off, Aunt Mirriah adds, "be sure and Answer this letter right Back."

In the first letter, Pearl Thompson wrote Eartha from Vero Beach, Florida,

"Mrs. Martha M. White will you please let me no where I can get me a Little offerin girl ar boy from 12 month or 2 years old let me no by return mail I am Pearl Thompson."

In Pearl Thompson's second letter from the summer of 1930, she wrote,

"Mrs. Martha M. White I written you afew days ago asking for information about offerin children I haven got any children an would Be glad for one are two the white Supendent of the white offerin home Sent me your name an said you was Very inrested in the colored offerin and sent a Picture of 2 white little girls I am a Colored woman and desire colored children if you have them are know where I can get one are two Please let me know By Return Mail if I can get them are if I cant get them are if I have to come for them or can Send me the Picture."

The next day, another woman wrote Eartha, "Can you give me any information where I can find a colored boy that needs a home? I would rather have an orphan for I would know that he was worthy, but any good, rugged, strong boy 12-14 year of age would answer, that I could teach our way, and give a good home until he was of age. I want one that can save me steps and do errands about the place, and be generally useful."

I can't help but wonder if all of these letters are written by women, if any of them is written by a man through his wife. Each is signed by a woman.

Some of the letters ask for a child to replace a lost baby, just as Eartha was supposed to be her mother's 13th child and first to live. Some of the letters sound like they're asking for a servant. Some of them ask for a strong boy to do chores. Some ask for a teenage girl.

Often, I can't figure out the legitimacy or the sincerity of a request. I worry about what may've happened to children requested in certain ways. Sometimes I wonder if the children and grandchildren of slaves requested adoption in terms that echoed advertisement or inquiry for the purchase of people as property.

Very few records at the Clara White Mission attest to Eartha's responses to such letters, though those that exist indicate thorough reviews of applicants and their living situations.

In 1930, a representative from the Humane Society, writing from the Hotel Burbridge downtown, ends a letter with a P.S. that says,

"Where I was at Fernandina [north of town], a very nice colored man told me of three motherless boys that he was anxious about, ages about 7 to 12, not going to school, they are his near neighbors I understand. He said they were at—said always around there—8th and Escambia and growing up wild. He wanted me to look them up. He said it was half an hour walk from where I was. I do not know the Fernandina streets, he did not know children's last name, by time I had gotten a conveyance would hardly have had time before bus left to try to find the children, and if I went over and tried, I hardly know what a stranger like me without any authority could do to help get them to school. If I could find them which in limited time seems doubtful. I wonder if you know anyone in the town who could hunt them up. The man who told me of them was so kind and so anxious about them."

A November 1932 letter from the Children's Home Society of Florida informed a woman named Ida Dixon, "We do not handle any colored children. I would suggest that you write a letter to Eartha White."

For Mother's Day, the Mission collected flour and flowers, and offered both to needy mothers and their children during a program called the Golden Rule Observance.

44

And who was that little boy, and who was that baby, in that 1930s' picture published in *A Pictorial Review of Activities Conducted under the Auspices of the Clara White Mission*? How long did they live at Eartha's "Orphan Home"? Who adopted them? And what did they do with the rest of their lives? Who loved them and whom did they love? How long did they live? Is either of them alive today, some 80 years later? And if that little boy is now an old man, does he have any idea where he came from? Does he know this picture of him was published? If he saw the photograph today, would he know that little boy had been him? Does he remember Eartha White? And who deserted these two little malnourished children in an abandoned house?

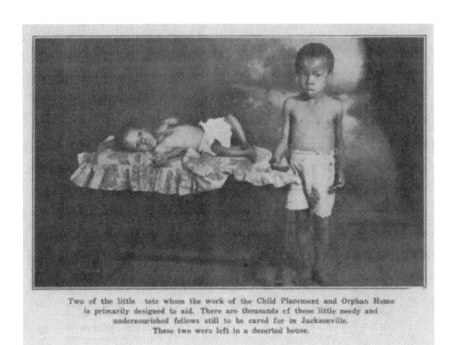

Two of the little tots whom the work of the Child Placement and Orphan Home is primarily designed to aid. There are thousands of these little needy and undernourished fellows still to be cared for in Jacksonville. These two were left in a deserted house.

And who in anger turned mother and child out by themselves in retribution, as though the infant in this second

1930s' photograph had asked for this beginning, as though any mother should have the possibilities of loving her child curtailed when she gives birth?

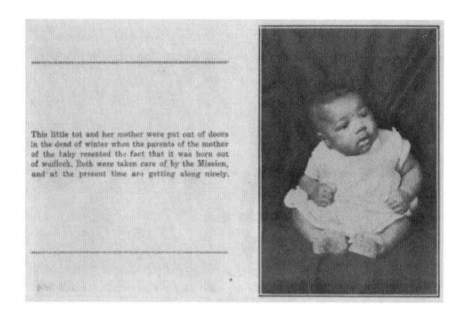

This little tot and her mother were put out of doors in the dead of winter when the parents of the mother of the baby resented the fact that it was born out of wedlock. Both were taken care of by the Mission, and at the present time are getting along nicely.

On April 20, 1957, Miss Clarice M. Blue wrote Eartha from Staten Island, New York, with a most unusual and lovely request, one that must have appealed to the musician and singer in Eartha, to Eartha as friend of J. Rosamond and James Weldon Johnson, to Eartha as erstwhile opera singer, to Eartha who left behind thousands of blues and classical music and opera records scattered throughout the Mission when she died, to Eartha who attended the January 1952 Marian Anderson concert at the Duval County Armory.

Miss Blue wrote Miss White, "I would like to know if it is possible to get a piano reasonable. I am interested in a little girl with a broken home who likes music. I would like to get her the piano if possible."

45

September, 1931.

Leroy Daniel Singleton, adopted to "Aunt Daisy" and Uncle Cornelius Robinson, one of the many orphans to pass through Eartha's child placement services, wrote to her first from New York City and then from Palatka, Florida.

Though the apparent purpose of the letters is to ask Eartha to sell a piece of property for him, Leroy spends much of the 14 handwritten pages of his first letter complaining about his adoptive aunt and uncle and his preacher. He swears to Eartha that he doesn't like to gossip, but that if he can't share such feelings with his godmother, he can't share them with anyone.

He says he understands Eartha has extensive experience in real estate and she can take any share she desires of the profits from the sale of his house.

He says his Uncle Cornelius won't help him at all. "I don't think that he has ever did any real hard work in his life, only once did he ever hold down a job and that was during war time and I guess he done it to keep from going to war, he has never worked before that and never since. I guess you think he's a big man in the church."

Leroy says he asked his Aunt Daisy why his uncle "didn't get a church like the other preachers that started out with him," but says, "My Aunt Daisy have got a mind like a child, he wouldn't do my mother like he do her."

He says, "My Aunt Daisy gets up early in the morning to cook for him and where's he going? not a place in the world, he do the same kind of work that I used to do when I was ten years of age."

It was Leroy's grandfather's property that his uncle held. Leroy contended that white people would have made the uncle sell the property and split the proceeds amongst the heirs.

"Were he to do this he would be compelled to go to work, he know this and always refuse to talk of selling saying, that he can get more later on. In speaking of my grandfather's property, the only reason that I think he attend church so much is because they send him to different places as a delegate and he should get that job easy as he's the only man in the whole church who have the time to spare, the rest of them have to work."

Leroy says that if Eartha were to give his uncle a job, Cornelius would never forgive her for it. He owed all the banks in Palatka, never repaid loans, and constantly put Leroy's property, inherited from his grandfather, up as security against his debts.

Cornelius had borrowed from Leroy's mother, and when she died, he borrowed from Leroy's father, and when he died, he borrowed from Leroy, who was very young and already working hard, and whom Cornelius made to fear the loss of his bequest.

"Every time that he borrow he would say that he would pay it all back as the money that I loan him would help him to get more."

Then Leroy asks Eartha to consider his status as her godson and as an orphan she'd helped in the past.

"Well you know I was saving my money for a future but with him borrowing like he did I couldn't save a dime and some times he kind of made it plain that if it was not for him I couldn't get along so good being an Orphan but I fooled him, one day I pulled out and have been gone for a year and a half."

Last winter, he traveled to California. Presently, Leroy writes from New York, but his "aunt" and "uncle" live in Palatka, and Cornelius has previously written Eartha about selling some property for them in Jacksonville's Murray Hill neighborhood.

Leroy asks Eartha not to respond to Daisy's real estate appeals, since his aunt only parrots his lazy manipulative uncle's demands, and he further asks Eartha to inform him of any requests Daisy makes of her.

Three months later, just before Christmas, Leroy writes to Eartha from Palatka. He's back home, he's desperate, and he doesn't understand why she hasn't responded. Was it all the bad things he said about his aunt and uncle and his adoption?

He says, "I am real surprise and I feel real bad that you did not answer the two letters that I wrote." He checked at various places for misdelivered mail, and asked people who knew Eartha if perhaps she were sick or too busy.

"I put this letter in the bible and said an prayer over it before I sealed it because on this loan do all my hope and happiness lie."

I can find no evidence of what Eartha thought about Leroy Daniel Singleton's case, or of whether she ever responded.

January, 1932.

"My boy Isiah Breaker I wrote him several times and could not hear from him My aunt wrote me stating the boy was getting along all right but he was not well and did not look well Mother broke the letter open and read it an we both prayed and worried to the Lord to help us."

Eartha's "sincere friend" in Clearwater, Florida had demanded then that her aunt in Newark, New Jersey send "her boy" down to Florida right away.

Ora had been lucky, she tells Eartha, that her boy was sent straight home to Clearwater, without having to change trains, his voyage "encluding meals," for $25.

Ora happily describes "the boy" as "fat," saying he "looks well and was dressed very nice a nice fur coat he had 1 suit case one nice hand bag," but says, "his mind was very bad he was not him self at all so I made the boy go to bed and rest a while."

Mrs. Ora Williams says she'd then taken him to the best doctor in Clearwater, "and he said to keep the boy home no visitors no schools no books he said the boy so young had studied to hard he had to many things on his mind."

And then she comes to the crux of her concern.

The doctor had taken the boy's blood. He'd seemed so nonchalant about it, but the blood was the life and identity, the vital force. This doctor had taken the blood and all the true problems had arisen therefrom.

"Dr said he had not got the returns back now it seems very strange that a Blood Test takes from Dec. 26 1931 till Jan 5th 1932 and if I had of known that it would have to be sent to Jax it was sent to Tampa or Jax so I decided tonight to write you, so you could please do me this favor keep your eyes open and your ears listning.

Then Ora refers to possible changes of name for "the boy" and demands of Eartha that she explain arcane knowledge about concerns of the "State Board" for information the missing "Blood Test" might reveal.

"I gave his name as Isiah Breaker as Same as befor because to change a name looks suspicious and will get you in serious trouble and that old trouble long ago is forgotten for it was nol prossed and thrown out so please write me a good consoleing letter and tell me why the State Board holds that Blood Test of Isiah Breaker it went to Tampa or Jax Fla why cant they sends the returns back they cant do nothing to the boy For he was set free."

Ora Williams demands that Eartha be the eyes and ears of Jacksonville, "for there is nothing to low for crackers to do."

Then she appeals to Eartha personally.

"The boy," she says, is "18 years old Very Neat Clean," and is "so much help to me in waiting on mother he cleans up and cooks and will do anything you tell him Would you let him remain here in Clearwater with Mother and I. I dont see why of course I would not like for his life to be stolen from him for nothing."

Mrs. Williams calls all these items to her defense because she cannot see "why they want to hold his Blood."

She prays "the Devil wont get busy again" and reminds Eartha that "no one in Jax knows the boy is heer in Fla."

In a postscript, Ora says, "I did not mention to the boy the delay of the Blood Test neither mother for he is sick and has had enough worry in his younger days for his head to be white and my aunt just made a slave out of him and would tell him you cant go back home?"

The doctor says his "lungs heart urine Physical condition is wonderfull only so young studying and thinking so hard and it was so sad the morning he arrived my mother said to him grandmothers baby did you want to come home O he broke down in tears and said O grandmother I wanted to help Aunt Ora take care of you but she—[Ora's aunt]—would take my money."

In a January 1932 letter, on the outside folding of which read, "Read this First," Ora Williams tells Eartha, "The boy is improving nicely and is a lot of help to me he cleans up cooks and helps to wash. I did not get any returns from his Blood. So I wont bother any more I dont know where they sent it to Tampa or Jax and I am not going to find out Will you please pray with me that nothing turns up of the past tense some time I will bring the boy over to see you when I can catch a good motor car over to Jax."

She signs off, "From your devoted and sincere friend."

The inference across these letters is Eartha's instrumentality in Ora Williams's adoption of her nephew and Ora's constant concern that someone else in the family might lay claim to him. *Someone* might claim him through closer blood relation, that secret language, and her lack of understanding of who received the results of "her boy"'s blood tests and where they were sent raises her anxiety to paranoia.

But she assures Eartha that Isaiah works so hard for her and brings her comfort, while Ora's aunt in Newark only treated him like a slave.

My concerns about the legitimacy of some of the letters Eartha received, asking her for specifically described children in need of a home, are apparently not unfounded.

On a cool early February night in 2014, I leave the lovely bed-and-breakfast that Dan Schafer and his wife run in Jacksonville's Riverside Avondale district, holding several folders of notes, old letters, and meeting minutes Schafer was kind enough to loan me after he'd dug through old files and boxes.

In these notes I soon find a faded copy of the Council of Social Agencies' minutes from a July 20, 1944 meeting at Jacksonville's Seminole Hotel, introductory notes indicating the Florida legislature should address "the baby racket," though this term, as scandalously tragic as it sounds, is not further defined or explained.

In 1950, a Tennessee state investigation shut down the Tennessee Children's Home Society, privately run for a quarter century by the nefarious Georgia Tann, who threatened impoverished single mothers and had their children kidnapped from nursery schools in order to sell them to wealthy Southern families.

If outfits of child-racketeering were conducted through, or indirectly on the backs of, such apparently noble agencies as orphanages, Eartha's reaction was to create a "school for delinquent negro girls."

Rather than simply match orphans with those who requested children by gender or strength or ability to contribute labor, Eartha's new school could keep children, and specifically girls who might be otherwise exploited, close to her, and allow her to help them toward adulthood.

The minutes note that Eartha was "appointed as chairman of legislation to secure from the legislature an appropriation for a school for delinquent negro girls."

Eartha had helped organize a group of Jewish, Catholic, and Protestant women to appeal to Duval County to allow the school.

When the County claimed they couldn't do anything to help "unless legislature told them they could do so," Eartha organized a diverse women's group to appeal to the state legislature, and "although they were very busy they said they decided to present this as a joint appeal here and the thing went through."

Despite Eartha's legislative victory, she told the Council of Social Agencies that such current facilities as the state prison farm at Starke, Florida, were insufficient. She also protested the presence of a home for needy young girls being housed adjacent to a state prison.

Eartha referred to certain legislative precedents that had fallen short 30 years before and offered to obtain data from court files on the numbers of young girls who needed care.

In undated directions from the middle 1940s in the possession of the Clara White Mission, Eartha dictated that someone—perhaps it was Grayce Bateman in her earliest years working for her—

"Please write a recommendation to the Parental Home Board Duval County: '1st requesting that one of the present buildings on Jessie Street be opened at once for the Care of Negro Girls.

'2nd that Miss Lula Braden be given the position as Cook or dietition [sic].

'3rd that Miss Clementine Days be given the position as teacher having the preference of those who have been previously recommended on account of her Musical Ability and Already she has the endorsement of Supt. King.'"

In the same 1944 meeting, she argued for "a place in this city to put temporary [sic] insane persons," other than "in the County Jail."

Eartha was almost 70 years old, and by general historical consensus, the Civil Rights Movement wouldn't begin for another 11 years.

But in 1944, she still had her hand in almost every Progressive concern in the city of Jacksonville. Her concerns with criminal justice focused on the reasons for crime among the least fortunate, and her long history of helping black children, and in particular black girls, had led her to respond to the threats of a "baby racket" by extending her orphanage services toward schools for young "delinquents."

49

I've been following particular social and political trajectories, but I need to back up to show a wider range of Eartha's enterprises and passions.

While teaching part-time in Bayard, when the century was still new, she'd taught school at Stanton in LaVilla and worked part-time as secretary for the Afro-American Life Insurance Company.

With almost Puritanical frugality, she'd managed to save enough to open a dry goods store, make it profitable, then sell it. She'd started, operated, and sold a janitorial service, then a laundry that advertised, "Put your duds in our suds. We wash anything but a dirty conscience." Almost all profits went into charity work and further investment.

She raised money for the segregated black cemeteries the city's white civic leaders would never consider maintaining.

She convinced the City Council of the need for a playground and park in the Oakland neighborhood near the Old Folks' Home. She had already accumulated the property.

She organized the Boys' Improvement Club, and channeled black teenagers into athletics and the arts with her "Save 1,000 Boys from Juvenile Court" movement, for which Eartha wrote and produced a didactic "side cracking Minstrel" play called *It Pays to Go Straight.*

As founder of the Boys' Club, she warned parents that "the 'Cops and Robbers,' the 'Shoot-Em Dead,' and the 'Double Pistol Packing Gunman' games played today will give them the courage to use these weapons at the least provocation later."

She became an active member of the local chapter of the National Negro Welfare League and the official historian of the Jacksonville chapter of the National Negro Business League and later the National Business League.

When Eartha met Booker T. Washington, author of *Up from Slavery* and early promoter of the idea of black empowerment as self-reliance in the face of monstrous white oppression, she was already practicing what he preached.

Long before Stokely Carmichael and the Black Panthers made "Black Power" a radical political slogan in the 1960s and '70s, Martin Luther King thought of black empowerment as black business and political enterprise. And long before King, Washington influenced people like Eartha to do for the black community what no one else would do for them.

Most people now consider Washington a conservative "accommodation- ist," a charge that caught momentum after the 1895 Atlanta Compromise, an agreement written largely by Washington to bridge black and white Southern leaders. The compromise was that blacks would submit to white political rule while whites guaranteed blacks basic legal rights and educational possibilities. Obviously, the latter didn't happen, and the compromise asked far too little for Southern black people.

Some say the progress of Civil Rights in the 20th century makes the Atlanta Compromise look more backward than it really was and that political thinkers and agents must operate in the historical terms of their time.

For Eartha, in the first decades of the 20th century, Booker T. Washington represented the possibility for black people in Jacksonville to have as many of the rights and services the city's white residents received as Eartha herself could secure for them. And she embraced all of it—black business, black political organization, black ownership, black leadership and back service to black people, though she also never turned away whites who needed her help.

When Eartha helped charter Jacksonville's chapter of the Negro Business League, she brought Booker T. Washington to town for a banquet and speech attended by 2,500 people.

Eartha had accompanied Abraham Lincoln Lewis of the Afro-American Life Insurance Company to Boston to help create the Negro Business League in 1900. It elected Washington its first president.

I've mentioned that Margaret Murray Washington, wife of Booker T., visited Eartha and the City Federation of Colored Women's Clubs in Jacksonville in March 1913, and the two women visited black public schools, Bethel Baptist Institutional Church, and Eartha's Old Folks' Home, where Margaret with her flower-laden purse and her draped black hat visited the old men, some of whom had been dropped off, anonymously, in the middle of the night, at the Old Folks' Home's wooden front porch.

50

Eartha visited state and county prisoners, brought them cigars, and conducted Bible study with them.

Throughout her life, Eartha worked with and for prisoners, and though she may have waxed didactic, I've seen nothing to indicate she judged the prisoners or condescended to them.

At UNF's Eartha White Collection, I've read letters from prisoners, as well as numerous case histories and court documents.

Such cases include young men who shot or stabbed a friend or rival.

They include the 19 year-old girl sick with a kidney infection, whom someone reported to the police as an indigent old woman. She'd been abandoned by her husband with their two year-old daughter and her eight year-old sister, behind on rent and unable to work.

Such cases include the baby who was left alone in a back yard, whom a "junk man" come to reclaim scrap metal found eating potash on a back porch.

Such cases include the woman with three small children whose husband suddenly "stopped eating altogether" and started staying out late. When she found a gun she didn't know he had and appropriated it for her own use, since she felt unsafe without him at home at night, he told her he wanted the gun back, but did not want her or their children. Then he began to threaten her. She told Eartha, "I have to leave. I leave to keep him from killing me."

By 1933, Eartha had been orchestrating Sunday religious services at the Duval County Prison Farm for a quarter century and Vaudeville performances for years.

In 1945, she protested a girls' reform school being built at the state prison at Raiford, Florida, arguing that the purpose of such a school should be to steer girls from a criminal future, while the placement of the school at the prison would effectively tell these girls that crime and prison were foregone conclusions.

In the summer of 1954, while Civil Rights supporters across the South worked for the abolition of prison labor and prison farm systems, Eartha protested the abolition of the Duval County Prison Farm.

Sociologists, historians, and activists have written of how prison labor replaced slavery after Emancipation. As Scott Reynolds Nelson points out in his wonderful book about that folk hero and black legend John Henry, famous for his strength in driving steel in the construction of America's railroads, blacks with little or no legal recourse were often falsely arrested and assigned to prison labor. In this light, prison labor was frequently seen as a transfer of slave labor from private possession to state ownership.

But Eartha didn't see the case of the Duval County Prison Farm that way. The prison farm wasn't just a farm, but also contained a paint shop and metalworking facilities.

Eartha's philosophy of doing good was always rooted in the earth. The residents of the Old Folks' Home worked a garden there, and Eartha helped the indigent at the Mission to harvest vegetables and fruits from farms, gardens, orchards, and vineyards all over Duval County. The prison farm regularly donated cabbage or lettuce or carrots grown and harvested by prisoners to single mothers, orphans, and the homeless.

For Eartha, the idea of people who had done wrong, broken the law, or hurt someone else, working the earth as rehabilitation went directly to the heart of her philosophy, identity, and sense of purpose. After all, an old prophet had supposedly named her for the earth, to be a "storehouse for the people."

But her middle two names were Mary Magdelene, the name of a destitute woman who'd redeemed herself by coming to Jesus and washing his feet—in that ultimate display of humility—with her hair and tears. Some Gothic art shows Mary Magdelene covered in hirsute redemption flowing from her head to her feet. She's often represented as having been a prostitute and the Books of Luke and Mark claim that Jesus exorcised her of demons.

Though various stories have his disciples telling Jesus not to debase himself by letting such a woman into his presence, Jesus demonstrates his grace, as he almost always did, by favoring the debased and the poor above the privileged. And he says in the Book of Matthew, "It is easier for a camel to go through the eye of a needle, than for a rich man to enter into the kingdom of God."

No wonder Eartha ministered to prisoners and never condescended to them. Though that grand story of Eartha's naming features two old men who argue over whether the child should be named for the earth or for Mary Magdalene, the character of Mary Magdalene herself is an archetype of the earth. Between the conflicting versions of her story, Mary Magdalene was a woman who sold her sex, "poor as dirt," but redeemed herself by prostrating herself to the earth, and cleansing that part of Jesus's body—his feet—that constantly met the earth—with the vegetation of her hair.

As the earth always pro- and re- creates itself, so did Mary Magdalene. As the earth always redeems its death with new life, so did Mary Magdalene.

And in 1954, Eartha argued that abolition of the Duval County Prison Farm would send those criminals currently rehabilitating themselves through working the earth into the county jail or out to state prison. Eartha told the Duval County Commission that she had visited prisoners at the farm for half a century, that she knew the farm, knew the prisoners, knew the renewal.

She lost the fight.

A quarter century before, a county prisoner named Willie Elron had written Eartha, worried sick about his children—

"Sence I have be in here there has Ben something hapen to my oldes Daughter and I wanto see if you could help get her in the hosPittle if so i will aPreashite it very much Now Mrs White i have Ben struglin with them Everry sence their mother Died and had no help with them until this Last Past six months my mother had them for a while and my sisterinLaws went and got them they kept them about four weeks i Bought grociers and Payed Rent for all of them to stay and they got mad with me Because i would not Let her have fifteen Dollars to By her man some cloths and they Put my kids out in the street at 12 oclock at night."

In July of 1930, Willie writes, "Laws i want them again and i Dont want them to have them Because they are not the Right wimen."

At the end of the letter, he says, "i want to take care of them Because they are mine and i will all take care of them."

He implores Eartha to go to his daughter, to whom this unnamed bad thing has happened. "Please," Willie Elron pleads, "Willie Mae Elron is her name."

And that's all. I put the letter down on my dining room table and look to the window darkened beside me. The names dissipate into the night and the city's past and the loss of time, with only this one proof of Willie's enormous feeling and love and sadness. I'll never know exactly what happened to his daughter who bore his name, and what, if anything, Eartha was able to do for Willie and Willie Mae.

In January 1945, 15 years and thousands of letters later, Eartha reads a desperate note a man named Henry Johnson sends her from Pensacola, Florida.

He tells her, "I am in a very unplesant position was beet very searious and framed by a bunch of negroe pimps I donot know anybody hear if you be kindenoufe to write JudgeMASON."

He ends by saying, "I am helpless with out a friend in this town, I will never need you worth then now."

Complaints against Eartha and her mother for helping white people didn't come from black people who clamored for equal service and representation.

It was white people who complained about the Whites helping whites.

White civic leaders asked why this supposed daughter of a former slave was so impudent as to serve poor whites with food and shelter and told her to "send the whites" to another shelter and "keep the blacks."

Eartha said, "When a man is hungry, if he needs clothes, white or black, I'm going to give it to him."

As so early in her life and in the century, she'd come to establish services for orphans, for alcoholics, for the homeless, for those old and incapable of taking care of themselves, Eartha saw no need to separate black people and white people.

She saw how Jacksonville kept LaVilla contained where its own citizens could come for alcohol or prostitution, though Eartha herself had taken an oath of abstaining from alcohol and had been part of the Jacksonville Civic Round Table's influence in illegalizing prostitution. Still white Jacksonville sequestered vices in LaVilla. And she saw no point in denying help to whites who found themselves as destitute and desperate as many of the blacks who came to her doorstep.

Nor did black leaders have a problem with Eartha's helping white people who needed her. Only the city's leading whites, amidst whom her father resided, objected to Eartha White helping whites who needed help wherever they could find it.

Occasionally, the few white civic leaders and local patricians who knew or suspected the truth of her origins rolled their eyes or threw back their heads or laughed or groaned at the irony of Eartha's last name or her mother's maiden name.

White.

English.

The names themselves ironically hinted toward things common residents should never know, though many suspected and many gossiped.

And what that Clara was born on the Fourth of July under a political system that denied her citizenship in the land in which she was born?

Perhaps the United States of the 1840s—some sources say 1845, some 1849—had not yet proven itself worthy of Clara.

If Clara was born in 1849, Zachary Taylor had recently become the 12th American president and would serve for a mere 16 months until he died of vague intestinal problems, the whole time vacillating on the question of slavery though he owned slaves in Kentucky.

Meanwhile, Clara English White and the United States of America shared birthdays.

*

And when Clara was nine years old, she saw her mother sold at auction in the center of Jacksonville. Jacksonville's City Hall would later occupy the same ground where Clara's mother was sold away from her—or at least, that's another story, the location can't be proven.

I've seen two old sources that refer to Clara seeing her mother Jane sold at the northwest corner of Ocean and Forsyth Streets, but I haven't found the source(s) of those sources.

I remember the Haydon Burns Library, which now sits abandoned on that corner, awaiting renovations by the Jessie Ball duPont Fund, a political endowment that does much good, including funding the Clara White Mission, established by Old Southern Aristocracy.

I loved the basement. It smelled musty. It was full of piles of newspapers and microfilm and microfiche machines. There were so many metal cabinets and what seemed like a million metal drawers full of microfilm rolls. When I worked on stories where I had to dig into the minutiae of the past, spinning through rolls on microfilm machines, I felt like I was in the basement of history looking up all the world's secrets.

And when I volunteered for Learn to Read, Inc., I met my student at the Haydon Burns Library twice a week. She was 27 years old and didn't know the alphabet. She had three kids. She had a husband who was 20 years older and treated her like a daughter. He said he would do anything to support her. He was going to turn her life around. He left her two months later. She missed meetings for two weeks. Then she came back and said her brother had AIDS and her five year-old son had a broken arm. She started to cry. She had forgotten what she'd learned of the alphabet. She showed me a lot about what it meant to be poor.

*

In 1965, architect Taylor Hardwick said he wanted to make the library "a place of serenity and delight." Hardwick also designed downtown's Friendship Fountain and the butterfly-winged "milk houses," small drive-through Skinner's Dairy buildings that, though they closed decades ago, still dot the Jacksonville landscape and now operate as flower shops and chicken wing shacks.

When the City closed the library, "Save the Library" bumper stickers appeared on various Volvos around town, but when the City first planned the library, city leaders tore down the Beaux-Arts style City Hall designed by Jacksonville's most beloved architect, Henry John Klutho, to make room for it.

I once interviewed a man who said he stood across the street and watched them tear down City Hall. It had a big, beautiful copper dome and a clock on top. The inside of the dome was covered in murals. And when they took down City Hall, he saw the giant canvas of the murals fluttering all ragged and torn over the wreckage underneath.

Ironically, Klutho had designed the city's first public library on the northeast corner of Ocean and East Adams, diagonally across from his City Hall demolished for Taylor Hardwick's library. The first public library building still stands. It has fluted columns capitaled with busts of Shakespeare and Aristotle.

In the 1990s, Jacksonville's City Hall was moved into another Klutho structure, the St. James Building, considered his masterpiece, one block north of Hemming Plaza and its Confederate Soldier on a pedestal in the center of downtown.

*

But what would you find on the northwest corner of Ocean and Forsyth prior to Klutho's City Hall, on this same site where Clara was said to see her mother sold?

Through most of the 19th century, private residences stood here. The mostly forgotten 1891 Pine Street (now Main Street) Fire destroyed the buildings all around it, and the Great Fire of 1901 included this corner in its sweeping devastation once again.

I find an 1856 Jacksonville slave auction notice for five "likely" Negroes—were there questions of Indian "blood" or were they too "white"?—"Boys, Men and one Woman" to be "sold on Thursday next, the 14th inst. [the current month] at the COURT HOUSE."

But the courthouse was located at the northeast corner of Forsyth and Market, not where Clara is said to have seen her mother sold. In fact, despite the Great Fire, part of it remained embedded in a very modern building until less than a decade ago.

*

In the 1950s, a government services building at this corner of Forsyth and Market was remodeled and dubbed the Lanier Building. In different form, it had served as the county armory, fronted by a five-story castelled tower, built in 1902. The 1901 fire had left the exterior walls of the County Courthouse largely intact here, and it was these fire-tested walls that were covered in the construction of the armory a year later. It had been the Courthouse since 1886, when the previous Courthouse building, burnt 15 years before in the Civil War, was reconstructed. The original Courthouse was built right here in the 1840s.

If Clara did see her mother sold at auction, I suspect it was here at the northeast corner of Forsyth and Market. I walk up and down Forsyth and try to imbibe these long-gone possibilities in the winter beginning 2014. It wasn't the site of the future City Hall. It was the site of the original County Courthouse.

The Courthouse was the only public building in Jacksonville through much of the 1800s. This central street corner housed government services for more than 150 years.

Walking east on Forsyth past the Florida Theater, I come to stand in an empty parking lot on the site of the original Courthouse.

Though its foundations went back almost to the beginning of the city, the City—notice the difference, please, the *city* and the *City*—demolished the Lanier Building a decade ago in exchange for one more empty space downtown for inefficient parking.

Clara English White was born on the Fourth of July. She was not English. She was not White. When she was nine years old, she saw her mother sold.

All the decent citizens of Jacksonville should come together at this empty parking lot at Forsyth and Market Streets to light candles for Clara.

53

I stood at the double tombstone in the Old City Cemetery. Just northeast of downtown Jacksonville, between the southern boundaries of the once white neighborhood of Springfield and the once and still black neighborhood of Oakland, the cemetery was founded in 1852, 20 years after the city was chartered.

Clara's side of the stone is on the left, Eartha's on the right.

Retired schoolteacher Mary Mungen Jameson, the fourth grade teacher of the current director of the Clara White Mission, Ju'Coby Pittman, remembers the way the Old City Cemetery was racially demarcated when she was a little girl.

A tall wire fence separated Section Six, where black people were buried, from the rest of the cemetery. Before she was 10 years old, Mary came to the cemetery regularly to help her mother tend the family plot, and she'd see the white kids on the other side of the fence. A white caretaker lived in a small wooden cemetery shack, and Mary remembers seeing his children playing among the graves. The black kids and the white kids stared at each other through the fence.

But the fence failed its purpose. Section Six continued southward on one side toward the Confederate section of the graveyard. Behind the Confederates were smaller slave graves.

When I stood before Clara's and Eartha's graves, I stood on the white side of where that tall wire fence once extended. Today there's a single paved lane that runs east-west in place of that segregating fence. In "Jim Crow" Florida, Clara and Eartha White were undoubtedly "black," though Clara was a former slave, and Eartha's secret father was a wealthy white man who'd impregnated a black family servant.

Almost adjacent to Eartha's and Clara's graves, Confederate descendent organizations have renovated a little gazebo and emblazoned Confederate names.

Throughout the Old City Cemetery, these groups have re-memorialized graves of Confederate soldiers. This tiny old cemetery that almost no one visits is one of the few places those proud of the Confederacy still have largely to themselves.

And Clara's and Eartha's double grave will always be larger than anything the Confederate apologists could provide—in that irony that Clara and Eartha are buried on the white side of the former black-white line.

The black Whites are on the white side through to which Mary Mungen Jameson, when she was a little girl, could only peer through the tall fence that separated children.

If Eartha's mother had been her biological mother, Eartha couldn't have loved her more.

She'd seen mothers who felt no responsibility toward their children, whom they'd just happened to bring into the world. But Clara had loved her deeply and actively, and Eartha sought to be for this city what Clara had been for her.

Clara loved Eartha with all the love she could have offered the 12 children she'd lost. She gave to Eartha what she would have given to 13 children. Baker's dozen. And that was the size of Eartha's love for the desperate people of her city, to whom she was Mother Eartha.

A 1971 magazine article said succinctly, "She is the good earth."

And so when Clara died in 1920, in her middle 70s, Eartha lost the life partner who showed her how to marry the community. It was hard to think of Eartha without Clara, but two paradoxical truths remained.

Eartha had always been on her own. Four and a half feet tall, she was always larger than life. She never seemed to believe she might not know how to do something. What she wanted to do, she did, because it wasn't for her that she wanted to do it. Though she was clearly Clara's girl, she was clearly her own from the beginning. She was never (but she was always) her mother's daughter.

Tiny Eartha seemed bigger. She was bigger than Jacksonville. She was bigger than her parentage. Her benefactors in the Old Folks' Home and the Home for Unwed Mothers and the County Stockade thought Eartha was big like an Old Testament figure—Moses, Noah, Abraham, Job, or maybe the Reverend Henry Harrison—but with a New Testament kindness.

Eartha came from some larger place to live and love and work in this little place called Jacksonville. So some people said.

But the other truth was that Eartha was her mother's daughter, wholly, entirely. Clara had given toys and clothes and food and care and medicine and advice and love and comfort and kindling and social and political solidarity all Eartha's life. It never seemed to be an effort. The giving came automatically, organic. The community always turned naturally to Clara. Without question. And Eartha absorbed what people later called humanitarianism from her infancy.

"No night was too cold or dark for her to help any one in distress. She began to fail in health last July and in Feb there was a consultation of physicians held which gave her the true condition of her self on July 4th her Birthday she took her bed. And with a continued weakness bore her illness with patience to the end which came at 10 minutes of Seven on Tuesday July 20.

"After her daughter had give her a bath, she folded her arms and breathed her last. She gave every one full assurance of her resting in peace. She said she had done all the good she could for everybody. She had give up her child who had given her everything she wanted, that her work was finished.

"Death was nothing more than someone handing you a package or crossing the street."

SOME SAYINGS OF MY MOTHER

This little book is dedicated in memory of my mother /
whose life was given in service to others.

CLARA WHITE

Born July 4, 1849 at Amelia Island, Fernandina, Fla.
Died, July 21, 1920 at Jacksonville, Fla.

*

ANYTHING YOU MIGHT GIVE WILL BE USED FOR
MISSION WORK.

*

"Leaving the Mission building at eleven p.m. before
going home I went to carry a sick member of the Mission,
Mrs. Dora Joseph, living on Cleveland Street, a bottle of milk,
and to see if she was comfortable for the night. I fell from the
walk between the sidewalk and the car, striking and
fracturing my right arm on the running board of the car.

"I was a 'shut in' for weeks, but friends came to see me,
bringing fruit and flowers, and doing everything they could to
make me comfortable. But while confined in bed, my

thoughts were centered on plans for the further improvement and building up of my work, the Mission."

Then Eartha writes, "A thought came to me that the day before my mother died, she made this expression—'Death is only a step.' I began to ponder that thought in my heart."

*

Then other recollections of my mother's sayings came to my mind, some of which are as follows:

You will miss me when I am gone.

A humble child will taste the grace of God.

When grown-ups are talking, children should be seen but not heard.

Every cloud aint rain. Every goodbye aint gone.

Every shut eye aint sleep.

Nothing goes over the devil's back that doesn't buckle under its belly.

If you play with a puppy, he will sure lick your mouth.

Any old dead fish can go down stream, but it takes a live one to swim up.

It's a long road that doesn't have a turn.

There is a first time to everything.

You will reap what you sow.

What you do in the dark will come to the light.

You can run but you can't hide.

What don't come out in the washing will sure be seen in the ironing.

Where there is so much smoke there is bound to be some fire.

The more you stir the fire the more it will smoke.

If you fall don't wallow.

A true friend will stick to you through thick and thin.

See and don't see; hear and don't hear.

Fine houses don't make homes.

There are some things money can't buy.

Every old sow will go to her wallow.

New brooms sweep clean, but an old one know where to find the dirt.

Don't cast off old friends for new ones.

Don't make a wound and you won't have to worry about the healing.

Be careful how you treat strangers.

Today is someone's last sunset.

Watch your friends. Your enemies can't hurt you.

It is a poor rule that doesn't work both ways.

My father knows.

God has his eyes on you.

God said he would never see the righteous forsaken or their seed begging bread.

When you are talking about someone else, someone is talking about you.

Be careful how you put your foot on the cross; your foot might slip and your soul get lost.

Every dog has its day.

Don't know, don't hurt.

Still tongue makes a wise head.

Empty wagons make lots of noise.

You may go, but you will come back.

You may run but your sins will find you out.

A good name is rather to be chosen than great riches.

You will never miss the water until the well runs dry.

Birds of a feather will flock together.

It's hard to teach old dogs new tricks.

Birds fly high, but they must come down.

Every tub must sit on its own bottom.

The Lord will provide.

Everyone must stand in the judgment for themselves.

Don't speak evil of anybody; open your closet and you will see a skeleton.

Take your burdens to the Lord and leave them there.

Blood will tell.

It's better to be born lucky than rich.

Trouble ain't for one.

Six feet of earth makes us equal.

A burnt child dreads the fire.

If it wasn't for the bitter, you would not enjoy the sweet.

Every rose has its thorns.

Pot can't call kettle black.

A friend is one who knows all about you and loves you just the same.

Every pain ain't to tell the doctor.

Every crow thinks his young'un the whitest.

Coming to see me ain't like living with me.

You must be born again.

Every dog that will bring a bone will carry one.

Do all the good you can in all the ways you can, for all the people you can, in all the places you can, while you can.

Remember, that behold he cometh quickly and his reward he shall bring with him, and shall give every one according to their work.

Don't loan money and you will keep a few friends.

PART THREE

LaVilla Gazetteer Interlude

Because see, there's things happening in this place, she said, things happening here that will keep re-happening.

And if one day LaVilla's not here, it's because LaVilla lived too much for Jacksonville.

She leaned in close to my face and her eyes were big when they looked into mine.

I looked down the block, shotgun shack porches, wooden porch railings, tin-sheet roofs. People laughing, sitting on porch steps. Somebody singing "Honeysuckle Rose."

LaVilla's tight, she told me. It holds you. You feel its folds and its turns all around you. Even though it's only so many blocks this way and that, you get to know a place like that. You know it personal and intimate because it's always all up in there with you. It's like a womb. Or it's like a brain with all them folds and wrinkles. It's a soft maze.

Now, it ain't no place is perfect, but this place has friends and food and music and togetherness all inside it. And wherever you go in its streets, it puts its arms around you.

She said that one day a white man with white hair in a blue-gray business suit would assassinate LaVilla.

She told me that if LaVilla could hang on and if LaVilla could go on, then one blues song sung in a back room with no windows, and that room behind and inside a back room with no windows, or a torch song sung in the cool air and moonlight, would get a new refrain in 50 years and 150 years. And more. African tunes and tones moved through slave fields right here in LaVilla and all over Jacksonville and the swamps around town, and the blues was born of the place where spiritual notes was struck of physical degradations, and all would keep on going in patterns in this place, in recurrences in these streets—

—unless some assassin set out to wipe it off the face of the earth, LaVilla would reseed itself, through cycles of destruction and creation, for hundreds and hundreds of years, maybe longer.

And this night would not die. Despite that the present time's always lost before it happens. Because tomorrow's come. But tomorrow moves today back through it.

Which, she told me, 's part of how she knew who a place was. Time was time, but more than that, time was place. LaVilla showed her that everyday.

Her voice had a lovely lilt and her hair was full of flowers made of pearls and beads. Tembleques, she said.

I asked her name. She wouldn't tell me.

She told me not to be silly. The stars and the trees were not silly. And these LaVilla streets contained and cared for everything, and I felt like a little boy, late at night, when all the world's mysterious but maternal love envelopes him dark and strong and benignant.

Old wood smells sweet, buckles outward, attic windows overhead, house risen from the Civil War, 1865 or '75.

Two blocks away, strong two-story-tall Corinthian columns hold up an attic that leans toward the street. A palm tree grows up through the roof from a second-story balcony.

Dormer windows in the alley and streetcar tracks curving 'round the theaters. Strange tall man in a top hat.

Three blocks north, where bay-windows bulb over an alley. Five blocks east, where a cupola of a witch's hat crowns two-story porches. Streetfront patterns, six blocks northward, one front porch fight, porch after porch of laughter, gossip, Biblical advice, shotgun shack after shotgun shack, the clack-clack-clack of the train tracks.

And in the middle she tells me a woman named Eartha,

beautiful but tiny, too-cool outlaws imagine her on their arms, she's so pretty, so pretty, but she belongs to this whole LaVilla.

LaVilla is Eartha at its heart. Mother City to the larger city outside. Jerusalem and Mecca.

62

In the streets so long ago were answers to questions that wouldn't be asked for a long, long time.

LaVilla self-suffices. It produces its fuel from its own death. It burns itself forward.

It builds new jazz from a fire in Freedman Gothic wood. Scroll-turned arabesques on the third-floor porch. A six year-old boy looks through these porch rails across the LaVilla night, and his skinny black legs swing freely above the street. The moon's uncannily large and it's red, harvest moon above West Ashley.

In the red moonlight, morning-glory blooms and orange blossoms crushed across the rock and sand and soil, mashed and pestled and distilled-pure through alembic-of-LaVilla.

Houses of grand rot. I see Eartha, young and old at the same time, spirit of place, personality of this geography. I know that when she's gone, no one will truly imagine the quiet gravity she bore. I know.

All air is ghost and present-day is history.

I turn a corner. The next block subsumes everything else. The Middle of the World.

I step through music from vaudeville and music-hall— the Two Zulus, acrobats and contortionists and the human corkscrew, and William's Wonderfully Educated Ponies, who stand on the stage and talk to the audience.

The Rabbit's Foot Company dances and jokes and sings songs called "I Didn't Ask, He Didn't Say, So I Don't Know" and "Do Your Duty, Doctor" and "Cannibal Love" and "I Am That Hen Roost Inspector Man."

I descend through a trap door in the wings, come across a wine cellar, move into the earth, walk subterranean stone steps, up wooden stairs into an old house embedded within a brick warehouse where a reader sits above the men mixing leaves and rolling Cuban cigars, and the reader dictates newspapers and fiery speeches from Cuban revolutionary José Martí.

In an old slave cabin turned into a tavern, a blind man play a blues harp and a Jew's harp, and a woman shoots him through the heart.

Early February, 1922. An itinerant preacher named R.A. Crump writes to Eartha, reminding her of his last sermon in Jacksonville.

In early March of the same year, he writes, "I forgot to ask whether you were married. You remember that quite a number of suitors were in line when I last visited you. Rehearse what I told you about the 'Old Maid Stuff.' Have been trying to make out but the situation grows worse with the dawning of new 'Bachelor Days.' Came to the conclusion that the 'Man without a Lover' is as the 'Man without a Country.'"

Crump shifts from asking about Eartha's marital status and complaining about his bachelorhood to asking for a job in her laundry.

"How is the laundry business? What consideration could you give me for the position of 'janitor'? Desire a job with lots of work in it and very little of worry."

Crump ends his letter by asking, "What have you decided about a trip to the North Pole this summer? To see you again would be splendid. But you have the Dear Old People to attend. How are they?"

The letter to Eartha's mother is undated. Albert Sammis must have written it in the late nineteen-teens.

He calls Clara "Mother," refers to someone named "Hunny," and speaks lovingly of Eartha.

"The balance of Hunny's things is here. Eartha can have anything she wants & me two when ever she gets ready."

He tells Clara of an upcoming carnival in Tampa, where he lives, and says, "Tell her to come and spend that time with me I will make it pleasant for her I will have a lady in the house so she wont be alone with and old batchelor. let her come mother dear. you can trust her with me. let me know in your next letter if she will."

1920. 233 Eagle Street.

"but when I think of you there: so faithfull to your duty. and there is nothing I can do to help you. it makes me feel somewhat a Slacker. pleas remember my love that albert and everything thats albert's is yours. O how I wish you could lern to feel and think that way of me. remember no matter what happens you are not alone. you will have one that will die for you if nessesserie."

And 1929. West Eagle had become West 1st Street. 233 W. 1st.

"Dear Sweetheart.

"arrived home safe found Everything OK. Enjoyed my trip to Jax so mutch you was so nice to me hop you got your business fix alright I am ancious to know about it pleas be carefull with yourself and business. As you promised you would. Cool this morning. Hello Miss Lucky love and Kisses

"yours

"A."

And 3-4-29.

"I have the blues. I have bin home alone all after noon. Thinking of you the world seams so lonely with out you. You are Every thing to me. With out you, life is not worth living. I think of you all the time. And when I get home its worst I wonder what is the matter I could not love you anymore O I hope we wont have to live away from Each other always.

"I truly hope you got your business all straight if that Jew will take the lot for what you owe him let him have it we will loos money on it but we can make it back on some thing else. That is business. Be sweet Love & Kisses"

And 9-21-30.

"Dear Sweetheart

"yours recived found me wel glad you are alright. Wish I could see you glad you are being encouraged you I here nothing but <u>hard</u> <u>times</u>.

"I had a policy for accidental death for $10,000. Ten thousand dollar. Had it made payable to you if anything you will get enough so you wont have to worrie. The only worrie I have is about you."

*

"Your Rail Road fair both ways is always here for you"

*

11-8-30.

"Dear Sweetheart

"inclose you will finde $1 one dollar for your Birth day wish you a happy one hope you live to see many more <u>Sweet heart</u>. <u>why</u> <u>dont</u> <u>you</u> answer my <u>letter</u> hope you are well and every thing going good with you the oranges and grapefruits lemons are most all ripe they are most all ripe they are Early this year wish you could get them no Express-office here.

"love and Kisses..."

66

LaVilla was where everything happened. Though Asians and Middle Easterners lived here too, it had always been mostly black since its days as plantation and then as its own town. When Jacksonville—present downtown east of LaVilla—annexed LaVilla in the late 1800s, Jacksonville increased its population and political power. It also became mostly black, anathema to wealthy Southern whites, though the city's almost always been close to half black.

By law, black meant outlaw. LaVilla was where sailors came ashore. LaVilla was where to find the liquor. LaVilla evolved the red-light district, the tenderloin. And it was packed with rows of shotgun houses built by former slaves, some of whose parents had been slaves right here in LaVilla.

LaVilla teemed. In that hot, humid, wooden, densely-populated place, it made sense that the word "culture," not just the "high culture" of Opera or European Impressionism or High Literature, really meant "controlled growth." So "culture" takes prefixes and forms "agriculture," "horticulture," "vermiculture," "arboriculture."

And LaVilla's culture cultivated itself.

West Ashley Street was the heart of it. Mississippi came to town. Harlem came down South. Chicago came to West Ashley.

And Eartha would establish her headquarters in LaVilla.

The Bijou Theatre, 615 West Ashley, featured locally shot motion pictures, contortionists, blackface acts. The Colored Airdome Theatre, 601 West Ashley, offered black comedians, "Oriental" impersonators, minstrel performers who called themselves Zulus and pimps and "Black Bottoms."

Across the street from the writer Stephen Crane's "common law" wife's brothel, the Hotel de Dreme, stood the Strand Theater, and across from the Strand was Wynn's Hotel, or the Finkelstein Grocery, or Genovar's Hall—several incarnations in the same building—where the biggest jazz acts played in the 1920s. Larger-than-life figures like Louis Armstrong came and stayed at Wynn's.

On the same block were nightclubs like The Bronx, The Top Hat, Manuel's, the Lenape Tavern downstairs from the Wynn, and the Hollywood Music Store. Big Band shows came to the Knights of Pythias Hall, and small and big bands both came to the Ritz around the corner. Other musicians played the Roosevelt, the Frolic, even Nick's Pool Parlor.

LaVilla's cigar factories were bally-platforms for Cuban insurgents like José Martí, who came in the 1890s and spoke to workers while they rolled tobacco. The cigar factories had a tradition of leader-readers who read newspapers and political tracts to the workers while they prepared cigars. The leader-readers in LaVilla's cigar factories became conduits for the radicals who agitated for Cuban independence from Spain.

I stand in the middle of a street of demolished buildings, no cars, and close my eyes and imagine the night sounds on this one city block in the 1920s.

Blind Blake is one of the few local musicians from that time whose recorded music survives. He sang about LaVilla's main corridor in "Ashley Street Blues," and I can hear it in my head.

Eartha was always at the heart of black Jacksonville. Eartha stood at those convergences of the city where people most needed help.

There was no other place for her to base her operations than the Middle of the World at the Heart of LaVilla.

There was no place else for Eartha to live her long life for others than in the center of gravity of black life in North Florida. There was no place else to make of herself the Storehouse for the People, to build herself around the people who needed her, no place else for men from far distances to centralize and idolize and fall in love with her.

Oh Eartha! Oh Albert Sammis!

Eartha White belonged to everyone but the men who wanted her for their own.

I walk up a slight knoll covered in grasses and dog fennel. Across the street is an unofficial trash dump that slides straight downhill into McCoy's Creek.

The surrounding streets contain worn-out century-old shotgun shacks, small tracts of public housing, empty brick churches from the 1890s, and small brick factories and warehouses.

I stand here in this weeded land. It's a thing I frequently do. Drive out to obscure parts of old town and stand where something significant to me once stood to see what I feel, or feel what I imagine.

It wasn't until local writer Sharon Weightman Hoffman conducted some pointed research that we knew where Blind Blake lived. The mythical ragtime bluesman lived right here on Stonewall Street one year. Census documents have him living on one side of Stonewall with Anna in 1927 and the other side of the street with Rosa Lee in 1928.

When Sharon first went to the latter vacant lot, she found a pile of garbage—burst trash bags, old whiskey bottles, rotten pieces of plywood. On top of the trash sat "a box of old traveling shoes and, believe it or not, a busted-up, cheap-ass guitar that somebody had decided to dump there. Since Blake was noted for his sense of humor, I thought it was a pretty good cosmic joke on his part."

On Stonewall Street in Jacksonville's Brooklyn neighborhood, a couple blocks from LaVilla, Blind Blake sang about a "four-legged woman crazy 'bout a cross-eyed man."

I stand beside a discarded tire and a pile of roof shingles Florida's subtropical growth seeks quickly to reclaim and adapt. I base the house I imagine on the shotgun houses in which I've been.

A blind black man sits on a window box by a low street-front window in a dirty undershirt and red suspenders and experiments with rag rhythms.

It's the early 1920s. Rain threatens. The heat withers the walls and palmettos and sagging porches. The swamp crawls up out of itself, crawls all over itself, calls itself Jacksonville, Florida.

Hey hey hey hey / Hey hey hey hey
Hey hey hey hey / Hey hey hey hey. Hey.
My Stonewall Street gal make me feel this-a-way.

You call me in the mornin'. You call me late at night.
You call me in the mornin'. You call me late at night.
You swear that you love, but you sure don't treat
      me right.

I got the blues so bad, I can feel 'em with my
      natural hand.
I got the blues so bad, feel 'em with my natural hand.
I been your dog ever since I been your man.

I'm gone grab me a freight train, ride until it stops.
I'm gone grab me a freight train, ride it 'til it stops.
I ain't gone stay 'round here and be your stumblin'
      block.

All over Brooklyn and LaVilla, musicians play with tunes.

I walk from Stonewall Street over the railroad bridge that separates LaVilla and Brooklyn. Both neighborhoods are ghost towns, though Brooklyn will feature substantial new development along Riverside Avenue in the next couple years.

LaVilla's a ghost town because Jacksonville paid millions of dollars to destroy a few thousand old houses and buildings to remove poverty and crime and open up real estate. Brooklyn is a ghost town because between LaVilla's fatal "renewal" and Riverside's re-gentrification, people forgot Brooklyn existed.

68

The DeLoach Furniture Company on Broad Street in LaVilla, whose building once housed the Richmond Hotel, admits almost no one to its upstairs ballroom, the whole floor in decay for decades.

A small group of my community college students visited DeLoach in the spring of 2013 as part of a "Legend Tripping" scavenger hunt project. Legend Tripping is a sociological and folklorist term for the visits young people make to places about which stories and urban legends abound.

The scavenger hunt project in my Legend Tripping classes asks students to work in teams to find and document old places across the city. They work from clues like "the mausoleum of the African princess in the city's oldest cemetery" or "the statue that glowed red in the 1901 fire."

My student Rachel Duff stared into a begrimed mirror in the upper floor ballroom and thought about how her idols Billie Holiday and Ella Fitzgerald had looked into this same glass. Her stare was superimposed on theirs.

So strange now to listen to the emptiness and silence of old wood and brick and imagine the music and mirth that sounded in these same streets.

I vividly remember walking Jefferson Street in 1991. I remember the skeletal woman with crazed eyes coming at me and grinding her hips, a sickly woman behind her asking me frantically to come into a falling-down house. I remember feeling scared and sad and, inexplicably to the young working-class-white-me of the time, terribly guilty.

Soon thereafter, the city funded Mayor Ed Austin's $235 million River City Renaissance plan, which included the destruction of almost 50 square blocks of LaVilla.

I take everything historical personally now.

I mourn everything I've missed, every building and life that could have been reclaimed.

Into the Petri dish of intensive and organic LaVilla culture, Eartha brought her particular personal lifeforce and purchased the Globe Theater and made it the headquarters of all her enterprises.

"All roads lead to Rome," and all Eartha's interests and the forces that surrounded them led to LaVilla, the "Harlem of the South," the "Blacksonville" at the heart of Jacksonville, and West Ashley, the "Great Black Way," as opposed to the "Great White Way" that was Broadway and all its lights, was the street that coursed through its heart.

69

City directories for the late 1880s and the 1890s list Squire English as stevedore and livery at Ashley and Bridge (now Broad) Streets in LaVilla.

English was the wealthiest black person in Jacksonville and carried his own political clout. When the Liberian writer and diplomat and early pan-Africanist Edward Wilmot Blyden visited Jacksonville in 1889, he stayed at Squire English's home.

Blyden spoke to the "sturdy workmen" he met in LaVilla and shared his message that the best life for a black person in post-slavery America was to emigrate back to the "homeland" and start a new life in Africa.

Not surprisingly, *The Florida Times-Union* editorialized that "Blyden was the heaven-appointed medium for solving the Negro problem."

Squire English, descended from the same slave-owning family as Adam English, Clara White's father, ran a produce market on the site where the Clara White Mission stands today.

70

Here's the lineage:

After Squire English ran produce markets and liveries here, a Boston entertainment promoter and entrepreneur named Frank Crowd financed the construction, in 1908, of a three-story building at 615 West Ashley that became the Bijou Theater.

The Bijou showed silent films including a version of Shakespeare's *Taming of the Shrew* and locally shot and produced films by early Jacksonville silent film studios. Vaudeville acts included a contortionist, an acrobat, and George Riley, "the foolish mirth-maker."

Soon, next door at the corner of West Ashley and Bridge, where the Mission would take over the Hollywood Music Store building in 1990s, the Colored Airdome Theater brought fierce competition with tap dancing, "coon shouting," orchestral ensembles, films, and the minstrel "Two Zulus." The singing and dancing "Too Sweets" and the comedian "Long Willie" always brought down the house.

A popular song called the "Jacksonville Rounders' Dance" played in both theaters, though community opposition to the word "rounder," meaning "pimp," pushed the songwriter to rechristen it "The Original Black Bottom Dance." Either way, the dance that accompanied the song was called the "Pimp's Walk."

In 1910, head-to-head with the Colored Airdome, the Bijou closed its doors and reopened as the Globe Theater, with expanded seating and orchestra space and a newly organized Globe Stock Company.

That autumn, a minstrel blues musician named Franklin "Baby" Seals played the Globe for two months, singing his original composition of "Shake, Rattle, and Roll,"

44 years before the white rock n' roll band Bill Haley and the Comets recorded their version.

Entertainers later famous, like the tap dancer Bojangles Robinson and "Mother of the Blues" Ma Rainey, then booked as a "coon shouter," played the Globe. The Globe staged dramatic Vaudeville performances with titles like *A Trip to Coontown* and musical "farces" like *Stranded in Africa.*

There's poisonous irony in the fact that "Jim Crow" was a stock character in Vaudeville blackface acts, a racist stereotype stealing chickens and watermelons—his name best known now as the whole code of racist "Jim Crow laws" the South enacted against black citizens in retribution for its losing the Civil War—and that black audiences supported so many of these "coon" and "Zulu" entertainments.

Frank Crowd became self-reflexive enough in 1914 that he wrote and staged a play at the Globe that featured a black newspaperman dealing with corrupt white politicians "and the duplicity of members of his own race under their influence."

The play marked a conscientiously different direction for the Globe, a striking rebuke of Booker-T.-Washingtonism, and was attacked resoundingly enough that Crowd soon rebranded the theater as the New Globe. But the Globe had begun a steep decline amidst the rise of new venues and theaters along bright and bustling West Ashley.

The Globe lasted for almost two decades, putting on thousands of acts before its demise. Shortly after the Globe closed, an investment group turned it into a grocery, but banks soon foreclosed.

Then Eartha White bought it and turned it into the Mission she named for her mother.

71

Ironically, Eartha helped keep alive LaVilla minstrelsy longer than anyone else.

But perhaps black support for minstrelsy is less surprising considered as precursor to 1970s' "Blaxploitation" films aimed at black audiences. In fact, mistrel shows, so embarrassingly racist now, often included references, puns, and jokes that whites just wouldn't get. Black people were made to feel like insiders in performances that brutally satirized them.

The *Silas Green from New Orleans* variety show had traveled the South and repeatedly hit LaVilla since 1904. Part minstrel show, part revue, *Silas Green* was the biggest traveling black troupe and featured big names like Bessie Smith, Nipsy Russell, and Gatemouth Brown.

In the late 1920s and early 1930s, Eartha brought the *Silas Green* show to the Mission for yearly Christmas Eve performances. As Peter Dunbaugh Smith says in his history of black music and culture in LaVilla, "Every year on Christmas Eve [...], Eartha White would entertain the entertainers as they celebrated the holiday with her."

Katie Abraham, a *Silas Green* dancer, later recalled, "After every show, we went straight back to the car, every night except once a year. We always played Jacksonville, Florida on Christmas Eve and that was the one night we got to go to the dance."

72

After the Globe went out of business, the building was home to a mercantile company, a grocery, a casino, and a hotel. All three floors had balconies that stretched the building's width.

Since banks refused to lend Eartha the money—she was black, she was a woman, she wasn't wealthy—she solicited the funds to build the Clara White Mission in the old Globe.

In 1933, Charles H. Loeb, a journalist later called "the dean of black newsmen," wrote that the Mission's "community center atmosphere is an outgrowth of the regularly held religious meetings, supplemented as they are by meetings of outside groups of young people, social clubs, the Lyceums, Red Cross classes, Domestic Science class, old fashioned quiltings, mass meetings and sewing bees by members of the Needlework Guild, affiliated with the Mission. These activities aid immeasurably in creating for the Mission a social atmosphere that assists in banishing fear of tomorrow from the face of Jacksonville's unemployed masses."

Even when a fire destroyed part of the Mission in 1944, Eartha not only contracted Henry John Klutho, the city's best known architect, to rebuild it, but she continued to live upstairs.

After the reconstruction, Eartha rented space to a dentist, a radio station, a barber, a jeweler, and the regional office of *The Pittsburgh Courier*, the largest black newspaper in the country.

The Red Cross used the building for health and safety classes. Local black colleges and business institutes held "adult night school classes" here. The Mission operated an employment agency and held a free reading room with more than 500 books.

Every day at noon, the Mission's workers and volunteers served lunch to the hungry and homeless and gave away old clothes and shoes.

If they had nothing else to do with the Clara White Mission, many of the city's wealthiest donated money each Christmas for the annual Merry Hearts' Club celebration. Just as Christmas was the one time of year many wealthy people thought briefly of the poor, it was the time of year the poor were made most aware of their poverty.

Eartha used the funds to buy food and toys for poor and homeless children. The Mission sent volunteers downtown to department stores to ring bells and wear Santa hats and ask for any small donation, any widow's-mite dropped into their baskets.

And every year Eartha made the city's poorest feel less alone at the enormous Christmas party she threw.

Bethel Baptist Church historian Camilla Thompson remembers when she and her sisters accompanied their father who volunteered at the Christmas celebrations. More than 75 years later, she laughs and says, "I would be mad because I wanted to stay at home with my new Christmas presents."

Clara had shown Eartha all her life how to be the center of a community's giving, and for 40 years Eartha made and kept her home on the second floor of the Mission she'd named for her mother.

As all roads lead to Rome, 613 West Ashley was Eartha's Rome and Jerusalem, and as Clara had been the center of Eartha's life, Eartha named the center of the community, to which she now offered herself, for her mother—just as her mother had named her, according to the mythos, for Mother Earth.

Throughout the Great Depression in the 1930s, through desegregation and Civil Rights from the 1950s through the 1970s, and when black business and enterprise and homeownership itself spread to further parts of town in the 1950s through the 1990s, as LaVilla turned on itself and self-destructed in the 1960s through the 1980s, and as the city that had absorbed LaVilla a century before decided to decimate it wholly in the early 1990s, and as Jacksonville subsequently mythologized LaVilla as the cultural-center-of-gravity-it-once-was, 613 West Ashley survived and remained the HQ.

When Eartha was 97 years old, she still went to bed in her room on the second floor of the former center of jazz and the blues. In 1974, she went to bed in the center of black desperation after years of the city's flight from itself to the suburbs.

Over the decades, Eartha went to bed on the second floor to the sounds of Big Band jazz and Dixieland, the blues, gunshots, the ringing in her ears of speeches by James Weldon Johnson, Martin Luther King, John Fitzgerald Kennedy. Through the late 1960s and early 1970s, she heard despair at night, but also laughter and singing.

At the turn of 1974, Eartha was the tiny, bird-like, Old-Testament-but-New-Testament saint at the center of town. She died in January. I was born in June. I so wish I could have met her.

PART FOUR

Heartbeat of the Body Politic

73

The newspapers said it was the duty of white women, in the year women received the right to vote, to support the political party that would protect the interests of white people in Jacksonville and throughout the South.

In 2014, it's hard to imagine the political party affiliations as they existed along racial lines in the South at that time. All my life, I've associated black Southerners with voting Democratic and white Southerners with voting heavily Republican.

When I was growing up during the Reagan and first President Bush years, I had no idea that white Southerners had once mostly voted Democratic and black Southerners, when and in what limited ways they could vote, supported Republicans for almost a century.

The reasons aren't hard to understand. Black Southerners supported Republicans for so long because Lincoln had been the first Republican president. They felt so indebted to Lincoln and the Emancipation Proclamation that black towns and neighborhoods were named after him, as were black leaders like Abraham Lincoln Lewis of the Afro-American Life Insurance Company.

Meanwhile, Southern Democrats voted for and enforced a whole regimen of anti-black segregationist laws. Since the South had lost the Civil War, they would sure as hell make it hell to be black in the South. They were called Dixiecrats, and the Jim Crow Code was their own.

The end of this century-long Southern political party affiliation came when Democratic President Lyndon B. Johnson signed sweeping Civil Rights legislation in the 1960s. When he signed the Voting Rights Act in 1965, a quarter million black Americans registered to vote for the first time.

When he'd signed into law the Civil Rights Act the year before, he correctly predicted that the Democratic Party had just "lost the South for a generation."

As far as many white Southerners were concerned, their fellow Dixiecrat, LBJ, had committed racial treason.

When the 19th Amendment granted women the right to vote in 1920, a Jacksonville judge urged white women to do their racial and patriotic duty and vote Democratic. To do so would honor, thank, and repay the "white men of the South who for 50 years past have done all in their power to protect you from the unmorality, savagery and beastly" qualities "of an inherently vicious black" population.

It's no wonder that as Eartha led numerous black and black women's business and social organizations in Jacksonville, she also led the Negro Republican Women Voters' Alliance.

74

Eartha worked hard to register black women voters in Jacksonville and Duval County.

As was so often the case in Jacksonville's political history, white politicians were scared of the sheer number of black people in town. And now they were scared of the number of black *women*. If the city's black population had all the voting rights that whites had, racist white politicians wouldn't stand a chance.

The Fifteenth Amendment to the Constitution in 1870 guaranteed the right to vote regardless of race. That meant Southern politicians immediately thereafter began working on laws to counteract the amendment.

One of their solutions was a poll tax, a tax on your vote. Such legislation usually included loopholes that excluded many if not most white citizens from having to pay, and of course more whites were able to pay such a tax than blacks anyway.

1920 newspaper editorials insisted white voters pay their poll taxes if they didn't want to live in a city run by blacks. The majority of Jacksonville residents who were registered to vote, in fact, were black, but most black residents hadn't paid their poll taxes. The city's whites couldn't afford to lose one vote.

And now that women could vote, both political parties and both races fought to register as many women voters as they could.

When Eartha went door to door registering black women to vote in LaVilla and Sugar Hill and Hansontown and Campbell's Addition and Oakland and other segregated black neighborhoods, she counteracted a Dixiecratic effort to register every last white woman to vote Democratic.

Sometimes, walking across streetcar tracks in the streets paved with bricks toward another line of shotgun houses where she knew several potential new women voters lived, she must have felt a new sense of power and hope well up from deep within.

When she walked through a neighborhood like Sugar Hill, she saw beautiful new two-story houses in Neo-Georgian and Colonial Revival architectural designs, and she knew the black doctors and lawyers and political and civic leaders who lived in those houses.

Residence of Mr. and Mrs. A. L. Lewis, 504 West 8th Street, Jacksonville, Fla.

So when black women came to registration offices and officials responded to them by suddenly and peremptorily closing up shop, taking hours-long lunch breaks that began early in the morning, or being inexplicably and mysteriously busy behind shut blinds, the lines of women standing in the late August heat grew longer and longer, and Eartha went up and down the lines with buckets of lemonade and led impromptu choirs of waiting black women in hymns and songs like the Johnson brothers' "Lift Every Voice and Sing."

75

But it was even more complicated. In fact, the voter registration of black women was also part of a larger calculated political strategy to get black men to vote and to vote Republican.

Surely white citizens and city officials wouldn't be as likely to threaten and harass black women who showed up to vote as they had black men in the past. If for no other reason, they'd look even more brutal and ugly and petty.

And more black men would vote, because men would accompany women voters to the polls to keep them safe.

The counteraction came from the Ku Klux Klan, which ramped up its activity across the South.

VALDOSTA KLAN-OPEN AIR CEREMONIA
KNIGHTS KU KLUX KLAN
VALDOSTA, GA. OCT. 10, 1922.

In Jacksonville, the KKK planned an election-day parade. They would march outside lines of black voters in white supremacist solidarity, dressed in their white robes and white hoods.

The day before Halloween, an NAACP telegram sent to the Duval County sheriff, the mayor of Jacksonville, and Florida's governor said, "Advertized purpose of parade is to prevent trouble on election day. Real motive terrorization and intimidation of colored voters. Instead of prevention will likely lead to trouble and perhaps bloodshed, responsibility for which would rest upon city and county."

Though black people showed up at the parade and yelled at the people in the hoods, they resisted Klansmen's instigations and protested the parade without violence. And voted.

Though thousands of black voters showed up at the polls and Republican numbers greatly increased, official campaign results erased all but a few new Republican votes.

Eartha and other activists made election-day counts and estimated that between 3,000 and 4,000 black voters had been turned away from their chance to vote. She collected the names and addresses of "qualified electors who stood in line from 8 a.m. to 5:40 p.m."

Though they prepared cases on behalf of black people who were denied the vote and planned to present them to the United States Congress when it next reconvened, Eartha told NAACP officials that many of her claimants were afraid for their safety and refused to speak publically.

Community activism had worked to turn out the vote, but the political machine refused to reflect it. The Ku Klux Klan had their parade, but they didn't hold back the black vote and they failed to incite violence they could blame on black Jacksonville.

Still, black political activism in the city required a long-term resolve to bear and buck the racial terrorism of the KKK and the white power structure.

76

But, again, it was even more complicated. Since poll taxes had been designed to dampen black voter turnout, and since black Republicans hoped newly legal voter registration of black women would also increase black male votes, Eartha wrote letters urging black women to have their husbands pay their poll taxes.

Black women's pressure on black men might counter the negative effect of poll taxes on black male voters.

From a later standpoint, what's troubling about Eartha's poll tax letters is that she advocates what the taxes fund, without differentiating between taxes white citizens would pay for basic services and taxes black citizens would pay, *as the cost of a vote*, but also as remittance for a separate and inferior service.

For example, Eartha's letters ask, "[D]o you know that out of the pole [sic] taxes our children are schooled? And do you know that our men are criticized for not paying their pole [sic] taxes."

Counterintuitively, Eartha writes that black men should prove their independence by paying their poll taxes. "Be independent men. Don't wait until the day of election and allow another man to pay your taxes."

She challenges black women "to see by our efforts and our influence how many men we can get to be men."

If black voters pay poll taxes, the logic extends, they guarantee themselves the right to demand better schools, education, and Civil Rights.

Eartha's poll tax letters defended this racist method of reducing black male votes at the same time women would be allowed to vote in presidential elections for the first time.

Ascribing to older conservative ideologies while espousing new progressive directions under the aegis of the retrograde is hardly a new rhetorical maneuver. I'd like to believe that's what she was doing.

More than two decades prior to the Civil Rights Movement, Eartha admonishes black people to be "independent" by subscribing to racist policies in the hopes of participating more fully. Not that she ever laid it out this way. These were the cards she was dealt. She understood how best to play them.

Nor was she alone in these admonitions. Mary McLeod Bethune likewise told black voters in Daytona Beach, "Eat your bread without butter, but pay your poll tax!"

Exhorting black women to make "their" "men" pay their poll taxes would, by playing by the rules of the current system, allow black men and women both to vote, and thus take the majority vote from that white almost entirely conservative majority, allowing for the first time the possibility of repealing policies like poll taxes.

All her life, the rhetorical genius of Eartha's apparent conservatism was the way it worked constantly to subvert and supplant the dominant racial conservatism it so often mirrored. Eartha would never have said any such thing. She understood it too intimately to do so.

As a reminder of just what black people were up against, in 1922, Eartha became the Florida director of the National Anti-Lynching Committee and pushed for anti-lynching legislation 17 years before Billie Holliday first recorded "Strange Fruit."

"Southern trees bear a strange fruit, / Blood on the leaves and blood at the root, / Black bodies swinging in the

Southern breeze, / Strange fruit hanging from the poplar trees."

I love the regal and magnificent magnolia that rises mightily behind my house. I love its fecundly open and broad fragrant blossoms. I almost wrote "blooms," but these are blossoms. They deserve the full lush lustiness of the word that hasn't been foreshortened.

But sometimes when I look up at that magnolia, I hear Billie Holliday sing, "Pastoral scene of the gallant South, / The bulging eyes and the twisted mouth, / Scent of magnolia, sweet and fresh, / Then the sudden smell of burning flesh."

How can a single black woman be rhetorically successful in that world?

And as *she* lived *her* life in *her* time, and I live mine in mine, I am trying to understand Eartha according to the terms of her own life; I can't expect her to operate according to the terms of mine.

77

Lift every voice and sing, till earth and Heaven ring,
Ring with the harmonies of liberty;
Let our rejoicing rise, high as the listening skies,
Let it resound loud as the rolling sea.
Sing a song full of the faith that the dark past has
    taught us,
Sing a song full of the hope that the present has
    brought us;
Facing the rising sun of our new day begun,
Let us march on till victory is won.

The greatest victory for Eartha and for black "Jaxons" or "Jacksonvilleans" in 1920, and certainly for newly though limitedly enfranchised black women voters, was perhaps not even the consolidation of voter registration and political networking, but the power of solidarity and community activism.

Eartha couldn't have foreseen the long-distance changes coming. In 1920, she couldn't have foreseen the Civil Rights Movement and Lyndon Johnson's Civil Rights legislation.

Given her loyalty to party affiliation, it would also have been hard to forecast black political loyalties switching to the Democratic Party.

Either way, it's hard for me now, a 40 year-old white man writing her ode 40 years after she died, to imagine Eartha, in 1920, imagining a black political loyalty that would last at least from Johnson signing the Civil Rights Act of 1964 to the election of President Barack Obama in 2008. Black leaders in that 44 year period remained as solidly Democratic as black leaders had been solidly Republican for almost nine decades of Eartha's life.

78

I sit at a table by a window in the UNF library's Special Collections room, census records and copies of Dan Schafer's and Eartha's own handwritten notes before me. I try to counter what vision I've had of Eartha so far. I'm trying to question the Romantic rhetorical stances I've taken in my questioning, my research, my writing.

I accept that it's impossible for me to write an objective and somehow "true" account of Eartha White. Nor will I ever be an historian. Though I've published stories about Jacksonville's Public School Number Four, Hemming Plaza, the architectural achievements of Henry John Klutho, and a long (too long?) study of the conflicting stories of Jacksonville pseudo-serial-killer Ottis Toole, I've always predominantly thought of myself as a writer of poems.

I say this in humility. Bill Slaughter, one of my most loved UNF professors, said he didn't presume to be a poet, though he had published collections of poetry. He called himself an experienced reader and a writer of poems.

Though I don't measure up to half a Bill Slaughter, I think of myself in the same category.

But this book also comes from a white Southerner often embarrassed by the South, personally dishonored—and honor codes are a big thing in the South—by my own parents'—and god, how I love them!—religious and cultural conservatism. In 2014, my father is personally offended that anyone would want to change the name of Nathan Bedford Forrest High School.

And I remember being a little boy, I think I was four or five years old, sitting with my parents at S & S Cafeteria at Wilson and Blanding Boulevards on Jacksonville's westside, this would have been 1978 or 1979, and pointing to a couple who had just entered and saying aloud to my parents, "Look! There's some niggers!"

I never heard that word at home again. Young as I was, all these years later, I am mortified as I viscerally remember my parents' embarrassment and shame.

I embodied their embarrassment immediately, and I carry their shame around in my gut to this day.

I don't remember if it was my mother or my father who leaned over me and said, "They don't like to be called that."

79

"One of the first things we did with the recording machine when Zora got it on loan from the Library of Congress, we went to Eartha White's mission, located in the heart of the black ghetto in Jacksonville, a soup kitchen, and they provided not only soup, but clothing and lodging. An old folks' home. It was the only thing going, really, for Afro-Americans, the only place they could go. Many ex-slaves were living there and eating there."

Stetson Kennedy was speaking to National Public Radio, in the last years of his life, in 2002.

Kennedy had written about the South from his Jacksonville base since 1942 when his *Palmetto Country* was published in the American Folkways Series, evolving from fieldwork he did with Zora Neale Hurston and Alan Lomax for Franklin Delano Roosevelt's Works Progress Administration.

The WPA was one of FDR's innumerable Great Depression projects that put Americans to work. It employed artists and folklorists and writers to collect the nation's folk stories and music and art, in whatever ways they could, intangibles that might otherwise have disappeared forever.

Kennedy became most famous for infiltrating the Ku Klux Klan, working undercover, inside the organization, and publishing his findings in a 1954 memoir *I Rode with the Ku Klux Klan*, which French existentialist philosopher Jean Paul Sartre soon thereafter published as *The Klan Unmasked*.

Zora Neale Hurston grew up in Jacksonville and Eatonville, Florida. She's most famous as the Harlem Renaissance novelist of *Their Eyes Were Watching God*.

And Alan Lomax was a folklorist and musicologist who traveled with his father John, most famously across Texas and the South, but also across much of the rest of North

America and the Caribbean, collecting folk songs with cumbersome recording equipment in the 1930s, after having begun the Archive of American Folk Song in 1928.

In the late 1930s, Roosevelt's WPA allowed these three larger-than-life figures to travel across the back roads and into the jungle hamlets of Florida to preserve the cultural remnants that would otherwise have disappeared into the Florida Petri Dish.

But of course that's not entirely true. Strong patterns and streams from disappearing cultures entered what was becoming mainstream and pop culture in the 1940s and 1950s and 1960s.

But two liberal white men and one conservative black woman moved across the byways and swamps of Florida to record the connections between disappearing folk cultures and the times to come.

And when Zora got her hands on that rare recording machine from the Library of Congress, one of the first places Stetson, Zora, and Alan went was Eartha's Clara White Mission on West Ashley.

80

Late 1930s.

Kennedy: Now, what is your whole name?

Whittaker: Annie Whittaker.

Kennedy: And you're about 70 years old, are you?

Whittaker: Yes sir.

Kennedy: I see. Now what is the title of the song that you're going to lead?

Whittaker: It's called "Lord, I'm Running, Trying to Make a Hundred. Ninety-Nine and a Half Won't Do."

Kennedy: Now why did you—you say this song came from?

Whittaker: Just I'm'a—it just come to me and I sung it out of my heart.

Kennedy: Sung right out of your heart, huh?

Whittaker: Yes sir, I just—

Kennedy: I suppose that you've made this song rather popular. Now where is it sung today?

Whittaker: In Georgia, Florida, Alabama, and—

Kennedy: I see. Well, thank you so much. Now we're going to have the entire group sing with you, and you're going to lead them.

And Annie sang with a full chorus and gospel claps.

In 1965, Wilson Pickett recorded a distantly related and differently worded "Ninety Nine and a Half (Won't Do)," and Creedence Clearwater Revival sang Pickett's version at Woodstock in 1969.

In 1993, Diana Ross, the Queen of Pop, the Queen of Motown, recorded Annie Whittaker's own gospel blues version, originally recorded at the Clara White Mission not quite 60 years before.

And Annie sang:

I'm running low (Lord I'm running, trying to make a hundred),

Trying to make a hundred (Lord I'm running, trying to make a hundred),

Ninety-nine and a half won't do.

I'm praying loud (Lord I'm praying, trying to make a hundred),

Trying to make a hundred (Lord I'm praying, trying to make a hundred),

Ninety-nine and a half won't do.

Ninety-one

Ninety-two

Ninety-three

Ninety-four

Ninety-five

Ninety-six

Ninety-seven

Ninety-eight

Ninety-nine and a half just won't do.

And the next time Stetson, Zora, and Alan came to the Clara White Mission with their great big recording machines, Eartha stopped them before they could record the singing of a preacher named Stuckey.

And she said, "Hold it right there. We're going to have a little prayer."

Republican that she always was, she thanked God for these people and the Democratic president who employed them. She prayed, "Dear Lord, this is Eartha White talking to you again. Just want to thank you for giving mankind the intelligence to create such a marvelous machine and for a president like Franklin D. Roosevelt that cares about preserving the songs that people sing."

The Mission opened itself to the Works Progress Administration's activities throughout the 1930s.

The WPA operated a Mission sewing room, where it trained and gave steady employment to more than a hundred women during the Great Depression. In November 1936, a young woman wrote to Eartha, saying, "I am a skill dress maker and is still out of work I will be to see you on tuesday evening and you will not regret helping me." Eartha received such requests constantly.

The Mission operated cooking classes, ran art classes that produced exhibitions in the Mission's WPA Art Gallery, and served as local headquarters for the Federal Writers' Project.

At this time, Eartha wrote publically about bringing the Mission to the "point where self-help, rather than bare charity, could be the keynote of many of its activities."

She writes of the Mission's classes for nursing, home hygiene, cooking, gardening and canning, of its quilting bees and its employment services. Her goal was "to aid the dependent Negro in earning for himself some of those benefits that in the past could come only through direct charity."

The Mission offered numerous courses for the blind, teaching them "to cane chairs, do beadwork, make belts, read Braille writing," and find ways to earn a living "far above that of the street-corner mendicant."

On an early November night in 1932, 250 people came to the Mission to watch and participate in a quilting bee.

Quilting had been a social and political activity since before the Civil War, when quilts hung in windows offering secret signs to runaway slaves and activists on the Underground Railroad.

In quilting bees, women and girls had long come together and stretched fabric and patterns across large quilting frames, working communally on these expansive artworks that often commemorated major life and community events like weddings.

In 1987, more than half a century after the quilting bee at the Mission, work began on the world's largest piece of art, the AIDS Memorial Quilt. In the next two decades, quilters donated thousands of panels, each approximately the length and width of a grave, in memory of someone they loved who'd died of AIDS. The quilt grew so large it couldn't be contained in one place, and large segments of it toured college campuses, public commons, and other venues simultaneously.

Back in 1932, a *Jacksonville Journal* article about the quilting bee called quilting a dying art. Happily, dying arts often survive.

The article referred to the Needlework Guild, of which Eartha, "indefatigable welfare worker," was president.

The guild required "as membership fee, the making and contribution of two garments. The guild is divided into sections under captains or leaders who direct the sewing efforts of their groups. Mrs. Martha Green has organized the largest group, having 54 members who have qualified by donating two garments each made by their own hands."

Vocalists sang "Negro spirituals," to the accompaniment of a ukulele, over the stands upon which quilters hovered and worked with "deft fingers." Mission workers served plates of Hoppin' John, with black-eyed peas, rice, chopped onion, bacon, and salt.

Later that evening, more than 200 quilts, the products of the night and the recent work of the Needlework Guild, were exhibited as art in the Mission auditorium before being given to the poor to shelter them from the city's unpredictable winters.

Somewhere in the cold winter nights of early 2014, in Mobile or Atlanta or Newark or Scranton or Toronto or St. Louis or Boise or Compton, or half a mile from Jacksonville's West Ashley Street, the artisanal remnant of a 1932 Clara White Mission quilt warms somebody still, I'm sure of it, someone hungry and sick and lonely and excluded from exclusive America, someone who's trying to walk back or walk forward to self-respect and some decent standard of living, and to love.

83

In June 1933, Charles H. Loeb edited the first and apparently only edition of *The Friend*, which was to be published monthly by the Mission Publishing Company. It's unclear to what *The Friend* would have evolved, since the entire first issue consists of Loeb's report on the activities at the Mission, alongside his startlingly conservative views on poverty.

His editorial notes from the first page admonish the reader, "Ignorance of natural laws, misconception of the Master's motives, and general slothfulness of the masses have more largely contributed to the lot of the poverty-stricken masses, than all the political or economic plutocrats or 'bosses' in the civilized world."

In one fell swoop, Loeb blames the poor for their poverty, absolves social policies that benefit the wealthy over the poor, devalues the efforts of organized labor, and calls God the Master, just as Harriet Jacobs recounts, in *Incidents in the Life of a Slave Girl*, how white preachers wrote separate sermons for slaves in which obedience to their *earthly* masters correlated to obedience to the *heavenly* Master.

Loeb editorializes that "no true child of God has ever been seen to beg for bread. Poverty, suffering, disease and misfortune go hand in hand with doubt and fear. They can have no effect on the lives of those who know TRUTH and keep Faith."

But lest the reader think Loeb too judgmental of the sick or the poor, he clarifies that he does "not say that all who are poor and who profess Christianity are hypocrites," oh no, just that their faith is weak. Their "ingratitude has weakened the connection between the supplicant and the source." After all, Loeb says, our needs "are obvious to the Master," but apparently He won't supply them to those not already grateful.

After this editor's note, Loeb praises the Mission's function as community center, the numbers of people it feeds, and its health services. He even says the Mission shouldn't be thought of as a bunch of "notorious beggars," asking for charitable items to give the poor, but he doesn't say anyone's actually called it that.

Loeb was 28 when he edited Vol. 1 No. 1 of *The Friend*. Almost immediately thereafter, he took a job at *The Cleveland Call and Post*, where he worked selling ads, reporting, and working as city editor and managing editor.

Sometime after covering the Montgomery Bus Boycott 23 years after his momentary stint with *The Friend*, a Jacksonville blip between his working in New York and Atlanta, someone tagged him with the honorific "dean of black newsmen."

What did Eartha make of these mean and illiberal remarks about the poor? I've found no such sentiments in Eartha's own thinking. In fact, Eartha wrote about offering "the dependent Negro" ways of "self-help," while likewise giving relief to "hundreds of unemployables."

The Friend's masthead includes her name as Mission president, but does that effectually stamp Loeb's opinions with her approval, or did Eartha grant him editorial freedom, even in the name of the Mission? Was his editorial voice the price for having an up-and-coming Howard University-educated journalist focus on all the Mission's activities?

The single volume of *The Friend* concludes with a Bible verse from the sixth chapter of the Book of Matthew, in screaming and unnecessary capitalization: "FOR YOUR FATHER KNOWETH WHAT THINGS YE HAVE NEED OF,

BEFORE YE ASK HIM," and the platitude that "Anybody can shoo a chicken, but it takes a blacksmith to shoe a horse."

In 1936, Pearl Randolph, a field worker for the WPA's Federal Writers' Project, found Edward Lycurgis, 64 years old, living at the Mission.

Lycurgis was born less than a decade after the Civil War and the Emancipation Proclamation, but his story was collected in conjunction with perhaps the greatest work of the Federal Writers' Project, the 10,000-page compilation called *Slave Narratives: A Folk History of Slavery in the United States*, or the WPA Slave Narrative Collection.

MISS WHITE, EDWARD LYCURGUS and "LILY WHITE," a dog that led a blind man about the streets of Jacksonville for years and was bequeathed to Miss White upon his death.

Lycurgis told Randolph he was the only one left of the half-circle of children who gathered, literally, around their father's knee more than 50 years before to listen to the old man's stories.

How easily stories lose themselves. They disperse on sound waves into trees and fields and summers and winters. They're gone forever. But if one person repeats a story, he becomes that story's archivist and author and passes it to future tellers. How easily stories attain immortality.

Randolph described Lycurgis as "a lover of home, very shy and did not care much for courting." He never married and he lived at the Mission in exchange for whatever "piddling" jobs they'd give him.

His father George was born in Liverpool, from which he made his way to the West Indies. George bought Edward's mother, Julia, to give her "freedom" to marry him, perhaps a contradictory contract.

Julia was the daughter of slaves who belonged to the Fleming Plantation whose land is now Fleming Island, one of the wealthier suburbs of Jacksonville. In the South, almost stereotypically, wealth lasts long and spreads murderous roots.

George considered himself English, though he was a black man, because Emancipation of the British West Indies had taken place in 1834. During the Civil War, George lived aboard a blockade ship off the coast of Virginia, selling weapons to the North.

When the ship was captured, George told his children a half century before Edward repeated the story to Pearl Randolph, and in her 1936 rendering, "Me, I was a scairt man, cause I was always free, and over here dey took it for granted dat all black men should be slaves."

It's not clear how he did it, but George fled imprisonment and went South, rather than North, ending up in Florida. "I met many runaway slaves. Some was trying to get North and fight for de freeing of dey people; others was jes runnin' way cause dey could. Many of dem didn't had no idea where dey was goin' and told of havin' good marsters. But one and all dey had a good strong notion ter see what it was like to own your own body."

George came through the North Florida town of St. Augustine and showed his papers indicating he was a "free nigger." He told his children, "One day I went to the slave market and watched em barter off po niggers like dey was hogs. Whole families sold together and some was split— mother gone to one marster and father and children gone to others."

He said, "They'd bring a slave out on the platform and open his mouth, pound his chest, make him harden his muscles so the buyer could see what he was gittin'. Young men was called 'bucks' and young women 'wenches'. The person that offered the best price was de buyer.

"And dey shore did git rid uf some pretty gals. Dey always looked so shame and pitiful up on dat stand wid all dem men standin' dere lookin' at em wid what dey had on dey minds shinin' in they eyes. One little gal walked up and left her mammy mourning so pitiful cause she had to be sold."

Then George told his children their mother "cost me $950.00 and den my own freedom. But she was worth it— every bit of it!"

There's no indication in Randolph's 1936 renderings of Edward's Clara White Mission recollections of whether he thought that buying a woman for one purpose was better than buying her for another. Nineteenth century feminists thought marriage, the Victorian laws of which made a wife little more than the property of her husband, analogous to slavery. Then again, 1970s' black feminists like "womanist" Alice Walker thought feminism the reserve of upper middle-class white women.

Edward remembers his father saying that former slaves felt free from doing any work at all after Emancipation. "De po niggers went mad. Some refused to work and dey didn't stay in one place long 'nough to do a thing. De crops suffered and soon we had starvation times."

His father told them of his own hard times living off wild hog and cabbage palms. George had said there were black families scattered all through the landscape who lived mostly off any one plant in the woods they knew wasn't poisonous: pokeweed leaves, though the berries and roots will kill you, elderberries, dandelions, oxalis leaves and tubers, betony tubers, clover. Or, whenever they could kill a squirrel. Or a snake. A crawdad. Or cicada. Whenever they could fish.

85

Pearl Randolph also wrote about Wilhelmina Kiser and Mollie Peartree in a document she co-authored with Zora Neale Hurston called "Negro Folk Customs and Folk Lore."

Wilhelmina Kiser walked Jacksonville's streets "wearing robes embroidered with the scriptures." The self-described "spiritual healer and prophetess" sometimes wore a robe upon which she'd inscribed the Ten Commandments.

According to Randolph, the prophetess was "a familiar figure on the streets," but her house at 1031 East 15th Street, though "lovely" and "old," was almost entirely empty, since her white neighbors and Ku Klux Klan members had terrorized her and confiscated all her furniture.

Mollie Peartree wandered the streets of Jacksonville "in the purple garb of a nun." Everyone knew Mollie Peartree when they saw her, and many people believed her claims to heal sickness of the body and the mind through the touch of her hands and prayer.

People knew her commonly as Mary Magdalene, the name of the former prostitute who washed Christ's feet with her tears and her hair, and of course, the middle names of Eartha White.

Mollie said God had assigned her the purple robes and the name.

86

Along with the orphanage, Eartha ran a Milk Fund Committee to bring milk to poor children. She ran a Maternity Home and daycare service on Milnor Street near the Old Folks' Home. The free milk Eartha distributed to needy children through the public school system coincided with her campaign to ameliorate tuberculosis in black children.

Tuberculosis has been by far the most deadly bacterial infection in the history of the world. In New England, by 1800, tuberculosis was the cause of one quarter of all deaths and one of every 250 people suffered from the disease.

Even in the 21st century, when diseases like polio have come close to eradication, and there's great hope and progress for treating HIV / AIDS so soon after the full-scale AIDS panics of the 1980s, tuberculosis still carries, now mostly latently, in one of three people on the planet.

Jacksonville's black community died from tuberculosis in far greater numbers than the city's whites.

Early in the 1930s, Eartha took 86 children suffering from tuberculosis to American Beach on Amelia Island, where she had arranged for nurses and doctors to care for them.

Abraham Lincoln Lewis of Afro-American Life Insurance had secured and purchased the Amelia Island beachfront property to open a public beach that black people could legally enjoy during segregation.

And since Eartha's American Beach relocation of tubercular children saved several lives, she decided to open a tuberculosis hospital for blacks who couldn't receive health care in "white" medical facilities.

She opened the tuberculosis home on Milnor Street in 1936 after a black man's neighbors found him dead in a collapsing car barn with a can of beans in his hand. The car barn was his last resort, since people had been too afraid of his bloody cough to offer him any help.

Tuberculosis bacilli have been found in Egyptian mummies from 6,000 years ago. In the 1800s, people called the disease Consumption, because it consumed its victims. Because people didn't yet understand germs, infection, and transmission of disease, they frequently saw Consumption not only as physical, but as spiritual.

And in comes the mythology of vampires, supernatural manifestations of Consumption.

Both vampires and TB *consumed* their victims. Both seemed to feed on blood, the vital force. Both caused in their victims pallor and emaciation and bleeding and coughing. When Consumptives died, they could project their disease, as though from the grave, on living members of their family, or their community.

Eartha visited each of her tubercular patients. She quickly grew to know them and to love them. When Consumption consumed the women in her hospital, some of them became almost as small as her.

And though she boasted later of never having had the time to marry, surely she never forgot the fiancé of her adolescence, James Jordan, who wrote her long-distance letters when he could hardly sit up to do so. Constantly he coughed. Dramatically his energy drained, his weight plummeted.

"I am really not well but better than I have been and at work with Mr. Richard. When I get in at night I feel like doing nothing but going to bed."

[...]

"I am not get entirely well. Though lots better than I was when I wrote you last. And am looking better. I shall make an attempt to go to work to morrow in Richardson office. My old employee."

[...]

"But dear I keep so poorly and weak that when I get home at night and get a little supper and get through with other little things nothing suits but bed."

[...]

"Eartha dear you dont want any Photo now. I have lost 16 lbs. Then I havent the means at present any way. My Dr Bill keeps me to the mark. At present for 21 treatments it is 2.00 a day. The weather is very pleasant at present. Eartha I must say I am tired

good night

Write to me though

All sends love

I realy can hardly keep up some days"

87

"And for the sake of posterity, I understand that you have a story from your mother from an actual incident from before the Civil War. And now, uh, first let me say that I believe you told me that your mother was a slave, was she?"

"Yes."

The Federal Writers' Project recorded Eartha's recounting of a story from the late 1840s that sounds like a taboo avoidance of contagion, for as folklorist Michael Bell persuasively argues, the fear of the dead is often a logical extension of the fear of death.

"She was a slave, and, uh, about what year would you say that this incident took place? Approximately?"

"I should say…1849."

1849's the supposed year of Clara's birth, though some sources say 1845. Either way, Clara would seem to be too young to serve as the source of Eartha's ghost story.

"1849. I see. And, uh, where was this, uh, where, where were your parents living at this time?"

"My mother was living at that time in Amelia Island, Fernandina, Florida, where she was born."

"And now let us get this story recorded just exactly as you remember it, the way it was told to you. Now what is your name?"

"My name's Eartha M. M. White."

"And, uh, your residence, Miss White?"

"Jacksonville, Florida. 611 West Ashley Street."

"I see. Well now, go ahead and tell the story please."

"During the days of slavery, and my mother was a house girl, on this particular plantation on Amelia Island,

Fernandina, Florida, while serving dinner in the early evening, one of the family came home, almost falling off of his horse, ran into the dining room, frightened everybody, and when he'd come to his self, he began to tell an experience he'd had on the road. He said just as he was coming 'round the big road not far from the cemetery, his aunt stopped the horse. It was the horse was owned by her during her lifetime. The horse seemed to recognize her voice. Every strand of hair stood up on his head. And then he heard someone stroking the horse. And then he heard her voice. She said to him, calling him by name, 'Don't be afraid.' She says, 'I want you to meet me tomorrow at sundown.' And told him just where. 'I have something for you. I am your aunt.'"

Then the tape breaks and a half minute of static ends with the resumption of the story. "Just as she finished, the horse began biting, and he moreso than ever, he ran home, falling almost off of his horse. In the dining room where they were eating, frightened everybody,"—illegible—"'You're going to hear what she has to say and to get what she has to give you.'"

"And he said, 'Not me! She can keep whatever she has! I won't be there.'"

Clara always delighted in repeating this story, Eartha said, though the long deep dates were not quite right.

"Thank you, Miss White, that was awfully nice of you to go to all this trouble to, uh, to give us this story."

What now occurs to me would not have mattered to Eartha.

The paradoxes made her more than the sum of her parts and greater than her reconciled oppositions.

She was called "Mother," but she never married, never had children. She was called "Mother," and she was named for the Earth.

Eartha White was Mother Earth.

She was four-and-a-half feet tall and larger-than-life.

She was the daughter of a wealthy white man too cowardly to claim her, but she was considered black.

The Self of Eartha White grew so large in its function in community and culture and history, because Eartha White constantly gave her (self) away.

A journalist in the 1970s called the Virginal Eartha Jacksonville's "universal mother." She was both pure and, simultaneously, everyone's mother. But as mothers are hardly virgins, Eartha inhabited the paradox of becoming Jacksonville's Virgin Mary. She was the Immaculate Conception at the heart of the 50,000 black people who once lived downtown.

But she wasn't just Black Mother. She was the mother of the city's destitute whites. She was the mother of black and white, as she'd come from black and white.

Or, if you erase the wealthy white figure from her history, as was the original goal of everyone involved, then Eartha is the Virgin Birth of the Earth, a Gaian Immaculate Conception.

Instead, Eartha White converted her Genesis into a Blessèd Miscegenation.

Though an objective history is not my goal, nevertheless, I don't want to write a hagiography, the biography of a saint, another comparison to Gandhi, Mother Teresa, or Jesus.

Eartha was as human as I am.

While considering this humanization—and personally I relate so much better to people than I do to angels—I come across a criticism connected to political loyalty and affiliation.

I also find a first allegation, without any further corroboration, that the death of her fiancé, James Jordan, did not lead directly to her marriage to community.

The latter first.

In a 1976 interview, Ted Redding, longtime president of the local NAACP chapter and a board member of the nursing home, told Dan Schafer it was "common knowledge" within the black community that Eartha had "for years carried on a torrid affair with Tom Baxter, a saloon keeper with a place somewhere on Bay Street."

Schafer's notes say, "Baxter reputation poor. He had killed somebody. Saloon keepers in those days were really underworld figures. Baxter was very fair. Almost White."

The transcript notes end, "She was known as a philanderer in those days, but everyone respected her for the good work she was doing and soon she dropped all disrespectful behavior."

This brief note lies so far outside most references to Eartha I've found that I don't know what to make of it.

It makes sense to me that the daughter of a wealthy white man and his maid, raised as the only surviving daughter of a former slave, having grown up in the by-default-outlaw neighborhood of LaVilla, once a plantation and, by the time Eartha was a teenager, district of brothels and bars (and churches and synagogues), would experience and exhibit some non-white-mainstream wild desperation on her way to becoming a woman.

The official history is that Eartha was never anything but a saint. Official history is hagiography. Can hagiography be true? Or maybe the truth swerves toward Baxter?

It seems likely the Tom Baxter Ted Redding mentions was the son of LaVilla's Thomas Baxter, a younger man named John T. Baxter.

Census records from the 1880s list Thomas Backster or Baxter as being a "mulatto" with a LaVilla "liquor business" and a son named John T.

Redding's or Schafer's references to "those days" don't indicate which years, but Redding said Baxter had killed someone. John T. was close to Eartha's own age and he'd been arrested for a double murder at the end of November 1900.

On Thanksgiving Day, a 24 year-old police officer named Henry Raley tried to arrest a "drunken negro" named John T. Baxter. Baxter ran into a store at the corner of Davis and Forsyth. Raley placed Baxter under arrest, and before he knew it, "a mob of negroes numbering 'from twenty to fifty young men'" confronted Raley and demanded the black man's release.

According to *The Florida Times-Union*, the "mob" was called "the Bridge Street Gang." Bridge Street later became Broad Street. The newspaper said the gang had been walking about LaVilla, shouting and "annoying any lone Negress they met."

Already that night, said the newspaper, the Bridge Street Gang had thrown a Mulatto woman named Mamie Jones down on her porch, invaded her house, and broken her chairs, Chinaware, and lamps.

When gang members saw Raley with Baxter, they immediately surrounded him and threatened him. An ex-cop named Virgil T. Tucker came to Raley's backup.

Baxter, 20 years old, identified as the "leader" of the "Bridge Street Gang," pulled a gun and shot Raley dead,

before turning his gun on Tucker and shooting him in the shoulder and the head. Tucker survived, but Baxter also aimed his gun at a 51 year-old black man named Chandler Brooks, who'd come to help the white police officers, and killed him instantly.

The *Times-Union* said Baxter lived at 106 East Beaver Street and "could pass for white." His father was LaVilla's Tom Baxter "who keeps a saloon at Bridge and Ward Streets," now Broad and Houston Streets.

Though Baxter was sentenced to life in prison, his sentence was commuted to hard labor in a phosphate mine 40 miles from the state prison in Starke. It's not clear how long he was there or what happened to him afterwards.

Jacksonville police were furious that John T. Baxter wasn't hung.

92

Tom Baxter, father of John T., first partnered with a friend, James Cashen, to run a liquor and cigar store at Ward and Bridge in the mid-1890s. With the store's immediate profit, the two men soon turned it into a saloon. Baxter had been selling liquor in LaVilla since about 1880, however, from a boarding house he ran and resided in on Bay Street.

Baxter's prosperity rose rapidly. He bought Cashen's half of the saloon after the Great Fire of 1901 and moved it to a new building on the other side of Bridge Street, where in 1903, it became the Exchange Theater.

The Exchange was one more theater / club offering blues and jazz and Vaudeville acts and other entertainment up and down and around West Ashley.

The boarding house Baxter ran around the corner on Ward was one in a long line of euphemistic "female boarding houses." Baxter's was one of more than 60 brothels along Ward, now Houston Street, in what was colloquially known as "The Line."

When the six-foot tall, hatchet-wielding Prohibitionist Carrie Nation visited Ward Street in 1908, she called Jacksonville a "demonocracy" through which ventilated "over a hundred breathing holes of hell."

If Eartha really did have her "torrid affair" with a Tom Baxter, it must have been John T., the Baxter widely known as a murderer, who perhaps inherited some business from his father. Perhaps Redding conflated father and son, attributing the son's double murder to the father.

The official Eartha story is that after her fiancé died while she toured singing opera, she decided never to marry and immediately gave her life to philanthropy.

But isn't everybody more complicated than an angel?

In February 1975, a year after Eartha's death, historian Dan Schafer interviewed Eartha's goddaughter Vivian Chavez.

With a television blasting nearby, she told him, "And I know one day she sat and she told me, why, why, um, she worked as hard as she did, she said that she did…something…I can't think what she told me she did…but anyway she said she was criticized, you know, criticized by the people, I don't know whether the people at Bethel Church or what people, but she said then she made up her mind she was gonna be determined to, uh, to, uh, do more, you know, and from that she started out doing more…for other people."

I can find nobody but Theodore Redding who mentions any connection between Eartha White and LaVilla's Baxters.

UNF's Eartha White Collection contains two promissory notes from Eartha to Thomas Baxter, one in 1908 for $25 and one in 1910 for $90.

The collection also contains a promissory note signed by Thomas Baxter in 1909 to the Joseph Zapf Company, a beer, wine, and liquor merchant, for $150.00. There's no indication of why Baxter's note to a liquor merchant was kept amongst Eartha's receipts.

93

The myth held that Eartha's grandfather wanted to name her Mary Magdalene, after the woman Biblically present at the Crucifixion and the Resurrection.

The tradition that evolved about Mary Magdalene in Gothic and Renaissance art informs her identity as much as the Biblical information. She washed Jesus's feet with her hair or her tears. One Germanic Gothic sculpture depicts her hair as flowing from her head to her feet.

Storytellers and artists and theologians depicted Mary Magdalene as the woman closest to Jesus, also as a redeemed prostitute.

Heretical groups throughout Christian history and some contemporary Biblical scholars have seen Mary Magdalene as Jesus's secret lover or his wife.

Compare that mythical Eartha who never married, because she married her community, to Christ who, in the Book of Revelation, takes the consummate body of his believers as his bride.

When Jesus appeared to Mary Magdalene after his resurrection, he told her, "Don't touch me," or "Don't try to hold on to me."

Noli me tangere.

They're the words of the unattainable beloved to her hunter in Sir Thomas Wyatt's famous early 16th century poem, "Whoso List to Hunt."

If you include the (in)famous Madonna-Whore Complex of men who see all women as either Virgin Mother or Whore, maybe while listening to Charles Mingus's *Black Saint and the Sinner Lady*, you can say Mary Magdalene plays every woman's role available for Sigmund Freud, Sir Thomas Wyatt, and Christianity in general.

But none of their views gets us any closer to knowing who the person named Mary Magdalene really was.

Their views tell us how these men came to terms with women, but nothing about this particular woman.

Perhaps her community's views of what kinds of Mary Magdalene—the redeemed philanderer or the wife of the people—it saw in Eartha White tell us equally little about Eartha.

94

Redding called Baxter "very fair. Almost White." The other complaint I've found stems from reports that the primary public defenders of Eartha's reputation were middle-class black women.

In 2014, in the second term of the United States's first "black" president, whose mother was "white," the emotions and connotations of shades of black seem much less significant—at least to young progressive whites, but frequently also to young Asian-Americans, Latinos, and to many young black Americans.

Indeed, my wife, my age, Panamanian, is "white"— whatever that means (it certainly doesn't mean she came from the Caucasus, and neither did I)—it means, for her, German and English and Scottish—and Chinese and Filipino. She's had poor whites ask her if she's Cherokee, and Middle Easterners ask her if she's Lebanese.

But to compare my wife or even myself (German, French, Scottish, English, Irish—awfully damn white, but all nationalities are formed from tribes and ethnic hubs) to all the shades of so-called black a century ago in America, and especially in the South, misses the point entirely.

I've taught Nella Larsen's *Passing*, published in 1929, and James Weldon Johnson's *Autobiography of an Ex-Colored Man*, 1912. Larsen's novel follows Clare Kendry, who passes for white with her white husband, who doesn't know she has "black" "in her," and her later reunion with a childhood friend who still goes about as "black."

Just as film director Spike Lee introduced the sarcastic term "Magical Negro" to describe stock characters in fiction and film, black characters with secret spiritual wisdom, Larsen's beautiful and complicated novel is now thought a prime treatment of the "Tragic Mulatta," usually a character with a white well-positioned father and a black servant or slave mother. The Tragic Mulatta feels confusion and ostracism. She can't reach what white society should offer her, but she can't succumb socially to what being black might mean. She is, *fait accompli*, a failure at what she has the capabilities to be in either world.

In Johnson's *Autobiography of an Ex-Colored Man*, a musically talented "light-skinned" "black" man from the South attaches himself to a wealthy white man who hears him playing ragtime and hires him to play music at parties. Their relationship becomes intimate, at times homoerotic, but increasingly redolent of a master-slave relationship.

Johnson left Jacksonville for college in Atlanta when he was 16. He'd grown up on Ward Street, which, as he left LaVilla, was becoming the brothel district of the city. In 1906, he became diplomat to Venezuela, and in 1909 to Nicaragua. He married New York songwriter Grace Nail in 1910, and her bridal photo in Panama shows her wearing all white, holding a white parasol, herself very "fair," or maybe Latina—not that the word yet existed.

*

As I walk down Ward Street, today's Houston Street, a narrow road of empty lots with occasional brick and stone left over from Jacksonville's demolition of LaVilla, sometimes abutted with the backs of brick factory and warehouse buildings, I think about James Weldon Johnson's having grown up here.

The giant brick Stanton School, where Johnson had been principal, still stands on West Ashley, a block from the

Clara White Mission. It's the predecessor of the city's Stanton College Preparatory School, one of the half-dozen good schools in Jacksonville, which consistently ranks nationally amongst excellent public high school education.

I feel strange parallels, walking in LaVilla. My daughters attended middle school at LaVilla School of the Arts, established in the 1990s, whose campus cuts West Ashley Street, the former LaVilla Broadway, or "Great Black Way," in two.

Johnson considered coming back to Jacksonville after his diplomatic tenures in Central America, but a longtime friend told him that Jim Crow laws had made Jacksonville far more Southern than it was during the Civil War, when, though slaves were held in the city and its environs, much of the wealthy white population had recently been Yankee and identified with the Union.

He told Johnson not to come back to Jacksonville, that it was not the same town Johnson had known growing up, whatever its faults had been then. Even in the 19-teens, a man as educated and accomplished as James Weldon Johnson would've had virtually no rights in his own hometown.

I walk Houston Street, along which ran a child named James Weldon Johnson, and I think of my wife, Panamanian— meaning so many ethnicities, hair textures, nose shapes, eye shapes, skin shades. And I think about that bridal photo of Grace, Johnson's bride, in 1910, standing at *Panama Viejo*, I've been there, old Spanish Panama founded in 1519.

White as I am, I'm only so many shades more "white" than Johnson and his wife and my wife, and if Johnson served as model for his fictional *Autobiography of an Ex-Colored Man*, and if Nella Larsen's Clare was a "Tragic Mulatta," then so perhaps are most of the whitest of us.

I stood at *Panama Viejo* with the love of my life a decade before she became my wife, where James Weldon Johnson stood with his bride, each of us (even ruddy and bluish-white me) only so many steps from that untraceable line between "fair-skinned" and "dark-skinned" that for so long paralleled "black" class distinctions in the United States.

*

Perhaps more black people than white conspiratorially claimed that Eartha secretly benefited from her clandestine white parentage. Perhaps those shade distinctions contributed to Eartha's official sanctifications, even if Thomas

215

Baxters, father and son, were "very fair" and "could have passed for white."

Only a couple of people are recorded having hinted, all these years later, that any part of Eartha's past was "whitewashed."

But without corroboration, they stand on their own.

On their own in the vast field of ghosts who didn't quite appear.

The other complaint stems from an interview with longtime *Florida Star* editor Eric Simpson, conducted in 1993, a year before he died.

The Florida Star and *The Jacksonville Free Press* are the two primary newspapers that served black Jacksonville for more than half a century in the historical absence of the city's mainstream newspapers offering credible news to a black audience.

It's from Simpson that Abel Bartley speaks of Eartha White's black cultural elitism in a city election crucial to rising black power in 1947.

It's a stunning assertion. I read it in the context of those claims that Eartha was always wealthy, propped up by the anonymous wealthy family whose son "knocked up" the family maid.

Placing her parental lineage aside, tracing her financial transactions throughout her life, as Dan Schafer concluded, shows that what profits she made she channeled back into charities, and as I said earlier, though she had property assets at the time of her death, whatever wealth she had was thus limited.

But Bartley doesn't refer specifically to these rumors, and if Simpson did, Bartley doesn't relate it in his reference to Simpson's skepticism.

In Bartley's *Keeping the Faith: Race, Politics, and Social Development in Jacksonville, Florida, 1940-1970*, he speaks of Eartha's opposition to Jacksonville's first black Democratic candidate for City Council, Wilson Armstrong.

The last black city councilman had been George Ross, a Lincoln Republican, more than 40 years before Armstrong's candidacy.

But Bartley says a coalition of black cultural elites strong-armed Armstrong from becoming the first black city councilman in four decades and the first black Democratic councilman.

Armstrong was a "mortar mixer," and as a working-class black man, was easily labeled in the political climate and vocabulary of the time a Communist, since Communists were supposed to be the party of the people, the party of the workers. Working class and perhaps a political naïf, Armstrong succumbed to the common political tactic of painting your opponent "red" with Communism.

But Bartley's and Simpson's chief criticism of the campaign against Wilson Armstrong is otherwise concerned.

In fact, considering the racial and political climate of 1947, it's surprising that blacks in power didn't almost automatically fall in line to put another black man in power. They didn't.

This was the year that Eartha White and black leaders and activists across the state raised public awareness in opposition to Jacksonville's own Florida State Senator John Mathews's "White Primary Bill," which would have forbidden black people from voting in political primary elections.

(Jacksonville's John Mathews Bridge is the main connector across the St. Johns River between downtown and the city's large Arlington area.)

Eartha took different rhetorical stances with different politicians, indicating her political prowess. To Senate President Dilworth Clarke, she telegrammed this note, "Back in the dark days my people depended on you and your folk.

We are still depending on you to help us. Please do not vote for the so-called White-Primary Bill."

But to Governor Millard Caldwell, Eartha wrote, "If the whole world go wrong I believe you will do the right and will not support the so-called White Primary Bill, because it is not for the best interest of all of the people."

The two telegrams are worded so differently, but it's clear each message is tailored to its recipient. LaVilla's Ritz Theatre and Museum's Adonnica Toler tells me when she first read Eartha's letter to Clarke, she felt nauseated, but when she later read Eartha's letter to the governor, she understood the different tactics to which Eartha must adjust, and how difficult it would be to gain any voice at all in such a system.

The bill's greatest opponent was Florida NAACP leader Harry T. Moore. Four years later, on Christmas 1951, the Ku Klux Klan murdered Moore and his wife Harriette on their 25th wedding anniversary. The Klan's bomb exploded beneath the Moores' Central Florida house. They were later called the first martyrs of the Civil Rights Movement.

In 1955, Jacksonville's John Mathews, having lost his fight for a White Primary, became Chief Justice of the Florida Supreme Court, the same year that 14 year-old Emmett Till whistled at a white woman in Mississippi, and in retaliation, was beaten, had his eye gouged out, was shot through the head, and was dumped into a river with barbed wire and a cotton gin fan wrapped around his neck, the same year that Rosa Parks refused to give up her bus seat to a white man in Montgomery, Alabama, and accidentally sparked the Civil Rights Movement.

I drive over the Mathews Bridge about once a week. I drive over the Fuller Warren Bridge daily. Fuller Warren was a Jacksonville city council member and Florida governor. He was also a member of the Ku Klux Klan.

96

Bartley quotes Jacksonville Civil Rights leader Frank Hampton as saying, "The so-called Black leadership…were opposed to Armstrong because they felt he was not among the so-called sophisticated of the Blacks in this Community." Bartley says Hampton considered Armstrong a man of "nerve and courage," attributes he didn't feel Jacksonville's black leadership had at the time.

Armstrong ran against incumbent Councilman Claude Smith, and Hampton told Bartley he blamed Armstrong's defeat, more than 40 years later, on the opposition of Jacksonville's black leaders.

More specifically, Bartley says Claude Smith canvassed Jacksonville's black population to see what they most wanted in 1947 and what they most wanted was not a black representative in city government, but a pool in which their children could swim.

Not being able to swim in a municipal pool, according to this argument, seemed a more daily and tangible concern than political representation. It was a time when black families tried to counter for themselves and their children, even under segregation, the things they saw white families being able to do.

So Smith offered black leaders a deal.

"What the Black fifth ward residents wanted most was a swimming pool for their children. Smith offered to build a swimming pool if they stopped Armstrong. He offered a straight *quid pro quo*."

Bartley names Eartha White as among those black leaders who accepted the appeasement. Her latter-day critics would call it accommodationist, very Booker T. Washington of her to align herself thus.

But Bartley gets down to brass tacks. He says, "They opposed him because of his social class, not his political ideals. They did not want an uneducated laborer representing a middle-class and upper-class African-American ward."

97

Though it's hard to corroborate Bartley's *quid pro quo* corruption claim, the timing holds up, though that proves nothing by itself.

Wilson Armstrong lost handily in 1947. In 1949, the city purchased land just south of Hogan's Creek and just north of LaVilla for a blacks-only swimming pool.

In 1951, the city opened the Jefferson Street Pool, the only swimming pool in the city for black people. Families came to swim there and church congregations performed baptisms. Walter Whetstone met his wife there.

Walter sold life insurance and delivered telegrams for Western Union for 30 years. When the City of Jacksonville destroyed LaVilla in the early 1990s, he bought a couple of old buildings on Jefferson Street between Union and State Streets.

He decorated the buildings and the grounds between them with a long lifetime's worth of his collections— everything from old LaVilla restaurant signs to folk sculpture to trumpets and piano innards to wagon wheels to giant barber's poles.

Walter is one of the nicest people I've ever met. At almost 80 years old, he often sits outside in a business suit and welcomes passersby to come on in to his place and look around. Despite living through decades of segregation and injustice at the hands of whites, he always welcomes me when I walk up. His whole face lights up with kindness.

He calls his most-of-a-city-block the Whetstonian, says if Smithson can have his Smithsonian, then Whetstone can have his Whetstonian.

As far as I'm concerned, Walter Whetstone is Jacksonville's great outsider artist, "outsider art" being artistic expression created by people not trained and educated within the artistic discourse and its institutions (and confines). It's a more specific and hip current name for folk art.

Walter and Dorothy have been married for 53 years.

In the preface for Maura Wolfson-Foster's 2012 photography book *The Whetstonian*, Dorothy writes about how she met Walter at the Jefferson Street Pool in 1957. It was a summer Sunday, she remembers, about noon. Dorothy wore a two-piece suit and high heels.

When she left the pool to go to the movies at the Ritz Theatre, she heard Walter calling after her, "Young lady! Young lady!" They talked for a while at the corner of Jefferson and First Streets. Then the two of them went to the movies at the Ritz.

98

Dorothy writes about another day—

"Had to go to work that afternoon. That evening, almost time to get off, one of the workers told me someone was asking for me. I went outside. There was this beautiful shiny black car, parked right at the backdoor. It wasn't quite time for me to get off, so I called my father to let him know I had a way home. Well, Walter's brother was chauffeuring us to my house. When we got home, he wanted to meet my parents. I was so afeared, because I let a stranger bring me home. When we came in, my daddy was in the living room, in his favorite chair, eating watermelon. Mom was making sure the children were in bed. When my mom met him, she liked him, I could tell."

Dorothy writes—

"On about the third Sunday, he asked my daddy could he take me out. We went to his Aunt Ruth's that afternoon. We went to Mac's Half of Dollar, on Avenue B. Listened to some records: Little Willie John, James Brown, Aretha Franklin. It was a wonderful date."

Dorothy writes—

"After delivering his telegrams, he would get back off his run a bit early, so he would stop at Hemming Park. He would put his kickstand down and sit on his bike and wish he was able to sit on a bench in the park. But it was the law that Negroes weren't allowed to sit in Hemming Park."

Dorothy writes—

"In the process of delivering a telegram, riding along on a dark narrow road, the car light would appear, and there would be some young white guys, armed with bottles and belt buckles."

That's all she says. It's enough.

Dorothy writes—

"Walter would ride his bike out to my house" in rural black Dinsmore Pickett "(16 miles round trip), unless he got his cousin, Arthur Lee Schuler, to bring him. Soon he got his own car…a big green Buick, with a big shiny chrome front. I could hear it from the highway coming. Oh, my heart would do a flip!"

In 1959, Walter was drafted. Dorothy was eight months pregnant when Walter finished basic training.

Dorothy writes—

"We were married at his mother's house at 3211 Pippin Street. Then he went to Texas, and from there he flew to the base in Paris, France. Two years later, when Walter finally came home, Negroes were allowed to sit in Hemming Park."

99

One day when I visit Mr. Whetstone, he's sitting on the sidewalk watching the street, wearing a baseball cap that says "Whetstone Chocolate St. Augustine."

"So there's a Whetstone Chocolate in St. Augustine?" I ask.

He laughs and says, "Yeah. So I went there. And I got this hat. And I told them, 'You're Whetstone Chocolate, and I'm Chocolate Whetstone.'"

It's 86 degrees in early October, and he's wearing a long-sleeved white dress shirt and a purple tie.

It's been a couple months since I last came to see him. I ask him if he has any recollections of Eartha White.

"Oh yeah," he says. "I delivered her telegrams. Western Union. Different presidents used to send her happy birthday messages. A lot of cats lived in the Mission with her there. She was a little tiny woman. Never did nothin' but doin' good for others."

A few days earlier, I'd found an August 1929 letter from Jack Gardner Ross, former minister of Bethel Baptist, in which he chides Eartha for not responding to his letters, saying, "I have written you several times, and knowing you to be so remarkably fond of dogs, cats, mules, Jacks, etc, I felt almost sure of a line in reply."

Among the few dozen extant photographs of Eartha are shots of her with mules, horses, cows, various cats, and various dogs.

In July 1933, a friend named J.C. Bradley wrote from the Mission on West Ashley to Eartha on a trip to Chicago, telling her, "The work are getting along fine every body are playing they part to make it." Bradley made a point of telling

Eartha, "Jerry the big cat and Shukus the baby cat are jest fine." A little dog named "Boy" and another dog called "the big shot" were also doing well.

Meg Fisher, the Mission's current vice president, tells me, "Eartha loved animals just like she loved people. Eartha was full of love. And the Mission was often overrun with dogs and cats."

Meg mentions Lilly White, the dog an indigent blind man left Eartha when he died. Lilly White assimilated well with Clara White and Eartha White. In old photographs, Lilly White appears by Eartha's side or in pictures of the annual Christmas Dinner for the Aged and Blind.

Eartha always used the stairs—those same stairs down which she finally fell just before her death, though the elevator was installed 25 years before the fall—because she relegated the elevator to the use of her animals.

On April 29, 1948, the Mission charged 25-cent benefit-concert admission and filled its auditorium for the Mt. Ararat Male Quartette to sponsor the Clara White Mission Elevator Fund.

It wasn't long before Eartha starting using the elevator for food and water bowls for the animals. When other people used the elevator, they had to make sure not to knock against the animals' bowls, which always made Eartha mad.

In June 1955, Eartha wrote Grayce Bateman from London, but included animals at the Mission in her missive, "My love to all, especially Hound Dog, Boots, and Mickie."

When people donated old extension cords, Eartha cut them apart and used them for leashes so she could walk the dogs down Ashley Street.

Grayce Bateman, Eartha's secretary for 27 years and the second president of the Mission, says that when President Richard Nixon invited Eartha to the White House for a humanitarian award in 1970, she insisted on wrapping some chicken from the presidential dinner to bring to her cats back home.

And as I finish the previous sentence, my border collie Oliver, who's been lying at my feet for the past hour, starts whimpering in his sleep. I try to imagine what he might be dreaming. I watch his ribcage fill up with air, then let it loose in another dream-whimper, so I end this chapter to lie down with my dog on the hardwood floor and kiss his snout and pat his haunch and picture Eartha doing the same thing upstairs in the Mission 80 years ago.

100

For so backward a town, one of Jacksonville's most eminent white leaders from a family prominent back through the mid-1800s was also one of its most progressive.

Richard P. Daniel had wielded his law firm against racial discrimination, chaired the Duval County Welfare Board in the 1920s, helped found the Jacksonville Urban League in the 1930s, and offered legal counsel *pro bono*, as a friend, to Eartha White for years.

His uncle had directed the Jacksonville Board of Trade and published the city's leading newspaper in the 1880s. His son would become president of the city's wealthiest real estate company in partnership with the Stocktons, the same white family from whom Eartha secretly claimed her father, and would publish the city's two leading newspapers in the late 1970s.

The family's position seems a caricature of how power works in Southern towns, but Richard P.'s politics stand in contradistinction to the generation on either side of him.

When Frances Ewell, community activist and humanitarian, first came to Jacksonville in 1909, having just graduated from Vassar College, Richard Daniel was one of the first people she met. She met Eartha soon afterward.

"I recall him telling me then that Eartha was the best businessman in town." The emphatic irony of a century ago could easily be lost in 2014. Women weren't businessmen. The best man in Jacksonville business wasn't a man.

Frances Ewell said Vassar had "imbued me with the idea that I owed my volunteer services to the community," and in her liberal humanitarian pursuits, she found Eartha's work everywhere she turned.

Eartha never seemed to sleep and her every idea seemed shrewd and fruitful. "She'd say, 'I can raise $10,000 if you and

Mr. A and Mr. B and Mr. C and so on will match this sum.'"
Thus the only Miss among the Misters would fund a new
project.

On the other end of the fiduciary spectrum, "She also
shrewdly managed to have a pickup truck at the site when a
building was being torn down, and so collected planks, bricks,
plywood, you name it, for her expanding social program."

In between such extremes, Frances helped Eartha raise
money for the blacks-only money pool known as the
Community Chest, several other charities, and the Duval
County Welfare Board.

After decades of working with Richard Daniel and
Eartha White, Frances helped initiate the Urban League in
Jacksonville. Daniel served as chairman of the Urban League's
inaugural survey of Jacksonville's black community, and
Frances coordinated the survey and reported its results.

101

In 1946, Richard P. Daniel chaired the Jacksonville chapter of the Council of Social Agencies, which organized the Jacksonville Urban League the following year. It convened a small steering committee that included Richard Daniel and Eartha White and produced an important 113-page report called *Jacksonville Looks at Its Negro Community: A Survey of Conditions Affecting the Negro Population in Jacksonville in Duval County, Florida*. The survey director was Frances Ewell.

Among the findings the committee investigated was the fact that "the general death rate among Negroes in Jacksonville and Duval County is about 50% higher than the death rate among whites." The leading causes of death for black residents were heart disease, tuberculosis, pneumonia, and cancer.

Though the survey doesn't directly credit Eartha's Negro Tuberculosis Hospital, or Mercy Hospital, it reports that the death rate of "the great killer," tuberculosis, in the previous 25 years, had dropped by half in the black community.

There were 198 white physicians and 10 black physicians practicing in Duval County and often white doctors didn't treat black patients.

Eartha's Old Folks' Home next to the tuberculosis home on Milnor is the only institution listed for the care of elderly black residents. In January 1946, most "days of care" per patient were given free. Similarly, there were 2,043 free meals offered, and 1,305 for which pay was received.

In "Delinquency and Law Enforcement," the survey reported that in the previous four years, 82 percent of Jacksonville's homicides were committed by "Negroes," and of that, the majority were instances of black men killing black men.

Though white segregationists made use of such statistics, the committee concluded, "While it is clear that Negroes commit relatively more offenses than whites and are sentenced to prison in relatively greater numbers, it is well to point out that students of crime are almost unanimous in their conclusion that *race* as such has very little, if anything, to do with the actual amount of crime committed. Rather they attribute the excess of criminality in certain groups to such factors as economic conditions, health and housing, community environment, the administration of justice, and attitudes toward law enforcement."

The survey reported that black residents were afraid of the police, would rarely if ever ask help of the police, and as a result, generally had no respect for the police. The committee noted that Jacksonville's police force was entirely white, saying, "In cities where Negro police have been used, their use is generally considered to be very successful."

The Mission had worked to pre-empt community fears of municipal authority and address violent crime for decades. In 1933, in the heart of the Great Depression, Eartha had begun a "Campaign against Homicides" that included "Lectures on City Streets."

On Kings Road at Davis Street, the first program featured speakers on citizenship, followed by a "literary and musical program." Eartha planned between 12 and 15 street-corner meetings at various places throughout the city, featuring preachers, poets, singers, and choirs.

Early-1930s press releases and communiques with titles like "Mission Moves to Reduce Homicides" spoke of the difficulties of bringing education and ideas of civic responsibility to the masses of desperate people, claiming that "since the mountain refuses to come to Mohammed, Mohammed, in the form of Mission Workers and aides, will go to the mountain."

Other considerations undertaken by the 1947 survey committee included sanitation services, proper sewage, housing quality, public housing, access to housing loans, education, employment, and public transportation.

The survey notes, "White passengers seat from the front of the bus to the rear, while colored passengers seat from the rear of the bus to the front." On some bus lines, white passengers seated from the rear to the front, purposely forcing black bus riders, by default, to stand.

Eartha had ridden streetcars in Jacksonville until Jim Crow laws segregated them. From then on, she never again used public transportation in Jacksonville. She drove a buggy or an old car, and when the car broke down, she walked. But more than any other vehicle, she rode bicycles around downtown and the neighborhoods of LaVilla and Oakland and College Gardens and Brooklyn.

PART FIVE

From the Fire and the Springs

102

On July 11, 1947 the Jacksonville Council of Social Agencies met to form the Jacksonville Urban League. The meeting minutes end with Eartha reminding the committee that the rededication of the Clara White Mission would begin just two days later.

On July 13, a scorching hot and humid Florida Sunday afternoon, the dedication of the rebuilt Mission began with hymns, a dedicatory prayer, and the singing of "Lift Every Voice and Sing."

These kinds of summer afternoons could make you feel like the whole world was melting and sweating and oozing and sinking into the dense ever-rotting swamp in which Jacksonville had been built. But today, the resurrection, "that great gittin'-up morning" of the Mission declared otherwise.

In this part of the earth where the world grew older so much more quickly, the memory of the fire that severely damaged the Mission three years before dissolved into its rebuilding and rechristening.

Dedicatory ceremonies lasted from Sunday to Friday and included speeches from the mayor and former mayors, pastors of numerous local black churches, attorneys representing Civil Rights and humanitarian causes, state educational leaders, leaders of black insurance companies and business organizations. There was a lot of singing from numerous choirs and soloists, and a great deal of sumptuous eating.

*

If any direct record of the fire exists, I've not been able to find it. Though the Mission had been called the nucleus of both black culture and humanitarian aid in Jacksonville, and though the Great Depression had been the time the Mission helped the most people and offered the greatest number of activities and forms of aid, the fire that scorched much of the Mission after the close of World War Two strangely garnered little lasting comment.

How did the fire start? Who was in the Mission at the time? Who witnessed the fire? Did Eartha witness it? Was anyone hurt? Did anyone die? Who experienced the terror of the fire, and how did that person describe it?

Bethel Baptist historian Camilla Thompson remembers the fire. She says a firewall kept it from destroying the whole building. She doesn't think anyone was hurt and doesn't know what caused it, but she thinks it started in the kitchen, which was originally on the second floor.

After the fire, the balconies on the front of the Mission were removed, and architect Henry John Klutho, Jacksonville's Prairie-style genius, designed the reconstruction "as a personal favor" to Eartha. What, in fact, were the dynamics of any personal relationship between Eartha White and the city's greatest architect? The later architect Robert Broward doesn't even mention the Clara White Mission in his book, *The Architecture of Henry John Klutho: The Prairie Style in Jacksonville*.

*

That Sunday afternoon, Mayor Frank Whitehead offered dedicatory remarks, as did Eartha's friend, colleague, and legal advisor Richard P. Daniel, but other than Eartha's, the most prominent voice at the dedication was principal speaker Mary McLeod Bethune, founder of historically black Bethune-Cookman University in Daytona Beach 43 years previously, and personal advisor on race matters to President Franklin Delano Roosevelt.

A majestic irony infuses the Mission's 1947 rededications. The festivities surely occasioned the grandest moment the Mission had ever seen. They marked the Mission's enormous social and political prominence, clout, and connectivity. But though the Mission's now iconic status carried it squarely through to its near demise in the early 1990s and its subsequent resurrection as one of the city's most progressive humanitarian institutions in the 21st century, its 1944 conflagration and 1947 rededication marked a watershed after which Eartha's Mission slipped from being the greatest black cultural, social, and political enterprise in Jacksonville and much of Florida to a post-Depression and post-World War Two institution geared to the practices that had worked best in the past, though the coming Civil Rights Movement already accreted energy and volatility for its appearance over the historical horizon of the next decade.

A decade before the rededication, late 1930s, Eartha's Mission offered a wider variety of educational and vocational opportunities for black people, white people, poor people, people of various religious denominations and people of no religious faith at all, and served a greater number of people altogether, than did any mainstream, traditional, and assumedly white humanitarian and educational institution in the city.

A decade after the rededication, late 1950s, the most progressive black leaders, having hitched themselves to the stories of Rosa Parks and Martin Luther King. Jr., were beginning to see Eartha's philosophies and tactics as tired and retrograde.

But Eartha herself wasn't tired.

Mary McLeod Bethune, often regarded as Florida's greatest black female leader of the 20th century, died six months before Rosa Parks refused to obey that Alabama bus driver who ordered her to the back of the bus and unintentionally sparked the bus boycotts that most people consider the start of the Civil Rights Movement.

But Eartha lived another two decades after Rosa Parks's momentary decision, and at the time, Eartha was already 79 years old. Students of history often ask why Eartha wasn't more progressive during the Civil Rights Movement. Was she merely a Booker-T. accommodationist? Was she, in that most unforgiveable language of the time, a "black Conservative"?

So July 13, 1947, inasmuch as the date marks a dividing line between Depression-era black philosophies of "racial uplift" and later black intolerance of perceived "Uncle Tom" thinking in favor of the urgent push forward toward expectations no black people born in America could before have imagined possible, becomes a line of demarcation.

Four years before Mary McLeod Bethune died, she wrote Eartha—"my dear, dear Friend"—a letter wishing her a happy 75th birthday. Bethune said she knew of no woman in the entire South "whose life has been more dedicated to the purpose of uplift, nor whose efforts have been more untiring in the service of mankind."

A. Philip Randolph, the Jacksonville-born activist and labor leader, sent Eartha a more personal diamond-birthday letter, reminding Eartha he had known her "practically all of

[his] life," and saying she was "just as beautiful now in body, mind, spirit and soul" at 75 years old as she was when he first met her.

*

In 1940, Eartha had traveled to Chicago to meet with Randolph and others to discuss a March on Washington. In 1957, Randolph wrote Eartha to enjoin her help in writing about the "Negro History of Florida." In 1963, when she was 86 years old, Eartha attended the March on Washington for Jobs and Freedom.

Randolph had issued his "Call to Negro America to March on Washington" in his magazine *Black Worker* in 1941, and the movement came to full fruition 22 years later when Martin Luther King gave his "I Have a Dream" speech before the Lincoln Memorial. Eartha was there.

But Randolph's original idea for the march was also productive. It resulted in his meeting with President Franklin Delano Roosevelt and the end of legal racial discrimination in defense industries and the federal government. Randolph's friend and fellow activist Bayard Rustin criticized him for calling off the march after FDR met these conditions, but Rustin became the chief organizer of the 1963 march.

And though Eartha lived another 22 years after A. Philip Randolph wrote her that sweet 75th birthday letter, 40 years after her death, the Mission would win further federal awards for community leadership and service to the homeless, the poor, and the increased numbers of military veterans returning from America's wars in Iraq and Afghanistan.

It feels so strange to me, so embroiled as I am in cataloguing Eartha's and the Mission's social and historical evolution every step of the way, that I can't put a finer finger on the transition from the Mission before the fire, with all its services to desperate Americans before the Second World War and during the Great Depression, and the Eartha of the Civil Rights Movement, the downfall of LaVilla, and the post-Iraq-War Progressive re-greening of North America's cities in the new American Gothic of the early 21st century. But I'll come to the rest as soon as I can.

1947 was a turning point. The great ceremony. Statewide historical, social, and political recognition of the place the Mission had achieved in the center of the city and the center of the century, an almost magical convergence of points of power. At this nexus, this four-and-a-half-foot-tall woman stood behind a microphone and lectern and rededicated the institution she had named for her adoptive mother almost 40 years before.

103

In 1974, Betty Koehler, helping Dan Schafer with interviews and transcriptions, recorded an audio cassette of a phonograph, pressed almost three decades earlier, of the 1947 dedicatory services.

She says, "The records this tape is made from are in very poor condition and are difficult to understand in some places. However, Miss White's voice comes through quite clearly in others, and therefore I thought it was a valuable addition to the collection."

The original records were "the property of the Clara White Mission." I wonder where the original phonographs are now. If they survive.

At first I think the record's playing at too high a speed. The introducer, Lillian F. Hunter, speaks too quickly and her voice seems high-pitched.

She says it's her pleasure to introduce "a woman who has given her entire life to the welfare of others. I have never known, I'm sure you've never seen, such unselfish untiring work in the interest of human beings regardless of race, creed, color, or national origin. I love her. All of the citizens of Jacksonville love her. I give you the finest woman of our age, Miss Eartha Mary Magdalene White."

The quality of phonographic recording makes Eartha's voice sound distant, muffled, and slightly too fast. She says she won't have a funeral because she won't be there in her physical remains. She mentions several dignitaries in attendance, then an "interracial committee, who I depend, I depend, I depend, I depend, I depend, I depend," and there's an abrupt break from the skip in the record.

She says this meeting and this week-long event isn't about her. She asks her audience, "Will you tonight dedicate your lives to serving humanity?"

And then she sings. Eartha the former adolescent opera singer, the leader of the polyphony of her city, sings the song of the mission worker, poet, and songwriter Fanny Crosby, "By the Power of Grace Divine."

> Consecrate me now to Thy service, Lord,
> By the power of grace divine;
> Let my soul look up with a steadfast hope,
> And my will be lost in Thine.

> Draw me nearer, nearer blessèd Lord,
> To the cross where Thou hast died.
> Draw me nearer, nearer blessèd Lord,
> To Thy precious bleeding side.

What a shame this recording is warped and full of noise and seems to rotate at a faulty tempo. All the scratches, warps, whooshes, mufflings, and crackles become its music. These are the sounds of the distance of time. Listening to Eartha sing, it seems all history is distant, even the history in which we live, this moment. Everything is ghost. That includes the present.

Somehow then I stand in the present before Eartha White speaking to the crowds in the street in front of the Mission in 1947. The speaker and her audience face each other, bound up in one another.

None of them realize we're watching, you and I, all these years later, barely seeing but trying desperately to see.

104

"She had a lot of warmth. She was able to say thank you without being servile or fawning. You felt that you did things for her because she was really doing something for someone else."

I have to hand it to Sidney Entman. His 1976 reminiscences of Eartha, though initially gracious enough, make me more uncomfortable than those of anyone else I've thus far encountered.

"She was a one-woman personal agency that operated on the personal appeal, really, that she was able to achieve."

It's his voice, not his first few sentences themselves, that make me feel instantly defensive. He has an annoyingly patrician way of elongating the ends of words like "appeal" and "achieve" and dipping them down into condescending creakings of his deep voice.

In 1946, Sidney and Rose Entman co-founded River Garden Hebrew Home, which evolved as a Jewish-sponsored nursing and retirement center through several names over the next half century. In the middle of the 1950s, more than a decade before the Eartha M. M. White Nursing Home opened, Eartha sought Sidney Entman's knowledge and experience to help her turn the Old Folks' Home she'd established so many decades before into a modern institution that could better help more people.

Eartha's working with Entman testifies greatly to her ability to coordinate with individuals across socioeconomic, ethnic, racial, and religious boundaries in a time when Jacksonville was locked blindly into such separations.

Long before John F. Kennedy said it, Eartha had learned the point of that famous quote, "For of those to whom much is given, much is required." After all, Eartha knew her

Bible, and the Gospel of Luke told her, "For unto whomsoever much is given, of him shall be much required."

105

Listening to this 40 year-old audio interview with Sidney Entman, recorded five years before he died, I bristle at his smugness and admire the earthy pragmatism that allowed Eartha to put aside such condescension from people who might help her.

I also find myself surprised by the change in Entman's tone from the beginning of the interview to the end. Even his style of speaking changes. As he moves from patrician and patronizing early in the interview to a more matter-of-fact tone by the end, he likewise moves from a kind of two-faced racist criticism of Eartha to a grudging respect for her control of her enterprises.

He begins by criticizing what he perceives as her lack of political organization and by equating her charity work to slavery.

"Despite all her genius and talent," Entman says, "she never really was able to mobilize the black community in terms of a coordinated, a black-community effort, et cetera, et cetera. Whether it's a carryover of that old mentality of depending upon the, the, the, the Whiteys, depending upon the white community, the, the, the handout situation, from the old slave days, I don't know."

The word "know," at the end of this sentence, creaks up and down and up again condescendingly. He frequently interjects phrases like "As we see" and "et cetera, et cetera" and "So we begin to see."

He says, "It was always a source of frustration, to *me*"—his "me" creaks up and creaks down and lingers importantly—"It was always very frustrating, to me, ah, that, ah, there was no real concern of whether she was able to mobilize, rather than to inspire, et cetera, et cetera, a black-community concern in her enterprise."

Entman links Eartha's birth a decade after Emancipation to her unusual standing between white and black, but then calls her "mentality" that of a slave's, of someone who could do no better than depend on white charity.

"We've got to recognize, ah, that she grew up, that she grew up an in era, and she was the un*usual* black person who was able to mingle and commingle with the white community, she had entrée into community, white-community circles, whereas the rest of the black community never *had* that access."

Though he may, or may not, hint here at legends of Eartha's white paternity, he quickly condemns the entire black community as being the immature stepchild of white America, and lays that whole judgment on Eartha's shoulders.

"Now whether within her mentality and her makeup, personality, recognizing that her support depends upon her personal contact with the white leadership or whatever group she was in*volved* in, and the fact remains that the black community as such was not mature *enough*, or responsible *enough*, or concerned about these events, in terms of a unified effort, uh, because again, the, the, the, the personality makeups, of, of, of people, or a group of people oppressed and suppressed over the generations, et cetera, change their mentality, and et cetera, ah, so the fact remains, ah, it was so very easy to shift the responsibility for welfare for the black community and the black individual onto the white community, because they were so totally dependent upon white community support in all aspects of their, ah, their, ah, *lifestyle*."

The word "lifestyle" seems pejorative, even if it's unclear what Entman might specify in that word's place. If he's euphemistic, any perceptive reader of the time could probably fill in a number of blanks.

But the more glaring lack of understanding is Entman's reference to black responsibility under segregation, as though the United States, as though Jacksonville itself, had no responsibility for slavery, for denial of black citizenship, and for Jim Crow legislation.

His statement ignores the many black success stories in the arts, in business, in law, in politics, all of which were gained against a social and political system that sought to prevent such success.

Entman's use of the word "responsibility" is an irresponsible shift of the burden of proof from the wealthy and privileged onto Eartha, the adopted daughter of a slave, and Clara, a woman who had been sold from one white man to another in the center of the city.

He had JFK and the Gospel of Luke entirely backward.

Even worse, he flatly dismissed the great responsibility Eartha White carried on her shoulders for a century.

But it gets worse before it gets better.

Entman's interviewer asks him if Eartha saw the same kind of division of black and white that Entman himself expressed.

He says, "She was a very realistic kind of an individual. Ah, does it work? Ah, she recognized, the, the, the, the, the line of distinction."

He has a way of making even his stuttering sound studied and important.

"We talked about the ideals of, of, of, you know, all men being God's children, but also recognizing that you can't change, ah, social forces and social problems, and cultural distinctions and subcultures of the black, liberal, and all the other fragmentations of our society."

Even as he expresses his own self-protective and fatalistic view of history as stagnation instead of movement, he goes on to substantiate the premise of his interviewer's question.

"In our—"

Yes, he says "our."

"—nursing home venture, there was no doubt about it, there were white patients there and there were black patients, and there were no distinctions among admissions as such."

Even though Entman's just described history as stagnant—and therefore, really, non-historic, since history itself implies narrative movement, he answers a question about how he thinks Eartha probably responded to the increasing frustration and militancy of black activists in the late 1960s and 1970s.

I still hear in his voice the self-comforting cadence and tempo and condescending creak as he speaks for her: "She would not approve."

He gives his preferred version of how societies change and compares anything else to the Bolshevik Revolution. Of course, by then, rearguards had been comparing the Civil Rights Movement to that be-all-end-all bugbear called Communism for decades.

"It's the old story of social changes via a peaceful, long, evolutionary, ah, thing, or the *impatient* view that, uh, that, uh, that wants a change overnight."

Then he speaks for Eartha of the burden of proof.

"She also was a strong believer that, ah, the black people, in order to be *accepted*, must be *acceptable*."

After all, he seems to say, in America, white middle-class Protestantism is the norm, and anyone who doesn't conform is to blame.

"This is typical white, middle-class morality, and the level of a culture, ah, the fact remains the, the, the, the individual culture and the unique culture of the black people, ah, the unique culture of the Chicanos, or the unique culture of the American Indians are unique unto *themselves*, and within the mores and the moral, ah, status of the, ah, dominant white Protestant Christian community that we have here, ah, their mores are, ah, ah, are, ah, *different*, ah, their, their *value* systems are different, ah, we can, they are *condemned*, ah, for a *system* that is different, ah, not taking the responsibility or recognizing that they were responsible in the *first* place for the value systems which they have created within the society they live in."

From there, he swerves back to denigrating Eartha's practices and misrepresenting them in doing so.

"So we begin to see, ah, Eartha White trying to be a, a, a liaison between the white and black com*mun*ity. Now. Her, her, a good many of the black community would not *accept* her techniques, and her methods of, ah, because again, the, ah, again, it was the same old handout from Whitey."

When the interviewer tries to historicize Eartha, countering Entman's own claims to do so—he calls himself a "social scientist"—she asks about Eartha's being influenced by Booker T. Washington.

Every time she asks a question, Entman starts talking before her question is finished and immediately talks over her, then modulates his volume once she stops speaking.

"*I* would say, it was a more peaceful, evolutionary group of people as compared to some of the more militant groups that we see *today*."

When he's asked how long he knew Eartha before she died, Entman says, "Oh, *I've* been in the community for 28 years."

The pronunciation of the word "years" lasts almost five seconds.

He says without shame or decency that he'd known Eartha since once having a surplus of clothing and having his servant call Miss White to see if she could receive it.

In the middle of the 1950s, Entman says, Eartha called him to be part of advancing her Old Folks' Home.

"She was operating this slum nursing home, and I mean *slum*, but she was"—Entman laughs disparagingly—"doing a *good* job. There was compassion, there was love, there was warmth. It was dirty as hell and stank like hell."

There was no money, almost no government funding, and white nursing homes wouldn't take black patients.

He laughs again and says, "Nobody *else* would care for them."

The interviewer says, "Uh, what would you say to a statement that, uh, Miss White collected these, uh, elderly people when they had just, uh, not much longer to live, and, uh, stripped them of what they had?"

No attribution. The interviewer calls it "a statement," but whose statement is it?

Entman says, "They had enough. What stripped them of what they had was the fact the few dollars that they had we had to utilize, they had to become eligible for, ah, well, uh, well, you talk about what? $500? $600? If anybody had that much?"

And then, "Look, I'm being accused all these years we have what we have, sure, little old lady had a house, and we sold it for $3,000, and at the cost of $600 a month, for the last five years, $3,000 is a hell of a lot of money. And she could never understand, and we could never on God's earth convince her that we didn't steal all her money."

Meekly, the interviewer says, "The question was put to me and I wanted to ask it," but she's interrupted—

"If there was ever any money at all, it never went to the Eartha M. M. White Nursing Home. Nor would it go to any place else."

"In other words, you would categorically deny that she preyed on any—"

"No, no, no, no. Look, she may have had a few that had some money and they died and the money was left over and she continued using it, but, but that is perfectly legitimate within the framework of, ah, any non-profit organization, as such, ah, we have money that's left over by people, we utilize it for the best of our purposes."

Now his line of distinction between River Home and Eartha's nursing home seems to have diminished. In becoming defensive of Eartha's operation he's defensive of himself.

Because when he came onto the nursing home's board of directors, he says, they recognized, "from the beginning," that the Old Folks' Home had to go, we "had to start all over again fresh."

Entman says, "We, we, we, we, she, she, she was, ah, limited, limited, ah, ah, ah, ah," she controlled the checkbook and the board, a "very strong willed, powerful person, and, ah, at times she would listen to me, she would accept my professional advice and council, and then promptly, and to suit her purposes, deny everything we did."

109

"Ah, she had enough courage, when, when, when, we, when things came to a real, real tough impasse, and, ah, I made the recommendations that we have to borrow $10,000, or whatever it is, in order to, ah, carry on at least some basic standards, later on, it was only recently really, and, ah, I was terribly disturbed, because 90 percent or more of her welfare cases, they could not demonstrate expenditure or funds that would warrant getting the maximum welfare grant."

She bucked the state requirements, found several people to come onto the board to back the expenditure, people who never came back again, when "there were only three or four of us who were steady." She started with an individual's need, then found any way practically to meet it.

"There was nobody there, and it was a shifting population on the board, one month this one showed up, one month the other showed up, and there was no consistency involved here," except for a few members who represented old family, like Ray Knight, who supported Eartha because she was Eartha, and when he died, left $100,000 to the nursing home.

"She dominated completely the board structure. There was really no board. There was no elections. I don't know when we had elections, when we had a nominating committee, et cetera. She met you, and she decided you were a nice person, and she invited you to attend, and you came, once and maybe twice, and after that you realized there was no sense in doing it, there was nothing left to do."

When the interviewer says she's amazed not only that Eartha accomplished so much, but that she ever got started, Entman says, "She got started because I think she had her independent wealth, her sources of income, whatever it might be."

Entman rambles about Eartha's belonging to neither the "white" or the "black world," while everyone else I've listened to, read, or interviewed sees her as being comfortable with both. Contextualizing his with these other voices, he seems to understand her position toward race hardly at all.

"Because of her frustrations, the kind of life she led, ah, *inability* to be accepted in the, uh, unable to be *accepted* in the white world, and then she herself was not accepting of the black world, and she stood as a transition between the black and the white world, such as, and with a tremendous need to bring people up to her level, conscious or unconscious, up to her level of understanding, so that we can pass over the line into the white world, I mean, who can say?"

He says he knows he can never "emotionally, gut-wise, understand, uh, the mentality, personality, makeup, the motivation, the lifestyle, et cetera, of another minority group, whether" black or Mennonite or Chicano, "et cetera."

"As a Jew, living in Duluth, with a Jewish lifestyle, with our share of two thousand years of persecution" and "having been called a minority, and a rejected minority group for two thousand years," he says he can empathize with black people, "but at least I wasn't spat at as openly as they were spat at."

110

Tom Crompton's understandings of Eartha's successes, motivations, and political methodologies couldn't be more different than Entman's.

And Tom Crompton saw Eartha from the perspective of the heart of the city and the heart of black Jacksonville. He understood Eartha from the perspective of a teacher whose earliest memories were of going with his mother to work at the Mission.

He grew up during the Depression and Eartha gave his mother work as a seamstress and clothesmaker. At his mother's side in the Mission, Tom learned to sew.

Tom grew up with his mother and his sisters. His father wasn't around. Though sewing was considered a woman's skill, the sewing he learned at his mother's side helped him help his family then and provide for his children later.

In the classroom where he taught math at Robert E. Lee High School, one of the many schools named after Confederate generals in Jacksonville, he spoke gratefully in 1974 of his "training there at the Mission, when I was young, and I never turned it loose because Mom had a machine that was given to her by the Mission."

He says, "The machine was there at home and I had access to it there, and I continued to make much of my clothing and my sisters' clothing." He later made clothing for his own four children.

Tom remembers the Mission as the heart of town. The heart of black Jacksonville was the heart of Jacksonville. The Mission was City Hall for the poor and underprivileged. The Mission pumped life through all the hidden circuits of the city.

And on West Ashley Street were "all the movies, all the record shops, all the hot dog stands, the dancehalls, the bars after Prohibition, and all of this was in that immediate vicinity of the Mission, almost every person one time or another during the week would have reason to go in that area."

As Tom Crompton spent a lot of his growing up in the Mission, he began a long-evolving understanding of how Eartha knew the city, all the circuitry of the black community and its few clandestine connections into wealthy white Jacksonville.

111

"She had a way about knowing the ins and outs of the power structure."

So many mostly nameless helpers and workers at the Mission and the Old Folks' Home and the tuberculosis hospital and the Home for Unwed Mothers and the Boys' Club wondered at Eartha's interaction between worlds. From the limbo between the Jacksonville of the poor and that of the wealthy, of the black and of the white, she brought back what she could for "her people."

"We didn't know how she would be able to make all of this outside contact, but there were people like my mother who were around at all times, and they were willing to help, because what little they could do was as great to them as as-much-as Miss White was doing for everybody. 'I don't have an awful lot that I can do, but what little I can do, I feel good in doing.'

"That's the attitude that people took, and I think that was because of Miss White's influence, and because they were able to see the good that she was doing for the underprivileged. And during that time, there were very few who were not underprivileged."

And if rumors persisted that Stocktons or Daniels supported Eartha financially, other old wealthy families like the Knights and the L'Engles were known to have bequeathed money to the Mission, though not necessarily much.

Three decades before E. J. L'Engle left the Mission $5,000.00 to be paid in installments, Edward L'Engle paid Eartha $25.00 a month in 1932 to investigate black applicants for a private emergency relief fund. He also gave her flour. "When you have used up the six sacks of flour which you got the other day, let me know and I will give you an order for more."

Tom Crompton refers to the "8th Street Strip," the wealthy line of black residences that paralleled the "main drag"

Scenes in Exclusive Residential Sections of Jacksonville, Fla.

of West Ashley Street. The "8th Street Strip" was the center of Sugar Hill, where black doctors and lawyers and businessmen lived, just as West Ashley was the heart of LaVilla, the "Great Black Way."

*

And how Eartha negotiated the difference between Sugar Hill and LaVilla, between the 8th Street Strip and West Ashley, was what made her the most successful benefactor of black Jacksonville, and much of poor white Jacksonville too, for half a century and more.

Tom Crompton says, "Miss White did not live where she could have lived. She could have lived in that area"— Sugar Hill—"but Miss White lived at the Mission. She would spend 24 hours a day at the Mission or some of the other places that she had that were trying to help people who were underprivileged."

"And this is the thing that made the difference, I think, in Miss White's thinking. She didn't permit herself to become engrossed in the upper class and forget the lower class. Because her association was never isolated from the lower class. She slept, she ate, she worked, she taught with the lower-class people, and only with the upper-class people when she was seeking help or assistance."

When Eartha asked for assistance, she combined brilliant rhetorical strategy with a kind of perseverance that humbled wealthy whites and white political elites.

"She had the drive to be refused and come back again."

So often, workers at the Mission saw her disappear "into the field" to find ways and means for the Mission's operations, while, Tom Crompton says, "those of us who were at the Mission serving, we were trying to distribute it as well as could be, so that we would have enough to go around for all the people who would come in and get what little we had."

Eartha brought in so much, but the need was always so great. So food and clothing and medical care were "rationed out, so to speak."

He says, "We got to make sure that everybody who comes in, can eat."

Historian Camilla Thompson says, "She was so caring and so concerned for others, but she was also firm, and in some ways, she was aggressive. She'd say, and she knew just the right way to say it, 'I need two thousand dollars for such and such, and they'd jump and give it to her.'"

And as Tom grew older, he continued to sew and to help his mother and his sisters, and he continued to spend time at the Mission, where he repaired clothes and served food.

Increasingly, through the 1930s and into the 1940s, Tom Crompton began to wonder how Eartha not only mobilized the black community, but brought white people to some modicum of responsibility toward the black and underprivileged.

This math teacher at a high school named for a Confederate general understands so much more than Sidney Entman about how black politics and social progression worked in Jim Crow Jacksonville.

Crompton talks about "how people could get aid during that time."

He says, "The power structure of a community, of *this* community, especially—If you would go over to the City Commission, and you would ask for something for the blacks, if you represent the blacks, to keep you from wanting anything that the whites had, and it wouldn't really cost that much, they would grant it. Miss White knew this. Consequently, she would ask for certain things" and "they could see that they could grant it" to black people "and they wouldn't even miss it."

Eartha, with political and psychological and biological connections to both halves of the racially divided city, was able to step through black poverty amongst white wealth and back. During those bellicose and often lethal years, Eartha knew how to operate in the space between two mutually exclusive societies.

Though ostensibly apolitical, Eartha was a greater political operative than anyone else in the Jacksonville of the mid-20th century.

"And this is how she was able to get things. Because that structure, I think, was basically the structure of this community, right up until about '54. The powers-that-be had black leaders and those leaders, you would never get to the power structure but the leaders could, and they would go in and say what they want, and the power structure would say, 'We can't give you that, you know we don't have it. So go back and tell the people we don't have that.'

"Well, this is the type-thing that I say she had afforded to, to be told, 'Go back and tell your people we can't do that, because we can't afford it.' She *didn't* come back and tell the people that. She would wait the next day and then go and tell them what was needed for her people.

"So consequently, if you do this-type-thing repeatedly to the kind of person who's not listening to your need, then after while, they hear your need, and they will yield, and give you if not all of what you ask for, a great deal of what you ask for."

114

It was through these kinds of rhetorical maneuverings that Eartha had been able to launch the Old Folks' Home in the first place. It was through this kind of political savvy that she had been able to keep the place going.

Tom Crompton says, "In that small facility she had, she did the best she could there, getting medical attention as well as providing food and shelter."

Former slaves and the children and grandchildren of slaves could never rely naively on the goodness of white people, and what you accepted from those with means inevitably made them feel benignant and absolved them of criminality. No matter that later generations and wealthy self-conceived do-gooders would necessarily bristle at your methodology.

You had to be a double agent.

Later activists would have the hardest time understanding that.

Especially since your double agency must be contradictorily-but-sincerely sincere in speaking to those smug possible benefactors.

Tom Crompton says, "You don't get anything because somebody else looked across and saw you had a need. You get it because you have to push for it."

*

But even as I consider Crompton's smart and pragmatic comments about rhetorical necessities, I ask myself if each of Entman's seemingly condescending comments are equally racist. What if he's right that Eartha failed to organize the community and relied mostly on philosophies of accepting the leftovers of wealthier whites? It's my responsibility at least to ask this question.

I can't imagine that Eartha's connections to the white community will ever be fully unearthed and understood. But if a child of a wealthy white family did impregnate Eartha's mother—whether through a consensual sexual relationship, or as was so often the case, through rape—and if that family never publicly accepted its responsibility, if Eartha was intimately connected to two wealthy white families in this small Southern city—the Stocktons and the Daniels, if the former family paid her shut-up money for her manifold but humble humanitarian works, and if the latter family alternated between generations, as we'll soon see, from Confederate wealth to liberal activism to the most elitist wealthy "country club" exclusionism, and if Eartha relied in varying degrees at varying times through her long life on either family but died poor and having worked for no compensation at all for years, then is Entman right? Did "Whitey," also known as the Stocktons and Daniels, support Eartha just enough to shut her up and relay to "her people"— since she wasn't "people" of her mother's rapist's family—the pittances that would make them feel they got something, though only enough to keep living, while "Whitey" developed rich white neighborhoods and country clubs and ran city politics?

I want to believe I have some sense of how things work. I want to believe Tom Crompton, but I also can't help but believe there's more truth than can be proven in uglier possibilities.

*

Florida State University historian Maxine Jones encapsulates the difference in strategy, despite solidarity, between Mary McLeod Bethune and Eartha White.

"Bethune championed social justice and sought to remove the barriers that prevented Florida's African Americans from participating as full citizens" and "frequently spoke out against lynching, barriers to voting, insufficient funding for public education."

There's certainly no great distinction between the two women in stance. The key words in Jones's assessment are "championed" and "frequently spoke out."

On the other hand, "Eartha White accomplished much in meeting the needs of the black community with a leadership style quite different from that of Bethune."

Jones says Eartha "sought to dismantle racism and discrimination," but that "she was not outspoken and did not vocally challenge the system." Nevertheless, she used her influence with "powerful whites and policy makers to achieve for blacks those opportunities and services they were denied," and in the process, working behind the scenes, "she established a network of supporters across the state."

Then Jones makes a further distinction necessary in understanding Eartha. She calls her "cautious," without being automatically "accommodating," and points out that Eartha gained great political power in the early 20th century, a time when both race and gender prohibited so many from even voting in Florida.

Historian Carolyn Williams writes that black Floridians in the early 20th century responded to their political exclusion in different ways. "Some organized or revitalized political associations [...] Others involved themselves in civil rights organizations and activities. More than a few concentrated on economics. Eartha White did all of these."

115

Whatever the truth of Eartha's involvement in the construction of the Jefferson Street Pool by the end of the 1940s, she had already purchased Moncrief Springs, just north of Jacksonville's city limits, for black recreation in 1943.

Summer 2012. Empty fields by the railroad tracks, gin bottles in brown paper bags, a drainage ditch runs through it, no sign of all the things that were. All up and down Moncrief Road are housing projects, dilapidated cemeteries, liquor stores and churches with barred windows.

Big black and red letters on the side of an abandoned commercial building:

"STOP THE KILLING

THE CREATOR SEE YOU"

1950s, hundreds of black Christians in suits and long dresses and festive hats and dark pants and white shirts and ties and bowties crowd about the swimming pool. On either side of the pool run long covered wooden breezeways, and behind the pool, a big wooden arch centers the word, "BATHING."

The religious revival will last days and dozens of new converts will be baptized in the pool. The swimming pools are fed by the natural springs that give this place its name.

1875, poet Sidney Lanier writes in *Florida: Its Scenery, Climate, and History*, in the chapter called "Jacksonville in January," that "Several good livery-stables offer first-class turnouts, in the way of saddle-horses, buggies, and carriages; and there are two shell-roads which afford pleasant drives. A very good object-point for a ride is

MONCRIEF'S SPRING.

"This is a mineral spring, not yet analyzed, but said to be of often-tested efficacy in the cure of intermittent fevers and of agues. It lies about four miles from town, near a creek also called Moncrief. There is a tradition—of somewhat filmy basis—that a Jew named Moncrief, who had married an Indian woman, was once murdered by the savages for his money on the banks of this creek and that its name is derived from that event. The spring has been recently taken in charge by a company and many improvements made in its environment. The water is unusually transparent, and is first received in a circular basin 20 feet in diameter. Below this, well-arranged bath-houses, separate for ladies and gentleman, each 60 feet long by 15 wide, are being built. A restaurant, bowling-alley, dancing-pavilion, and race-course of a mile in length are also in process of construction. On the way to this spring one passes through the pleasant suburb known as Springfield."

Another story says a Frenchman named Eugene Moncrief buried nine chests of jewelry and gems by the springs, and left eight of them buried there when local Indians killed him.

He'd dug up one chest to decorate his Indian bride Sun Flower with its jewels, but within a year, the treacherous Sun Flower and her Indian lover Grand Powder had left Moncrief's scalp drying in the Florida sun.

Summer 2012. No race track now, no swimming pools, no bathhouses, restaurants, dancing pavilions, bowling alleys, no crowds of people betting on horse races, no religious revivals, no springs.

No springs inhabit Moncrief Springs. The name itself is a ghost in an overgrown field.

Whatever bathhouses were built at the 1870s resort were long gone by the time Eartha bought Moncrief Springs in the 1940s and had the springs diverted into swimming pools.

Before the Jefferson Street Pool, black kids and couples and families could drive just outside the city limits and laugh and swim and play games at Moncrief Springs. And as at the Jefferson Street Pool, religious congregations held large services here and baptized new converts.

When the last of Eartha's bathhouses were demolished in the 1960s, the springs were covered and converted into a drainage improvement plan.

The horrible irony of the destruction of the springs is that the quadrant now called 45th and Moncrief, an urban district (dis)served by the City of Jacksonville, still has limited city sewage infrastructure.

What was in the 19th century a resort area four miles out of town, named for its natural springs, is in the 21st century a long-desperately-poor inner-city neighborhood with inadequate sewage.

116

Eartha sometimes stayed overnight at the small cottage at Moncrief Springs, just over the city limit.

As Jacksonville expanded, and as city government merged with that of the county in 1968, Moncrief Springs disappeared into inner-city Jacksonville, just as its legendary springs vanished into city drainage.

Since most of Jacksonville's black population had always lived in the city proper and to the north, it made sense that black people would come together at Moncrief.

Eartha's Moncrief Springs bungalow also connected to a rear library and gymnasium from the days of the black recreation center. Over the decades, the two rear buildings increasingly housed her collections of books and historic documents and artifacts.

By the early 1960s, Eartha's financial difficulties had grown unmanageable. The springs fell into disuse and quickly became overgrown by Jacksonville's subtropical flora.

In the summer of 1963, *The Jacksonville Journal* ran a story called "Moncrief Springs—The Splendor Has Vanished." The story told of the mythical Indians Sun Flower and Grand Powder who so duplicitously dealt with the Frenchman Eugene Moncrief.

The story quoted "Miss White," who had "to close the pool" "for financial reasons," and said she had already "built a museum of Negro history on the grounds and hopes to establish a memorial park with complete recreation facilities."

The article accompanied photographs of the spring emptying into a concrete-walled container, and a "bathing" pavilion seen from a collapsing wooden bridge, everything overtaken by Florida's cancerous overgrowth.

The last photograph was of 87 year-old Eartha holding her head to the side and looking at the face of a sculpture who pointedly looks away from her. It's Grand Powder, the generic "Indian" who supposedly scalped Eugene Moncrief.

His sculpture looks exceedingly European. He looks far more French than Indian. Eartha's hands are placed on his waist and on his back, as though granting him his being.

Which of course she did. For a while, I'd wondered where the tacky bust of Grand Powder went. And who made him? How long did he reside at Moncrief Springs? How long after the springs were diverted?

117

Summer 2012. The abandoned Eartha White Memorial Boys' Club is what's left of Moncrief Springs. The windows of the earthen-colored fieldstone bungalow have long been boarded up. The boards in the back are loose and dislodged. The white paint on the wide wooden Doric columns on the bungalow's porch is chipping. The library and gymnasium that once housed Eartha's collections were years ago demolished.

When she died in 1974, kids broke the windows of the tiny cottage, crawled inside, and stole whatever they could. Men broke into the buildings behind her house and burnt Eartha's papers in barrels to keep warm. Because there was no exact inventory, it's hard to know what disappeared: albums and record players, jewelry and sculpture, old Bibles, photographs and personal letters.

For a while I'd wondered if they took Grand Powder, lost him down in the swamps behind the housing projects. Or maybe he'd traveled across the continent through buyers at yard sales.

Eartha's friends and volunteers rescued the historical documents and Dan Schafer orchestrated their safekeeping in a new Special Collection at UNF. Furniture and art were sent back to the center of the city and displayed at the Mission.

That's where I finally saw Grand Powder in all his garish tacky glory, perched on a pedestal of teak. Both Grand Powder and a large urn faced with the Seven Sisters, the Pleiades of Greek myth, are now shown as objects made decades ago in the Mission's ceramics classes.

*

Camilla Thompson was the project coordinator for bringing objects back to the Mission. Now 91 years old, she says Eartha obtained many of the objects when wealthy white families redecorated their homes. Though police found and confiscated some of the stolen items from thieves' houses and apartments, most of what disappeared was never reclaimed.

Several oak and mahogany pieces of furniture made their way back and are now displayed on the second floor of the Mission. It's plausible that some of the old wooden furniture came from the Victorian St. James and Windsor Hotels downtown where Clara had worked on occasion. A Victorian bookcase holds violin and harp guitar. Against one parlor wall stands a pump organ given to Eartha by a member of Duke Ellington's orchestra. There are Tiffany lamps, Abraham Lincoln Lewis's carved walking stick, dated 1916, a wheelchair from the original Old Folks' Home, and photographs of the Oriental American Opera Company.

In the early 1980s, Thompson coordinated art shows at the Mission that featured sculpture, painting, African art, and the photography of E.L. Weems. Ellie Lee Weems ran his

photography studio out of his home at 434 West Beaver Street in LaVilla and is now considered the foremost photographic chronicler of black life in Jacksonville from the 1930s through the 1970s.

Camilla Thompson owns the small Weems collection on permanent display in the Mission. The Atlanta Public Library System owns most of the rest, though Patricia Moman Bell and many other Jacksonville residents would love to bring his photography back home. Weems worked with sepia, black and white, and hand-tinted color. He photographed weddings, funerals, graduations, black Masonic ceremonies, and community and church events. He took personal portraits at his home studio. The metal sign announcing "Photos by Weems," which hung above the porch steps at his home and studio, now hangs above his photographs on the second floor of the Mission.

Thompson remembers frequently going to his house to sit on his porch beside him and look through his voluminous albums.

118

I'm standing on the sidewalk, looking at the rubble and the three Corinthian columns that remain.

A black boy with dreadlocks and neck tattoos rides up next to me on his bike and stops to look at whatever I'm looking at.

This is as close as he's ever come.

All through his childhood, he says, adults told him and his brothers to stay away from this place. They said someone had been murdered here. They said someone had had his head cut off.

Now he wonders if it's true, he says and looks at me, or if they were just trying to scare him and his brothers to keep them away.

He says he doesn't know who Eartha White was.

I nod toward the name on the column and say she was something like Jacksonville's Mother Teresa or Gandhi.

He nods meaningfully. But he doesn't know what else to say. And I don't know what else to say. For another moment, we face the broken columns together, him on his bike, me on my feet.

The three columns are beautifully capitaled and bear faded, hardly legible big blue words. The words on the first column are "Eartha White," the word on the second is "Memorial," and the words on the third column are "Boys Club" [sic].

I look at the boy on the bike. It's a moment full of the fact that he shouldn't find me here. I should fear him and he should resent and distrust me. Neither happens, and in their absence, I feel strangely close to him.

"The world's so beautiful, even when it's not," I say, before I quite know what I've said.

I feel him turn his face to me. A slow moment lapses and he says, "I never thought of it that way before."

I don't know at this moment that the next time I'm here, this land will be thriving and serving the community again.

119

In 1985, S.L. Patterson, the administrator of the Eartha M. M. White Nursing Home on Moncrief Road said most of the structures at Moncrief Springs had been knocked down several years before.

Patterson had read about the buried treasure beneath Eartha's sacred springs in a small Xeroxed 1980 book by Wesley Plott called *Antique Bottles Found in Northeast Florida.*

Plott owned the Purple Petunia in Riverside, a former gas station built in the "Tudor-Revival" architectural style of the 1930s, whose pseudo-half-timbers he'd painted purple. He had turned it into a flower and antique glass shop. He knew where to find 19th-century bottle dumps all over the city and he'd found thousands of treasures in them. He claimed to have dug up "an Indian" at Adams and Ocean Streets downtown and decided the ethical and respectful thing to do was to cover "him (or her) back up to sleep until ? There's a gas station on top of that site now."

In regards to the story of buried treasure, Patterson had told Plott, "My goodness! Don't tell a darned soul."

But Plott's little book on salvaging bottles ends with a page-and-a-half chapter called, "Hidden Treasures Just for You!"

He tells the story of Moncrief, his buried treasure, the one chest of which he dug up for his bride, and the treachery of Sun Flower. The book ends:

"Thousands of people visit the springs yearly. Springs are located across from Eartha White Center on Moncrief Road.

"With gold being from $500. to $800 an ounce, will you be the lucky person to discover the eight remaining chests?"

PART SIX

The Center Cannot Hold

120

Night. Early December and the winter is cold. Last winter it snowed on the city's palm trees. Two months from now, snow and sleet will rake across the North Florida oaks and freeze the banana trees black.

On the phone, a worried white woman said there was a man outside her window. A colored man. No, she said, it wasn't like that. She wasn't afraid of him. She was afraid *for* him. He was just sitting there beside the road, rocking back and forth with his hands cupping their opposite elbows. The night wind was so cold you could see through the window that it cut to the bone.

"Please come as quick as you can. My neighbor, my neighbor, she saw an old car stop beneath the oaks. Somebody stopped and dropped him off just at twilight."

When Eartha, Grayce, and a young nurse pulled up beside the weathered man lost and hunched into himself at the curbside in this white neighborhood, they could see him shivering under the streetlight.

Eartha and Grayce got out of that beat-up old station wagon—I've seen the Mission's meeting minutes where the station wagon's purchase was authorized—and hurried to the man's side. The white breath of the women and the stranger came together in the night, and Eartha saw he was much worse than she'd imagined.

Not only was he worn and haggard, not only was his clothing nothing but rags, but he couldn't stand up. The two small women tried to pick him up, and he weighed so little they could do it, but only when the nurse hoisted him from one side beneath the armpits could they get him into the car, where he said, pleadingly, "Thank you so much for picking me up."

He said he knew what cold nights could do to a man.

When he collapsed into the front passenger seat, the women could see why he couldn't stand. Where his feet should have been were only a pair of exposed raw nubs.

121

The women helped the stranger to the Mission door, where others came to help and got him to a warm bath. He found clean clothes waiting when he was finished, just a little bit too large, but clean and warm and comfortable.

Then Eartha and a volunteer brought him into the kitchen, sat him down, and gave him a bowl of hot chicken and dumplings. The Mission felt warm and safe against the continent-wide night outside.

He was so tired he could barely talk, though not so tired he couldn't eat ravenously. He said his name was Andrew.

Andrew had been desperate to do two things: get out of the South and find work. He left Savannah, Georgia, and rode with seasonal workers westward across North America. Somehow he found his way about as far across the United States from Georgia as he could be.

One freezing night in Spokane, Washington, where he'd taken day labor picking apples and baling hay, Andrew found himself locked outside of a barn in an orchard, where he'd never known such cold in all his life.

He didn't sleep all night. By morning, his feet were frozen and swollen and black as coal tar. At the same time, they hurt and felt like something other than him. They seemed to split in violent cracks like lightning forks up toward his legs where the pain was greatest. His feet were wholly other and alien, as though he had never known them.

After doctors in the hospital amputated his feet, he bumbled around Spokane on his stumps and a stick. He had no money. He couldn't work anymore. Though he had no living family members, all he had ever known was the South.

So drivers in the mountains of Washington State and Oregon were kind and gave him a ride. As were drivers through places in Utah and Arizona where the rocks were red and brutal and named after Hell and the Devil. Texas was bleak eternity, but surprisingly, more drivers gave him rides. Then the Southeast. Even Mississippi, Alabama, Georgia, he couldn't really remember the transit, but strangers ferried him back toward Georgia.

This country, he thought, was bigger than he'd ever imagined, and amidst all the hateful people were at least enough kind ones to get him home.

When Eartha began to solicit funds on her regular rounds to get Andrew a new pair of feet, she quickly raised the money for his artificial limbs and rehabilitation.

Forty-three years later, Grayce Bateman wrote, "Andrew was a happy man the day he stepped out on his new feet. He has worn out several pairs of shoes. Each time he has needed shoes, the rehabilitation center has replaced them."

122

The air had just turned cool enough that it felt clean the way it never did in the fetid humid summers. Louise had been waiting outside since before dawn. Her hair was filthy, her elbows and the corners of her mouth were chafed, most of her toes on her left foot stuck out from her worn tennis shoe, and her belly was swollen.

Just as first sunlight colored the sky over brick buildings and the highway, the tiny 75 year-old woman came down the Mission stairs and looked at the line of people already waiting on the sidewalk. Three people over the course of the week had recommended Louise go see her.

Louise sat slumped against the wall, at the head of the line, and looked at the old woman. Eartha came straight to her and looked into her eyes with a kindness Louise hadn't seen in a long time.

Louise said, "This old bum in the park tole me they call you Mother Earth."

Eartha called up the stairs for a younger woman who took Louise to a spare bedroom that held the first bed she'd touched in more than two years.

When Louise awoke early in the afternoon, she looked around the old room and, though she heard sirens outside, felt safer than she'd felt since she was a little girl. She felt at once like everything human that could happen had happened in this building and that this building was Mother Earth, where she would be safe.

Later that afternoon, she told Eartha and Grayce how she'd lived on the streets for two years, and about all the times she had believed, without believing, only with desperation, that someone who was supposed to love her did love her. The first hope was the woman who brought her into the world. Now Louise was about to bring someone into the world, and the last hope had been the stranger who did that to her.

Louise felt confused about what to expect from Eartha and what to expect from her baby. She'd heard about Eartha's Home for Unwed Mothers. She'd heard it was the only place desperate pregnant women, white or black, could go in 1955 to receive care and not be condemned in exchange.

"You have a place to stay. You have plenty of food. You have the clothing you need," Eartha told her in her room at the Mission.

Louise's baby would be loved and nourished and taken care of. It was a promise to her baby and it was a promise to her. She was desperate, lost. When Eartha spoke to her, she felt the universe personally looked after her.

So Louise moved into the Home for Unwed Mothers on Milnor Street and she worked in the nursery. As she cared for other women's babies, her own belly grew. A few days before Louise's water broke, Eartha told her to come back to the home and the Mission, to stay there with her baby until she found work elsewhere.

And on February 26, 1956, Louise gave birth to Maria. Eartha and Grayce and Vivian Williams, who worked with Louise at the nursery, and a dozen other women who worked for the Mission, loved Maria from the day she was born.

The baby came back to Milnor Street and West Ashley. She said her first words in Eartha's presence. She took her first steps on Milnor. Louise watched her stand up as happy as she might ever be in her life and triumphantly fall forward into a first step. Having caught herself upright on one foot, she dared the next, and then fell forward, catching step after step, magically, and even falling down she looked like a little girl who had suddenly found her wings and flown.

In Grayce Bateman's 1994 reminiscences, she says that Louise and her daughter stayed with Eartha and Grayce until Maria entered Kindergarten. She doesn't say where Louise went when she left the Mission, but that Eartha and Grayce kept up with Maria through elementary school, high school, even college.

After having lost touch with Louise and Maria for 20 years, and long after Eartha's death, Grayce happened to meet Louise again, she doesn't say how, but writes, "After completion of her school work, she applied for a position at the Eartha M. M. White Nursing Home." The year was 1994. "I gladly recommended her for employment. Louise has come full circle, for she is working at the Nursing Home where her career actually began in 1955."

When Louise had come to Milnor Street 40 years before, she'd come as a young woman desperate for her own survival and her daughter's.

Twenty years after Eartha died, Maria had graduated college, married, and moved away, and Louise had come back to Eartha to give back what she could.

When Louise came, Eartha had just returned from her most extensive travels since her days with the Oriental American Opera Company, 60 years before.

Her Grand Tour took her to Italy, France, England, Ireland, Belgium, the Netherlands, Switzerland, Jordan— which then claimed Jerusalem, which Eartha visited, and Egypt.

From Belgium, she wrote Grayce to give her love to the animals at the Mission and do her "best to keep things going" and said she was "taking in everything."

Then she said, "I have a woman in my room from Clearwater trying to talk me to death."

She visited Versailles in France.

She rode camels by the the Great Sphinx and the Pyramids in Egypt.

From Jerusalem in July, Eartha sent Grayce a post card of the Old City. She wrote one sentence on the back: "It is very hot here."

In 1960, Jaquelin James Daniel became president of Stockton, Whatley, Davin, and Company. J.J. Daniel, or "Jack Daniel," as he was often called, was the son of Richard P. Daniel, who had worked so closely and extensively with Eartha in the 1930s and 1940s.

Jack Daniel ran one of the largest and wealthiest companies in the Southeast. Its business was real estate and mortgage banking.

Though his father was one of the biggest white advocates for Civil Rights in Jacksonville in the first half of the 20th century, Jack Daniel led Stockton, Whatley, and Davin to develop one of the wealthiest, whitest, most exclusive neighborhoods in Northeast Florida. Deerwood Country Club is gated, patrolled by guards 24 hours a day, and proclaims "high standards" required for residency.

From a distance, it's hard to believe J.J. Daniel was the son of a progressive Jacksonville leader. From a further distance, it's also hard to believe that Jacksonville's progressive Richard Potts Daniel was the nephew of a Confederate army surgeon.

In the decades before 1960, however, Daniels and Stocktons had worked together, as they did in an American Red Cross drive to aid towns swamped by Mississippi River floods in 1927.

But other lines formed between the Daniel family and the Stocktons across the Jacksonville landscape, and Eartha touched many of those lines, even if clandestinely.

Less than a month after Eartha died in 1974, former city council member Mary Singleton said she knew Eartha had hardly died destitute. "But she died, I'm sure she's a wealthy woman, I'm almost positive of that."

Mary Singleton's election to City Council had been followed immediately thereafter by that of Sallye Mathis. The election of two black women to City Council sparked great fear in Jacksonville's conservative white community.

Though the fear of growing black political power led to Consolidation of Duval County and Jacksonville city governments the following year, expanding the white electorate from a shrinking white urban population, both black city council members, the first in 60 years, came to support Consolidation.

J.J. Daniel, principal developer of Deerwood Country Club, would come to be called the "Father of Consolidation."

Singleton said, "Miss White owned lots of property, but she would deny herself, uh, just to get to somebody who needed."

She told her 1974 interviewer, "Now I can tell you somebody who can give you some information. And that's Jack Daniel. J.J. Daniel. His father and Ms. Eartha White were, I, I don't want to use the expression 'like brothers and sisters,' but they were very, very close, in fact, uh, uh, yes, more than extremely close, and, uh, you know who I'm talking about—Stockton, Whatley, Davin—"

There's a strange splicing sound in the audio tape. You can hear the interviewer typing in the background. There's an extended silence. Then Mary Singleton says something about "how she ran that board," and says, "They can give you a lot of information."

If anybody at Stockton, Whatley, Davin ever gave anyone else information about Eartha White, there's no trace of it now. If the conservative Jack Daniel had anything to offer about his father's progressivism as response to inherited wealth, somebody—the Daniel family? the Stocktons?—

somebody's keeping a tight seal on it—as tight a seal as was kept on the Deerwood Country Club's early exclusion and admission policies. Or as tight a seal as is kept on who's allowed to live there now.

127

In that February 1974 interview, Mary Singleton says that historians should have contacted Eartha before she died. Only immediately after Eartha's death did historians descend on the Clara White Mission and the city's black politicians.

Eartha, Singleton said, could remember everything. She could remember everything back into times just after slavery.

The Mary Singleton interview was conducted a few months before I was born. Singleton died, tragically young, serving in the state comptroller's office in 1980. She was 54 years old. I was six years old. Four decades later, I listen to her interviews and am left with more questions than answers.

What had she meant by saying that Eartha and Richard P. Daniel were "more than extremely close"? She'd almost called them "brother and sister," but said that wasn't quite right.

I find myself staring down at a birthday card sent to Eartha from Richard P. Daniel's secretary Charlotte Sibthorpe, in which she's typed, "I shall always prize the beautiful Bible you brought me from your trip to the Holy Land," after which she scrawls in pen, "Thanks so much for sharing your delicious cake with Mr. Daniel and me."

What of the ironies that Eartha, born in 1876, believed her father to be Guy Stockton, and that Richard P. Daniel's son became president of Stockton, Whatley, Davin, and Co.?

What of the ironies that people assumed Eartha died wealthy, having been propped up throughout her life by a wealthy white family? A 1971 magazine article that headlined a claim that Eartha was "rich" said she had been given financial help and advice by "certain concerned white and black citizens in early Jacksonville."

In her 2001 master's thesis on Eartha, Carmen Godwin connected the article "to the story that the Stockton family gave Eartha money for her education, and later, for her humanitarian endeavors throughout the years."

Godwin refers to the "numerous black and white informants" who'd claimed "the Stockton family looked after Clara for years, providing her with money and property for covering up their family secret."

What of the ironies that Eartha began her business successes with laundries and real estate, while her apparent white father was brother to the founder of the largest real estate family business in North Florida? What of the ironies that Eartha seemed wealthy in land holdings in her last years, but "cash poor"?

What of the ironies that she lost property value in holdings along Moncrief Road on the mostly black Northside, after Stocktons and Daniels reaped exponential wealth for developing exclusive white neighborhoods on the Southside?

In 1960, the same year J.J. Daniel became president of Stockon, Whatley, Davin, a white man named Herb Peyton opened a Gate Petroleum gas station in the black neighborhood of Moncrief and 45th, and Interstate-95 slashed its asphalt wound across what had been the western portion of LaVilla.

Gate Petroleum later bought Stockton Whatley Davin's Deerwood Country Club and several other wealthy white neighborhoods into which residents had to buy and qualify (usually partially by being white) for membership. His son John Peyton served as mayor of Jacksonville from 2003 to 2011 and is now president of Gate Petroleum.

What of the ironies?

And what if the ironies aren't so ironic after all—that in Jacksonville, white is wealth and wealth is power and power is politics?

And the very worst theories about Eartha's power were that it was bought, or, even worse, that is was bred.

And apart from what can be denied or confirmed, after all this time, the ugliest ideas may be true, may be sexist or racist, or may be some combination thereof.

128

In Chamblin's Uptown, my favorite bookstore, I'm sitting across a café table from a young woman who's done her own research on Eartha White, but doesn't want me to use her name.

She says she knows all about the Stocktons and Eartha. She says there was never any significant money from the Stocktons. "There may've been a little bit of money, initially." She doesn't say how she knows.

"But the fodder is there for some kind of conspiracy theory, right?" I say, "You know, that the Stocktons gave hush-money, then supported her, that there was some kind of secret wealth. I mean, I'm not suggesting that's the case, but I'm saying, when people get the chance to make a neat pattern out of certain facts, they'll do it."

"Well," she says, "And I think people certainly have assumed that, and I don't think it's true, but I think that from time to time, she used relationships—"

Pause.

"—to build her capacity, I don't want to say to her advantage, but to the…"

Pause.

"Yes, she did," she says and laughs.

Pause.

"Well," she says, "but to the advantage of others. I mean, it really wasn't about Eartha getting anything from this, it was about accomplishing what she wanted to accomplish. You know, I think there were a number of relationships, gentlemen over the years that…that benefited her projects."

I mention the letters Albert Sammis wrote to Eartha from Tampa for almost a decade and Ted Redding's claim that Eartha had a "torrid affair" with the "underworld figure" named Tom Baxter.

"Yes, Sammis was," she says, "Was he white, or was he half-white?" She thinks for a second and says, "He was half."

She's never heard of Tom Baxter, but she jots the name down on a napkin, her eyebrows lowered.

She says, "That's a name I've never heard. I've heard Daniel, but then I also heard that Old Man Daniel might have been her father. Oh, and she evidently had a fairly intense relationship with James Weldon Johnson."

"Really?" I say. I try not to show my skepticism.

She mentions that Eartha toured in the opera company with James Weldon Johnson's brother Rosamond and says there are stories of "some things" being "fairly evident," but says she knows of no proof and isn't sure where the stories came from.

I suspect Eartha's fiancé James Jordan got conflated with that more famous James from Jacksonville.

"You do have to wonder," she says. "Everybody turned to Eartha, but who did Eartha turn to? She wasn't a god."

She thinks it's probably true that Eartha's and Richard P. Daniel's relationship was, in Mary Singleton's words, "more than extremely close."

"There was an incident where Eartha went to his daughter's wedding," she says, "because he *insisted* that she come, and she didn't want to go, and she, she was uncomfortable, but she got all dressed up and she went, and Richard's wife, in front of everyone, literally turned her back on her, so obviously there was something known to some degree, and it was a horrible situation. And she went because he insisted."

"So here is this woman," I say, "this single black woman who did all these amazing things, and there was this idea of her being wedded to the community…"

She says, "There was a whole *other* aspect," and she pauses and laughs, "to Eartha White."

I can't find any evidence for these assertions, but I don't exclude them from the narrative of my search. Their value doesn't inhere in their truth, but in the indications they give of how many ways Jacksonville responded to Eartha.

Was that "whole other aspect" extant mostly or only in the minds of people who could not and would not believe Eartha could do what she did by herself? Without secret wealth? Without white patronage? Without a man?

And is it, 40 years after Eartha's death, less urgent and more titillating for some of us to entertain these ideas, to fit Eartha to what knowledge of "human nature" we believe we've learned from celebrity gossip?

129

Jack Daniel developed the wealthiest and most exclusive residential enclaves in Duval County, spearheaded the Consolidation of Duval County's and the City of Jacksonville's governments in 1968, and published both of the city's newspapers in the 1970s.

Each of those endeavors infuses the others. Consolidation was supposed to be about solving the many systemic problems and corruption in city government, but it also extended services and the tax base to the new discriminative suburban neighborhoods Daniel was developing. And the implications of his control of both the city's newspapers?

Daniel's biography usually highlights his lineage from his grandfather and great-grandfather who both played large roles in early Jacksonville.

But some Jacksonville histories fail to mention Jack Daniel's father, Richard P. Daniel, the great liberal leader and friend of Eartha White, though the 19th century physician and civic leader Richard Potts Daniel gets frequent historical adulation.

Likewise, so-called histories of Jacksonville that give barest mention to the city's black community, which has usually numbered almost as much as the city's majority and has at times exceeded it, constitute no more than half—if not half-assed—histories.

Jack Daniel died in 1990. A quarter century later, I speak with an elderly friend of his in a stodgy bland dining room with a gargantuan fireplace. I was given an access code to drive through ornate gates into this "community," physically and personally reminding me that the root verb of "exclusive" is "exclude."

This singular and momentary admission reinforces the fact of my exclusion.

He tells me, "Jack was embarrassed of his dad." He's not the first I've heard say it.

Jack's friend speaks in the manner of an older man who's always had too much time and capital ever to have been hurried.

"I know that story," he tells me, when I mention the wedding of Richard P. Daniel's daughter, Jack's sister. "Look," he says. "I'll tell you what that was all about. Jack's dad had too much principle." He's not the first to tell me this story this way either.

"Much as Jack didn't like his dad's principles, no way would Jack think his dad had an inappropriate relationship with another woman, never mind Eartha White. Jack knew that. He heard the stories about his dad and Eartha White. He did. But no. I mean, no." He rubs the outer corners of his eyes.

"Look. Here's what was scandalous. Jack's dad gave free legal counsel to a colored woman. That wasn't less inappropriate than anything else," he says obtusely. "Do you understand? Let me see if I can make you understand," he says.

I look at him, waiting.

"After all that went between Jack's dad and Miss White, his dad's inviting Miss White to his daughter's wedding? I guess he did it to make some kind of point. The point didn't take. The point just didn't take. And I guess Miss White couldn't decline. So much for the all-powerful Miss White. But she must've known what she would encounter. She came anyway."

"And?" I say after a painfully long pause.

"Look," he says, "Jack had walked down the street in neighborhoods his own family developed, and he'd had people call out to him, call his name, and then call out his father's name, and then they'd turn their backs on him, right there on the sidewalk of the neighborhood his family had brought to exist. Can you imagine that kind of shame?"

I don't say anything.

"Jack's had all these people turn their backs on him because of his dad's support of Miss White. So then Miss White shows up at this wedding? The response is just math."

130

In October 2013, 30 minutes into my discussion with Ju'Coby Pittman and Meg Fisher, president and vice president of the Mission, I say, "I want to just throw something out and see how you guys respond. I've spoken with several people about this, and I've heard that during her life, there was lots of gossip and rumor, and I've seen Eartha's family Bible, where she writes that her father was Guy Stockton."

I don't know what to expect when I say this. I haven't expected as warm a reception from the current directors of the Mission as I've received. I understand that Grayce Bateman, who directed the Mission after Eartha, was very protective of Eartha's reputation, and I understand that a wealthy white person threatened litigation on nebulous grounds in the 1970s against anyone who might mention Guy Stockton.

But I push on. "And then later she formed several business partnerships with Richard P. Daniel, whose son later became the president of Stockton, Whatley, Davin, and I understand that in the black community at the time, there was gossip that her father was white—"

And both women nod their heads, eyes serious, and say, together, "He was. He was."

I'm surprised. "Is that generally believed here at the Mission that Stockton himself was—"

Both women nod and say, together, "Yeah, yeah."

Ju'Coby says, "Most people probably didn't know that, I don't know if exactly, if they thought he was her father?"

And Meg says, "Yeah, I think, I think it's pretty well—"

"I mean, they probably knew he was a white man," Ju'Coby says, "but they didn't know who he was."

Meg thinks that Eartha found out about her biological father shortly after Clara applied for benefits in 1896, following the death of her husband Lafayette, when pension investigators uncovered the truth.

That very year, 1896, when Eartha was 20 years old, she returned to Jacksonville from her opera tours upon her fiancé James Jordan's death, and four years later, the census referred to Eartha as "mulatto," a clear indication she knew her father was white.

*

It's easy to imagine what kind of emotional confrontation might have taken place between Clara and Eartha, these two women so wedded throughout their lives, Eartha naming the Mission after Clara, the two sharing a headstone after death. It's easy to speculate about the effects of this sudden knowledge on their relationship and on Eartha's relationship with men.

And when I ask about that great Old-Testament-style story of Eartha being Clara's 13th child and the first to live, and Reverend Harrison coming to name her, I have to pause because of the look on Ju'Coby's face—her furrowed forehead and fluttering eyelids.

"Should I just stop and read the look on your face?" I ask her, and I say, "I mean, it's a great story."

"Yes," she says, "it *is* a great story, and we *told* that story for years until we found out it wasn't true."

But there was a letter, Meg says, that the two of them found years ago, when the top stories of the Mission were full of boxes from floor to ceiling and wall to wall, and she's not sure where the letter is now, but it seemed to corroborate the idea that Clara had a daughter she couldn't take care of named Bertha, whom she "gave away," before receiving Eartha from the Stocktons. The letter, faded and moth-eaten, seemed to be addressed to someone in New Orleans, "and it seemed to suggest that Eartha had looked for her sister, and that maybe Eartha was speaking to Bertha?"

*

I asked to see the Mission's own materials for months. I was told they were kept off-site, that they were hard to access, then that they were in the back of the third floor but their archivist was hard to reach. I offered to do anything I had to do to get to whatever historic documents the Mission might have. If they were buried somewhere, I said, I'd tunnel underground with a toothpick, if that's what they required.

Four months later I emailed Ju'Coby, "I've got so many people speaking to me and speaking of the history. But I'm wondering, and other people are wondering, why you're not letting me at whatever records the Mission has. Maybe you're just too busy. Maybe you don't take me seriously. Or, maybe—and I really don't believe this—the Mission has something to hide." She put me in touch with archivist Patricia Moman Bell.

Through what felt like obfuscations, I was given to understand there are materials stored elsewhere, but that no one will get to them anytime soon.

Maybe letters between Eartha and Bertha exist. If they do, they'd be the biggest treasure any historian researching Eartha White could find. I don't think the Mission is actively keeping secrets, but I think there may be secrets the possibilities of which the Mission has not the time or resources to explore.

*

There's a moment of silence. I'm trying to connect several stories in my head, and finally Ju'Coby says, "You know, some of this stuff, it just doesn't connect." She pauses and says, "A couple years ago, one of the Stocktons' nephews came through here on a tour. And he didn't know."

"But we did tell him," Meg says.

And for clarification, I ask, "You did, or you didn't?"

And Ju'Coby says, "We did tell him."

And this Stockton seemed, they say, "kind of excited," though possibilities of the name being released in the 1970s met with threats of lawsuits, and Meg says, "He said, 'I'm not one of the rich Stocktons.'"

"Oh," I say and laugh. "Well, who know what *that* means?"

But the knowledge is out there now, historians and former Congressmen have talked publically about it. And if the black community, long ago, without reliable media outlets, had spread folk-news, some of that news may've formed conspiracy theory, but sometimes, if rarely, the kernels of conspiracy theory are the truth.

Eartha spent every Christmas Eve the same way for 40 years. She went with the choir from St. Paul's African Methodist Episcopal, and for 30 years with Grayce Bateman, to hospitals and nursing homes and prison farms. Everyone sang and Eartha gave Christmas candies and fruit to everybody she visited.

The whole group came back to the Mission late at night and, first thing in the morning, came together for a hot breakfast in the first floor auditorium.

By 10 a.m., homeless families came to receive free Christmas dinners of chicken and turkey, and volunteers took more dinners to those too sick or old to leave their homes.

The children started lining up on West Ashley hours before Eartha and her volunteers handed toys out to the lines stretched around the block at 2 o'clock.

Eartha and Grayce and several other women from the Mission visited Raiford State Prison just before Christmas every year. Eartha spoke to the prisoners in chapel each Christmas, and the prisoners often wrote her.

When entering the state prison, Grayce later wrote, "Miss White, as group leader, was searched first. As she stepped on the metal detector, the bell rang, so she had to be specially checked."

But though Eartha lived in the heart of Jacksonville, and though she was a single woman, a small woman, Grayce wrote that Eartha never carried "a gun, a knife, or any other weapon on her person."

She said, "The staves in her corset caused the bell to ring."

Though children stood in line for up to two hours, the giveaways lasted three and four hours.

Some children were so excited they could hardly contain themselves. Some of them were sad. A lot of kids felt strange combinations of jubilation and sadness, each waxing and waning against the other, sometimes altogether overwhelming and confusing.

When I was two years old and Eartha had been dead two years, *The Florida Times-Union* ran an obligatory annual blurb with two photographs under the headline, "The Happiest Kids in Town (Toy Giveaway)," no byline.

The first sentence reads, "If happiness were measured by sheer smile power, the Clara White Mission at 613 West Ashley Street probably was the happiest place in town."

The top image shows a beautiful four year-old black girl named Tasha Campbell wearing a tight-ribbed sweater, holding a baby bottle to the mouth of a white baby doll about half her size.

Terry DeLoach walks across the ruined ballroom in the wet August heat, as pigeons flutter frantically in a corner of the ceiling. The windows are boarded up and the ceiling slats are splintered and dangle patiently overhead.

There's a mirror in this ballroom into which thousands of black faces looked from the dance floor in 1923 or 1946. Some of those faces belonged to Ella Fitzgerald and Billie Holiday and Earl "Fatha" Hines and Cab Calloway and Ray Charles.

Lloyd DeLoach first opened DeLoach Furniture here at the edge of LaVilla almost a century ago. The furniture store was the central ground floor business. To their left was a pool hall and to their right a mortician.

Upstairs was the Richmond Hotel.

Walking through the old hotel hallways, looking meditatively in the heat at the green paint on door paneling, I feel a humility and awe toward how much this building has lived.

DeLoach stands tall and broad-shouldered. In his early 60s, his pate is bald and his beard is trim and white. He speaks with a deep, calm, kind voice and seems both professorial and like someone who's been surfing for 45 years.

"The sad irony is that LaVilla really started to implode after desegregation," he says. "White flight" wasn't just *white* flight. It was also the flight of the black middle and upper classes. "Then," he says, "in the '60s, there were all the race riots downtown, and there was just this violence in the air all around you."

In fact, the 1960s began ominously with the construction of Interstate-95 being barreled across the western portion of LaVilla and with Ax Handle Saturday, when whites in Confederate uniforms gathered downtown at Hemming Park, now Hemming Plaza, with baseball bats and ax handles and assaulted scores of black people. They wanted to take back the middle of the city in response to black sit-ins and protests at segregated downtown lunch counters.

The September 12, 1960 issue of *Life* magazine contained a photograph of a white policeman with a worried face holding the arm of a young black man named Charlie Griffin, whose face and shirt were covered in blood. Griffin stands in the middle of Laura Street less than a block from the Confederate Memorial at the heart of the city. Across from the church is today's Chamblin's Uptown, bookshop and café.

Rodney L. Hurst, a member of the local NAACP Youth Council, went to high school with Griffin. Though Hurst had actively participated in lunch-counter sit-ins at department stores like Woolworth's and W.T. Grant's, Griffin hadn't been politically involved. He'd been shopping downtown. Walking down the sidewalk, he'd looked up to see a complete stranger running at him and swinging a heavy wooden cudgel. When Griffin, a high school football star, tried to defend himself, several other men came down on him with ax handles.

Two days before, anonymous phone threats had been made against Richard Charles Parker, a young white man from Massachusetts who'd decided to sit-in with black students at downtown lunch-counters. Parker was a student at one of the two nearest public universities, Florida State University, two and a half hours from Jacksonville in Tallahassee.

At the lunch-counter sit-in at Woolworth on Hemming Park, a group of white construction workers approached the protesters but clearly singled out Parker. They stared him down, holding heavy wrenches and other construction tools in their fists. But Parker, Northeastern liberal, was also Massachusetts-tough. Though he wasn't about to back down, a number of his Southern black friends that day thought Jacksonville's whites were about to lynch him.

Somebody had called the Booomerangs, and they came over from their hangouts on West Ashley. They walked single-file into Woolworth and formed a stone-faced circle around their white brother. Then they escorted him safely into Laura Street and through Hemming Park. A crowd of young white men followed them. They called Parker the usual epithets—a "nigger lover" and a "race mixer."

Just as the Boomerangs would later escort Sallye Mathis and Mary Singleton, the first two female black city council members, to their offices each day, they escorted Parker north on Hogan Street and west on Ashley. The white crowd followed them until they got to Clay Street, heading into LaVilla, and there they turned back.

135

The Ku Klux Klan had held meetings at the multi-story Robert Meier Hotel on Hemming Park to plan that Saturday's events. An FBI informant named Clarence Sears had infiltrated the Jacksonville-area Klan and reported to Jacksonville Sheriff Dale Carson on their plans for that Saturday.

The Sears report quickly disappeared at the sheriff's office, not the only occurrence of its kind, and local Klan meetings demanded requests for knowledge of the "traitor in our midst."

Later writers said black people called Richard McKissick the "Mayor of Ashley Street," though he dismisses the idea with a wave of his hand. McKissick managed the Strand and Roosevelt Theaters on West Ashley, on either side of the Clara White Mission. When he showed up Saturday morning on West Ashley, black kids and older black men came up to him right away and told something was going on downtown.

McKissick called his boss and told him what he'd been told, but Clint Ezell had already heard what was happening. In fact, he'd heard that black people from several parts of town were siphoning through West Ashley toward the center of the city.

So the theaters and businesses and the Clara White Mission, all the buildings up and down West Ashley from downtown to the interstate, offered refuge to every black person they could shill inside.

Police blockaded intersections of West Ashley, searching storefronts and businesses, and were soon reinforced by between 20 and 30 police cars that shut off the perimeters of LaVilla, and downtown more loosely, and effectively placed the black heart of Jacksonville under lockdown.

The police shouted through bullhorns for complete evacuation of the streets, saying they would arrest anyone who didn't comply, including LaVilla business owners who had nothing ostensibly to do with the protests or the riots.

Rodney Hurst, a teenager then, saw violence he'd never been prepared to see. He saw white men walking the streets swinging baseball bats and ax handles. He saw a cameraman from a local TV news station knocked from the top of a car.

He saw one small Southern city come to the verge of Civil War, while only local black news sources and national media outlets were willing to report what was happening.

The DeLoaches, a white family who had lived and worked with black entrepreneurs in LaVilla and had met the black athletes and musicians who could stay in few other hotels in town but the Richmond, kept operating their furniture store through LaVilla's decline into poverty and violence and hardcore drugs.

"The hotel went down in the '60s," says Terry DeLoach, "because it seemed unconscionable then for it to exist. During segregation, it had always been an all-black hotel, but successful black people wouldn't want to stay in an all-black hotel anymore. They wanted to be where black and white people both could stay."

So the Richmond Hotel turned into a boarding house, where rooms rented nightly or weekly or longer for a few dollars and nobody asked any questions.

We walk through long-neglected hotel room after hotel room. I keep registering the room numbers in my head. 11. 19. 38. 41. I try to look through every window, though all of them are boarded up. I want to see through them to the people on the street in 1925. Maybe I'll see Blind Blake or Jelly Roll Morton.

When we first come up the stairs from the locked and metal-grilled door down on Broad Street, I'm ready to set down my bags and check in.

The battered and missing-lettered sign over the check-in counter says, "R OMS DA LY R TES INGLE $4.16 DOUB E $5.2 [T]V $1.00."

Behind glass on the check-in counter sits a dust-covered lamp carved with angels and grapes and filigree, which a friend later says looks like it belongs in a brothel. The ceiling is caving in.

In the 1970s, LaVilla became a very dangerous place, and the gravity that had made it a densely massive star of black business and political networking and blues and jazz before segregation made it a labyrinthine magnetic mass of desperation that culminated in the crack cocaine epidemic of the 1980s.

No wonder so many black people believed conspiracy theories that the U.S. government created crack as a way to destroy black communities in the decades following desegregation. The view from a place like LaVilla made such theories seem obvious. It was a kind of chemical warfare.

"And after the Richmond closed, the police wanted to use the top of this building to spy out on LaVilla," DeLoach says. Though I can't walk through the internal LaVilla political dynamics of the 1970s and '80s, I hear him saying, beneath what he's saying, that the DeLoaches were trying to be Switzerland in the war-charged atmosphere of the time.

The fire department, he said, did permit watches from the top of the nearby fire station and the message, "We know what you're doing and if you don't stop, we'll burn this place down," had the desired effect.

Around the corner from the former Richmond Hotel at Broad and West Ashley, diagonally across from the Mission, stood a bar and drive-through pharmacy intentionally or ironically called "Perks" (Apostrophe or not? It changes the definition. I'll soon find out, but while I'm walking with DeLoach, I don't yet know).

DeLoach says, "We fronted downtown. We were on the border between downtown and LaVilla. But by the 1980s, you could just disappear into LaVilla behind us. You could find any drug you wanted to find and never come out again, and if you wanted to be lost, no one would ever find you there."

He remembers being in the warehouse at the Church Street corner of the building, in and above what had once been a pool hall, and suddenly hearing an apocalypse outside the Richmond Hotel's old walls.

"I remember how cars would line up all the way down Broad Street on Friday afternoons to drive through Perk[']s." What happened there was obvious and blatant. Anybody in the city who wanted to know about it could do so, but everybody was scared to do anything about it.

But Terry DeLoach remembers the police coming in with a SWAT team and circling helicopters that zeroed in on Perk[']s.

"They'd told him if he didn't stop his trade, they were gonna take his place down to the ground." Now he's standing on the sidewalk outside the Richmond Hotel, looking at the empty lot across the street.

He says, "They followed through."

138

And it becomes apparent to me, as at certain previous moments, that LaVilla was a whole world. It had the gravity of a sun. So much good happened here, and so much bad. So much life. So much.

Terry DeLoach walks down Broad Street to the former Progress Furniture Company warehouse at 318.

On the first floor is sheet rock and carpet and an old barber shop setup with a couple of now-collectible barber chairs in all the patience of their lost time.

Up the stairs, the old warehouse becomes bare. Brick walls. Wooden slats. Boarded windows. And then a very strange thing.

We step through a door on the second floor and step from the warehouse onto a completely walled-in front porch.

Front porch ceiling slats. Windows that looked out the front of a LaVilla house a century ago.

This old warehouse was built right around an even older Carpenter-Gothic LaVilla house. The second floor of the house is intact inside the warehouse, completely invisible from without. The warehouse is old, but the house inside it is older.

The original decorative wooden porch brackets of the older house within are well-preserved against the right angles of the interior brick warehouse walls.

And inside the old house, back from the porch, are rooms in which people lived stories I can never know but only try to imagine.

The very idea of an older house preserved inside an old brick warehouse seems to model how history works, how history haunts. Always. That's its definition.

Trying to find Eartha White is like looking for, then through these rooms hidden inside rooms all over the city. Eartha White nesting-dolls.

139

Back in the Richmond Hotel, I stumble deep into the building's interior. I'm carrying a dim flashlight, but accidentally kick something in the darkness at my feet. I look down and see the hardened carcass of a pigeon.

Walking through hotel rooms and the corridors connecting them, I come to a different kind of window, one that opens out into an air shaft in the middle of the building. I can't help but love the metaphorical value of such windows. I've looked into them in beautifully restored old hotels in San Diego and San Francisco, but I've never before looked through windows into the ventilation shaft of a building uninhabited for decades.

I love the names for ventilation shafts almost as much as I love the things themselves. Air shafts. Most poetic of all, another purpose: light wells.

They were brilliant ways to ventilate old buildings naturally, before air-conditioning. They help me think of these buildings as natural expressions of the landscape, the way Frank Lloyd Wright thought of his architecture. Ventilation shafts rose up the interiors of tall buildings and offered a breeze and sunlight to the hallways and rooms.

This one suggests the present emptiness at the heart of the Richmond Hotel. It suggests the void at the center of things in some pseudo-Buddhist sense. It offers an embodiment of mystery at the center of whatever we think we know.

For how many millions of cars have passed this building, and how few of their drivers, if any, have given a second's thought to the tall empty central space that once brought sunlight and breath to a healthy, living structure?

I think about when Eartha White, 97 years old in 1974, fell down the stairs at the Mission. She broke her hip. Her heart gave out. She died within the week. The newspapers never said exactly how she died: she was just old.

And I feel sad that she died as the neighborhood fell down its own staircase, after she'd helped so many people and had seen so much death and life in LaVilla. I'm happy that her Mission endures in 2014, that it's now a multi-million-dollar non-profit charity. And I'm saddened Eartha died just a couple steps up from LaVilla's hitting rock-bottom.

Again, I want to look out the boarded-up windows of the Richmond Hotel and see a whole culture below me, masses of people, amongst them blues and folk and jazz musicians and hairdressers and bankers and bakers and preachers and poets, and, by name, maybe Ray Charles, maybe James Weldon Johnson, maybe Asa Philip Randolph, maybe Eartha White.

140

My daughter and I are spinning microfilm reels in the downtown library, digging back through *Jet* magazine to 1964. She hands me reels, I place them, and together we watch time fly backward.

The April 9th issue of *Jet* featured a story called, "What's Behind Jacksonville's Race Violence?"

It's been a pattern in Southern history, and the beginning of the 20th century made Jacksonville recalcitrantly Southern. Whenever large advancements were made for black people, whites retaliated with aggressive entrenchment.

Just as the Civil War ended with Jim Crow laws and the rise of the Ku Klux Klan in response to Reconstruction, the hopes of the Civil Rights Movement made many Jacksonville whites angrier than ever.

The difference was that this time, Jacksonville blacks got just as angry and didn't hide it.

The *Jet* story begins with Jacksonville police breaking down the office doors of the local NAACP. It says, "The violent police action was not disclosed in the controlled press releases emanating from the Florida city. Nor was there any mention of the kicking and beating of young Negro students, children and women or the wholesale arrests for unlawful assembly. The Southern city reacted violently to the Negro communities [sic] refusal to bow to demands that peaceful demonstrations to desegregate downtown restaurants and hotels be halted immediately by command of Mayor Haydon Burns."

A 1964 *Jet* subhead said, "Ambitious Mayor's Menacing Threats Triggered Riots." Any historian looking only at the city's mainstream newspapers would have little idea that any such racial violence occurred.

141

Black kids threw bricks at Haydon Burns's campaign offices.

Jet had referred to Ax Handle Saturday in 1960, which mainstream newspapers—or *white* newspapers, as most any black Jacksonville resident would have called them—hardly even mentioned.

Though *The Florida Star* and *The Jacksonville Free Press* and *The Pittsburgh Courier* reported the violence in the streets, *The Jacksonville Journal* and *The Florida Times-Union* had very little to say about racial tensions that erupted in all-out violence.

What the city's newspapers reported about racial violence in 1964 was mostly filed under crime news, but *Jet* gave the true magnitude. "A race riot brought the city, hailed as the gateway to Florida, to its knees for the second time in four years."

If local papers didn't contextualize the race riots they sparingly reported as crime, national publications referred to Jacksonville as buckling under racial difficulties twice in the early 1960s, in echoes of the city burning to the ground in the Great Fire of 1901.

Many of Jacksonville's black high school students had taken up Martin Luther King's call for nonviolent resistance, in the mode of Mahatma Gandhi, to protest for desegregation, just as Mayor Burns had decided to run for governor. Peace, he decided, was less important than order.

He said he would crush all efforts to desegregate downtown hotels. Such desegregation would cause whites to flee the city and leave it to the blacks. Burns would bring in unprecedeted numbers of white cops, burgeoned by his immediately deputizing 500 white firefighters as police officers to squash black protests.

More than 2,000 black high school and college students rushed toward the middle of downtown with chants of "Freedom" and promises to defy any authorities that denied their rights.

While the infamous 1960 Ax Handle Saturday has reached a kind of apologetic memorial status in the last several years, fewer people talk about 1964. Ax Handle Saturday probably wouldn't be so memorialized today if 1990s Jacksonville Sheriff Nat Glover hadn't been a young black victim in Hemming Park that day.

In the 1964 riots, police drove motorcycles through crowds of black protesters in downtown streets. Cops billy-clubbed kids. Black students called in a bomb scare at the New Stanton School, and angry black men threw bricks and firebombs through white-owned and "accommodationist" black-owned business buildings. After all, white supremacists had firebombed black churches and killed little black girls in "Bombingham," Alabama.

142

Eartha sat in a chair out in front of the Mission. She'd watched this city from its core for almost 90 years. She heard shouting and screaming from every direction. A mass migration of angry young men had rushed from LaVilla toward businesses and public squares downtown.

Then the mayor was standing before her. She could see he was desperate. How desperate must he be if he needed, in the midst of the greatest mass racial violence in the city since slavery, to journey to the heart of LaVilla and stand before Eartha White with hat in hand?

He said he had always come through for her when she asked him for help for her people. Now he had something to ask of her. Hers was the most powerful voice in black Jacksonville, but he thought she had never looked littler, more brittle, more frail.

Grayce, Eartha's goddaughter Vivian, and several other people in the Mission had warned her not to go outside. When people turn to mass thinking and instant mass action, any kind of unanticipated and unintended violence can happen. But Eartha had known about mass psychology since decades before most of those inside had been born.

So she watched West Ashley Street from outside the Mission, witness to however this thing might take place in the streets, and that's where Mayor Burns found her.

"I need your help, Miss White," he conceded. The city was its own organic animal, and even in all his political power, he was only a part of the larger organism. "I've helped you before, Miss White," he said. "I need your help now. I'm asking you to talk to your people and help me stop this rioting."

Eartha, so soft-spoken, so gentle, had not removed her gaze from his the whole time he'd besought her, and when he was done, she said, "You started it. You stop it."

When the Mayor left the Mission, he felt defeated. He felt angry. He felt jilted. I imagine that for a moment, as he slipped down invisibly into the back seat of the dark car that took him from LaVilla, he imagined news headlines announcing that Mayor W. Haydon Burns was gunned down in LaVilla upon retreating from being denied by Eartha White. One day, he might have thought, one day Jacksonville should take down this whole LaVilla menace, wipe it clean from the earth.

Jet reported that the race riots went on for hours. Black kids attacked white suburban commuters heading home from downtown businesses. White police beat and kicked young black men and women, and news spread through the black community in LaVilla and North Jacksonville that white judges were expediting sentences against blacks while mainstream newspapers were ignoring, or even worse, striking and deleting accounts of white vigilantism.

"In retaliation at the police measures, the Negro community exploded. Attacks against anything or anybody white skyrocketed. To get back at the white deputized firemen, youngsters started a siege of ringing false alarms, accounting for 50 such calls in a single night. The Negro neighborhoods were barricaded and put off limits to all whites. The Negroes warned that if 'one white officer fired a bullet at a child,' there would be blood running in every street of the town."

Newspapers reported what *Jet* said were "false stories" of young black men attacking whites. Police reports supported the idea that most of these stories, like that of one white person being bound to a tree and slashed with razors, were false, though why reports from Jacksonville's corrupt police department should be believed in certain cases and not others should be better documented and explained. As *Jet* said, the anger and violence in Jacksonville "reached pepper heat."

Forty years later Oprah Winfrey, the Southern Poverty Law Center, and media outlets all over the country refocused on one black woman shot on the sidewalk in the midst of Jacksonville's 1964 race riots. She was a mother of 10 who had nothing more to do with the city's race hatreds than being murdered for being black and walking down the sidewalk.

Johnnie Mae Chappell was 35 years old. She worked as a maid for a wealthy white family. Her youngest son was just four months old that day. She went to the grocery to get ingredients for homemade strawberry ice cream.

When she got home, she noticed she'd dropped or left her purse behind and went back to look for it along New Kings Road and Moncrief.

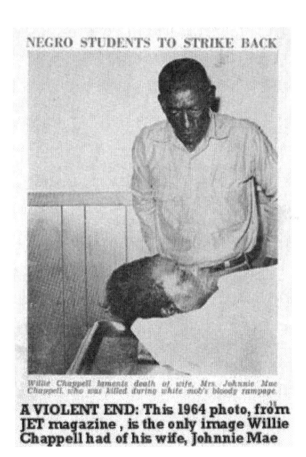

NEGRO STUDENTS TO STRIKE BACK

Willie Chappell laments death of wife, Mrs. Johnnie Mae Chappell, who was killed during white mob's bloody rampage.

A VIOLENT END: This 1964 photo, from JET magazine, is the only image Willie Chappell had of his wife, Johnnie Mae

Just as she walked in the dimming light along that intersection, four young white men, drunk and angry about black responses to segregationist law and order, had decided to drive through black Jacksonville with guns and beer, where they saw Johhnie Mae Chappel on the sidewalk.

Jacksonville's newspapers only mentioned the murder several months later, when it came to trial, in a one-column story buried deep within.

But shortly after the killing, *Jet* published a photograph of Willie Chappell, looking down at his murdered wife, "killed during white mob's bloody rampage."

Police interrogations buried for decades had one of the young men in the car, which one differing according to who told the story, saying, "Let's go kill a nigger."

In the years following the murder, the photograph of Willie looking at the murdered body of Johnnie Mae was the only image he had of his wife. Willie, a gas station attendant, couldn't raise his five sons after his wife's death. His daughters had already gone to live with relatives. His sons went to live in foster homes.

Jacksonville detectives Lee Cody and Donald Coleman had assumed someone was already working on the Johnnie Mae Chappell case.

When Wayne Chessman and Elmer Kato, two of the four men in the car from which the bullet came, approached the detectives at a hot dog and milkshake joint called the Freezette on the Northside's Lem Turner Road, the detectives were taken aback.

Chessman and Kato wanted to confess, but they wanted to confess that their friend J.W. Rich had pulled the trigger.

The detectives were wrong to think that someone was working on the case. They looked for a file, but no file existed. While they waited to speak to Chief Detective J.C. Patrick in his office, they saw papers shoved under the rug beneath Patrick's chair. One of the detectives reached down to see what the papers were and found they pertained to Chappell's murder.

Just as 400 black people had been arrested during race riots the weekend Johnnie Mae was shot, but almost no whites, Cody and Coleman realized they were witnessing blatant obstruction of justice.

The Florida Times-Union gave almost no coverage to the murder and little more to the trial.

The four boys in the car that night were indicted, but Rich was identified as the shooter. He said it was an accident.

The detectives were called to bring the gun into court, but couldn't find it in the property room where it had been stored. Nobody ever found the murder weapon again.

The defense claimed the killing was an innocent mistake. The boys were just out having some fun. They didn't intend to kill anybody. Surely the all white male jury could understand young men getting a thrill from driving fast cars and shooting guns. The bullet had bounced off the ground and struck Johnnie Mae by accident.

The jury was convinced. A juror named Bill Loos said he'd examined the bullet in court, though the gun had gone missing, and, from his knowledge of killing hogs, judged it a ricochet. One juror believed Rich should receive a sentence for murder, but the rest of the jury agreed the shooting was an accident.

Just like that Waylon Jennings theme for *The Dukes of Hazzard* said:

> Just the good ol' boys,
>
> Never meanin' no harm,
>
> Beats all you ever saw,
>
> Been in trouble with the law
>
> Since the day they was born.

And "Makin' their way, the only way they know how, / Just a little bit more than the law will allow."

In fact, it *was* just a little bit more. The one holdout for a murder charge changed his mind within the hour.

Rich was given 10 years for manslaughter, but paroled four years later. The other three good ol' boys went free.

Both detectives were fired within the year. For the next 10 years, Cody and Coleman fought to show evidence of corruption and obstruction of justice to four Florida governors, the Florida Department of Law Enforcement, and the FBI. Finally the political system wore them out and they gave up, exhausted, blasé, and saddened.

They gave up until Cody saw, in 1995, that Johnnie Mae's youngest son Shelton, four months old when his mother was murdered, had decided to push for the truth.

Before Willie Chappell died in 1995, having never remarried after the death of his wife, people sometimes asked him why he didn't pursue justice after Wayne Chessman, Elmer Kato, James Davis, and J.W. Rich got off so easily.

He said, "Listen. You ain't never seen a man hung by his neck in your lifetime. You ain't never seen a woman's belly split open. But I have."

If you hadn't been black in Jacksonville in the 1960s, there was no way you could understand it.

But long before that, his daddy, he said, sometimes had to drive his boys near where Edgewood Avenue crosses New Kings Road. His daddy always told his children to put their heads down when they drove through that wooded area.

But Willie Jr. couldn't help but look. He remembered seeing burnt Ku Klux Klan crosses in the woods. He remembered when he was a little boy, crouched amongst his siblings in his daddy's old ramshackle truck, peeking over his hand and seeing a black body hanging from a tree.

Just like in that Billie Holiday song. *Strange Fruit* hanging from the poplar trees.

And as an old man, Willie Jr., who had held his dying wife in his arms, said, "You will never forget that feeling."

Eleven years after Willie died, the writer Susan Cooper Eastman found J.W. Rich in the Triangle Bar on Lem Turner Road on the Northside.

Jacksonville's Northside has long been a strange region that epitomizes the city's ongoing racial segregation. Everything north of downtown to the Trout River and westward has for a century been primarily black. On the city's Southside, it's sometimes hard to imagine that 40 percent of Jacksonville's population is black and Latino and that black percentages have often been higher.

North of the Trout River, and especially where Main Street reaches into Oceanway, a largely rural area that sprawls, despite its name, nowhere near the ocean, the demographics not only turn mostly white, but historically Oceanway held a sizeable portion of the city's avowedly racist, even white supremacist rednecks. Early in the 21st century, Oceanway is opening up to remote new suburban subdivisions.

Lem Turner runs through parts of town almost entirely black into longtime hillbilly Oceanway and then through Callahan, the town just northwest of Jacksonville best known now as the region's meth capitol.

When Eastman asks Rich about Detective Cody, Rich snarls and says, "I wish he'd walk in that door right now. I'd kick his ass."

It's exactly what you'd expect him to say. Having no good alibi or intelligent rhetorical response, he falls back on weak threats of physical violence made all the more pathetic by the fact that he's 63 years old, limps on one hip, has "a gimpy right arm," and lacks a lower jaw from cancer.

Beneath the *Folio Weekly* headline for Eastman's story runs the tantalizing statement, "It's not hard to find the man behind one of Florida's most notorious race crimes."

Eastman paints the scene of the bar perfectly. It's cold outside, but the door is propped open. The Triangle is a one-story concrete-block building with burglar bars on the windows. She describes one nearby customer as having "a greasy wad of brown hair matted to the top of his head" and circles around his eyes that seem to be drawn with Magic Marker. And he's representative.

J.W.'s come to the Triangle Bar almost every day for 30 years, and he stays all day. He wears a camouflage ball cap with the bar's logo across the front. He shows up at 10:30 in the morning and he drinks until he goes home late at night.

Surely the Triangle takes a loss on J.W. It supports him financially, since his finances, if there are any, all go to the Triangle, and it nourishes him on beer.

Rich's Triangle co-drinkers say they've often found him at the bar crying, and they blame the wrongs that have been done him.

Rich says Cody bullied him to get a confession. He says Cody put a gun to his head in police headquarters and said he could shoot Rich dead that instant if he didn't tell Cody what he wanted to hear, and that Cody would get away with it, because he was a cop.

When Eastman first sought Rich out at his house trailer behind his barbed-wire fence, his ex-wife neighbor told her he was probably home, just passed out drunk. Confederate and American flags both waved tattered in the front yard.

On the barstool, Rich calls the woman he's believed to have murdered a "black lady," but he refers to most other black people as "niggers."

Rich tells Eastman he never fired a gun, but that all his friends in the car did. They were having fun shooting at street signs.

Then he tells Eastman that Willie Chappell was the true murderer of his wife.

He tells Eastman he didn't even know race riots had happened in Jacksonville.

1969. The Halloween violence capped a full decade of intermittent race riots in Jacksonville.

In her vast and sprawling 2010 folk-history, *Remembering Neighborhoods of Jacksonville, Florida: Oakland, Campbell's Addition, East Jacksonville-Fairfield—The African American Influence*, Mary Mungen Jameson writes about the race riots on Florida Avenue—now mostly A. Philip Randolph Avenue—in the neighborhood of Oakland.

At four in the afternoon on Halloween, a 23 year-old white man named William Simmons shot John Riley, 20 years old and black, outside the Pix Theatre on Florida Avenue. Riley was too close to Simmons's truck and looked suspicious. Simmons said he shot Riley because he thought he was trying to steal his cigarettes.

Riley looked first as his blown-apart leg and then up at the shooter and said, "You shot me! Why did you shoot me?"

Doctors would soon decide to amputate his leg. At the last minute, he'd tell them he could feel his toes, but two years would elapse before he could walk.

"It was a rainy Halloween afternoon and evening," Jameson writes. Florida Avenue exploded. Angry young black men set fires and looted the stores their grandfathers had founded along the main drag of Oakland. They'd grown up angry and frustrated and they didn't strategize or wait for logical targets. The police responded in full riot gear and sealed off Florida Avenue. Cars were set on fire, windows smashed.

Jameson writes of black residents along Florida Avenue helping a 61 year-old white businessman named Morris Biller, who'd run Bill's Clothing at 954 Florida Avenue for 15 years, sneak out the back door of a coffeeshop to Courtney's Auto and Body. Someone had thrown a garbage can through Biller's store window before running into his store and shouting, "Run for your life!" Biller's black friends got him to his car, and he fled Florida Avenue as fast as he could.

Jameson speaks of the death knell in black neighborhoods, and inner-city neighborhoods both white and black, brought about by a full decade of race riots. Suburbanization and white flight happened across the country, and such long and continuously burning racial tensions only sealed the fate of once-diverse areas like Fairfield, Oakland, and East Jacksonville. Likewise, the fate of LaVilla and Ashley Street and Eartha's own headquarters at the center.

The federal government supported mortgages for mostly white suburban developments, but denied them in America's cities, as did homeowners' insurance companies.

The process of denying service or charging exorbitantly for banking, insurance, health care, and even retail soon became known as redlining or credit rationing.

But all the angry kids in LaVilla and Blodgett and Oakland knew was that everything seemed stacked against them and they had no access to making things better.

Jameson writes, "Florida Avenue never recovered after the riots. Many shop owners closed their doors and these stores remained dormant. Structures deteriorated and were demolished." The process of redlining, denying black businessmen, even after decades of success prior to desegregation, access to mortgages and insurance in "high risk" neighborhoods condemned them.

Mary invited me to her home on a private drive off Moncrief Road, signed her book for me, talked to me about the process of her research and writing her vast and sprawling story-quilt of a book, which she worked on for at least a decade and which itself mirrors the shape of the city, then met me out at the "Mungen House," where she grew up.

Her grandfather built the house at 545 Jessie Street in 1928. When Mary's father died before she was a year old, her grandfather, Roane Mungen, committed to helping raise her in the two-story Oakland house. Though the house became a boarding house a few decades back, and now sits empty, it has "strong bones" and retains its original tin roof.

Though Eartha had lived with Clara two blocks away on Pippin Street at the end of the 19th century, and though Eartha first started the Old Folks' Home and the Home for Unwed Mothers and the Mercy Hospital for tuberculosis patients all on Milnor Street just up and east a couple blocks from Florida Avenue, Eartha's Oakland and Campbell's Addition traces are all but invisible.

But traces of Eartha must remain like the cobblestones and bricks just beneath the asphalt pavement of Eastside roads. Just as in front of the Mungen House, you can still see a carriage stone for stepping down from a horse-drawn buggy, I can feel what Eartha sought for single mothers and old men and the city's homeless before she founded and became the institution she named for her mother.

In August 1969, Arrelia—sometimes spelled Aurellia—Johnson turned 100 and Eartha threw her a centennial birthday bash at the Mission.

"Grandma Johnson," as just about everybody called her, had worked with Eartha since 1920, when she'd helped the cook in Eartha's original soup kitchen on Eagle Street behind Bethel Baptist.

She needed dentures, but she told people her eyes were good. She didn't think it remarkable that she had to climb 18 steps to enter her apartment at 964 Hogan Street over an empty storefront, where today sprawls the main city bus station. The apartment had a porch overlooking Hogan where she liked to spend the evenings with her dogs.

She claimed her diet consisted mostly of "greens and corn bread." She had a television, but it didn't work anymore.

The *Jacksonville Journal* staff writer who interviewed Arrelia Johnson asked her what she thought about "demonstrators and campus troublemakers."

She responded, "They just never got spanked enough when they were little and it could do them some good."

Arrelia Johnson lived for one more birthday. Her funeral was held on Halloween, 1970, a year to the day after the final Jacksonville race riots of the 1960s began.

Perk's epitomized LaVilla's most tragic and final years. Urban legends that the owner of Perk's had been gunned down in a phone booth were untrue.

I stood between the shelves just outside the Florida Collection in the downtown public library and searched listings in the bound volumes of newspaper indexes. Nothing.

But the 1980 city directory lists Perk & Loretta's Soul Lounge, 530 N. Broad Street. Then I found police reports and stories about Perk in his daughter's autobiography.

Perk's, as it was often called, didn't go down until most of LaVilla was already demolished and its residents scattered across the landscape. In the summer of 1996, undercover cops bought crack cocaine and heroin on several occasions at Perk's.

Perk was Andrew Preston Perkins, and his criminal record stretched back decades.

In the 1970s, Perk was arrested for a numbers racket he ran from the Soul Lounge. The FBI tracked Perk and his gambling partners in 1976 and 1977.

In a typical episode of the investigation, FBI agents watched Eddie Allen, Perk's pickup man, leave LaVilla, park his motorcycle outside an apartment complex on Old Kings Road on the northwest side of town and open the hood of a nearby car. In a few minutes, a woman came out of an apartment holding a cigar box into which Allen, hidden behind the car, placed a brown package. The agents followed the woman to the Cohen Brothers' Department Store on Hemming Park downtown, where they watched her spend the package's contents.

FBI agents searched numerous residences and businesses associated with Perk and found betting slips and lottery sales records at all but one of them.

151

What happened at Perk's in the 1970s and '80s echoes in strange ways today through his daughter, Kimberly Daniels, one of the most controversial politicians in Jacksonville's controversial political history.

Daniels has attracted national attention for her hysterical antics and wildly conservative beliefs since Jacksonville elected her to City Council in 2011.

She's said she's tired of hearing about the Holocaust, because Jews own everything.

Certainly, beliefs in black communities about conspiratorial Jewish ownership go back a long way. Malcolm X told an interviewer in 1963, "Walk up and down in any Negro ghetto in America. Ninety percent of the worthwhile businesses you see are Jew-owned. Every night they take the money out. This helps the black man's community stay a ghetto."

A half century later, Kimberly Daniels repeated the same ideas. While there are historical reasons blacks saw Jews this way—in many communities both groups were ostracized and black communities were the logical places Jewish merchants would operate—Daniels seemed merely to mimic old assertions.

Daniels has argued that celebrating Halloween can invite the demons that infest the holiday into your house.

She not only believes that gay people are possessed by demons, but she performs exorcisms to cast out the demons of homosexuality. She doesn't call them exorcisms though. She calls them deliverances.

"It's kind of crazy for me," she told a *Times-Union* reporter, "to be on the City Council and then I go home and sometimes I talk to people with demon voices coming out of them."

In a sermon aired widely before Jacksonville elected her to City Council, Daniels said she was thankful for crack houses, because without them, she wouldn't be here. She said she was a former prostitute and crack addict.

Then she said she was thankful for slavery, because if it weren't for slavery, she would probably be in Africa somewhere, worshiping a tree.

She later tried to explain what she meant by saying, "If slavery would not have happened, I wouldn't be living in the greatest country in the land."

152

In Kimberly Daniels's 2005 autobiography, *Delivered to Destiny: From Crack Addict to the Military's Fasted Female Sprinter to Pastoring a Diverse and Multicultural Church, Kim's Story of Hope is for Everyone*, she talks about spending lots of time at Perk and Loretta's Soul Lounge when she was growing up.

Perk was handsome and respected as a big man in aVilla. He had lots of money and lots of women.

I feel sad reading Daniels's account of how Perk's once-radical political ideals devolved into cold capitalist opportunism by the late 1970s and 1980s. I think of all the white anti-establishment types of the hippie 1960s, in accordance with the *zeitgeist*, who became uber-capitalists in the Reagan 1980s, again in accordance with the *zeitgeist*.

If you'd never been out of poor black neighborhoods by the 1980s, maybe you had to adopt your own Reaganesque (no-government-interference, make-profit-at-all-costs) attitude. If, in the late 1960s, you'd adopted a black-radical, Black-Panthers mentality, by the 1980s you became the inverse of white Reaganism, which was much the same as official Reaganism, but illicit.

In the 1960s, Perk was a prominent member of the Boomerangs, the same group who escorted Richard Charles Parker away from that Woolworth lunch counter sit-in. The boomerang refers to the idea that what goes around comes around, that the chickens come home to roost. The Boomerangs challenged segregation in Duval County, which had hardly changed despite the Supreme Court's 1954 *Brown vs. Board of Education* decision.

Less radical than the Black Panthers in Oakland tailing the police in cars full of shotguns in theatrical attempts to police the police, armed members of Jacksonville's Boomerang Gang personally escorted the only two black city council members to work each day.

Councilwomen Sallye B. Mathis and Mary L. Singleton both claimed powerful personal influence from Eartha White.

Though some black radicals threatened to burn down white businesses in the downtown area, some whites started to see the Boomerangs as a force for calming angry and frightened urban black people and keeping alive possibilities of reconciliation.

From the politically radical late 1960s, however, Perk's position as community leader moved from political activism and confrontation with white racists to making lots of money, building up his status, and intimidating opposition. Maybe the dichotomy was never that clearly defined.

But in the years between his political radicalism and his gambling enterprises, Perk ran for City Council. As someone who had fought for greater black power in the city, surely this campaign represented hope. Perk must have hoped his candidacy could make some kind of difference. Or was his political ambition just a function of his ascendancy to power in LaVilla and the black community?

Kimberly Daniels remembers seeing the political ads and placards calling for Perk's election to City Council. She was 13 years old. Now she runs a ministry called "Operation Boomerang" for people who have "fallen through the cracks of life."

She knew she was Perk's daughter, but Perk had never acknowledged her. It was an open secret. A lot of people knew so-called secrets about whom other people's parents really were.

153

Daniels claims her exorcisms of gay men and women come from her growing up with and learning to love the men who performed in "sissy shows" in her father's bar.

Several nights a week, Perk and Loretta's Soul Lounge featured drag shows. "Baby Kim" came to see the "sissy shows" regularly. She says she loved "her sissies." She lived close to the bar and several gay men and "transvestites" lived in the LaVilla apartment beneath hers.

In 2005, she said, "I loved my sissies, and ministering to homosexuals will forever be close to my heart."

But in 2009 she called gay people "an army of darkness." She offered prayers gay people could say: "I renounce the perversity of the lifestyle. I declare that I hate it," and "I renounce masturbation."

Another prayer says, "I renounce the witchcraft that comes with homosexuality / lesbianism. That which I have participated in knowingly, or that unknowingly would tie me to the demonic supernatural, is under my feet."

154.

I speak with the daughter of a long-time LaVilla businessman who kept offices in the "Black Masonic Temple," "The Most Worshipful Union Grand Lodge of the Most Ancient and Honorable Fraternity of Free and Accepted Masons of Florida and Jurisdiction" at 410 Broad Street, built in the 1910s.

She remembers coming to her father's office in the 1970s. She wasn't afraid of LaVilla at all, but she knew not to go near those intersections most notorious for drug sales and prostitution. She says LaVilla had become really "dicey."

She remembers a transgender person on the street who always greeted her father and seemed to have a crush on him. "My father was a handsome man. And he was an important man. And his stance and his walk and his clothing said the same."

But she was surprised when the transgender person greeted him and called him "Honey," and she was even more surprised when her father returned her welcome and treated her kindly.

As so many kids have so often done, she thought her father a rube. When the two of them got to his office floor and stepped off the elevator, she told him, "That was a man down there on the street."

As if he didn't understand.

Her next surprise was her father's saying, "You know what? If she could have been born differently, she probably would have."

155

I'm surprised I can't quite connect the dots when I find the October 1, 1970 testatory note from Andrew Perkins in a box of random and uncatalogued materials at the back of the top floor of the Clara White Mission.

"I Andrew Perkins owe Thaddeous Anderson the sum of $7200. In the event of my death before this amount is paid," Perk's wife would pay "the balance due out of my life."

Why had these notes been stored in a weathered cardboard box atop a shelf in a back room at the top of the Mission? What had happened that linked Andrew Perkins to Eartha White through this seemingly random document?

*

One of the gay men who worked at Perk and Loretta's Soul Lounge tried to convince Kimberly's mother to take her to one of Perk's campaign parties.

"Now you know that baby needs to be with her daddy in the time of his glory," he argued to no avail.

And then I think about the differences and similarities between Kimberly Daniels and Eartha White. I wonder what Eartha would say to her.

Growing up, Daniels spent so much time in her father's bar, one block away from the Mission Eartha named for her mother.

Kimberly Daniels couldn't say publicly who her father was, though it was an open secret in the community. Eartha White couldn't say who her father was, though a few people knew it without anyone publicly saying it.

Daniels constantly draws attention to herself, screams and rants on stage and behind the pulpit, while Eartha was as soft-spoken and persuasive as she was tiny. Despite having a following, Daniels disgusts and turns many people away. Eartha's humility and gentleness and kind soft voice inevitably drew people toward her. You just couldn't turn away from Eartha.

Daniels attained the political office she remembers her father seeking. Eartha never sought political office, though she worked behind the scenes and had greater political power, both locally and nationally, than either Perk or Daniels would ever achieve.

Daniels would become more radical (in the 21st century) than her more legitimately radical father (late 1960s) by exorcising gay people instead of providing armed escorts for black City Councilwomen. Daniels's radicalism reaches so far that it sounds like far-right-wing white-supremacist Southern conservatism. Eartha tried to figure out the greatest good for the greatest number. She was pragmatic, because her life's desire was to help as many people as she could.

Kimberly Daniels said she was thankful for slavery. Eartha's adoptive mother had been a slave and as a child had seen her own mother sold at auction in downtown Jacksonville.

I wonder if Kimberly Daniels would have told Clara White that she was thankful for slavery.

PART SEVEN

A Thousand Years Old at Dawn

156

Clara White Mission

613 West Ashley Street

Jacksonville, Florida

1971. Winter. It was harder for Eartha to make her way around the Mission. She wasn't old yet, she said. She was only in her 90s.

Several of her relatives had made it past 100. And hadn't Reverend Harrison, the old man who'd visited Clara to name the coming baby after Mother Earth, lived to be 117 or older (or younger)?

Maybe Eartha remembered Annie Whittaker recording that song saying that 99 and a half just wouldn't do, all those years before, and every day of Eartha's life had been at least that eventful.

It was cold this December night. She looked out that second story window from her bedroom in the Mission. *This* place had been *the* place. So much music and life. Now so much desperation. Even more than what she had seen in her childhood, when her mother had so recently been a slave.

Some stranger had come, earlier today, she hadn't the time to make it downstairs, and Grayce had brought her the sandwich the stranger offered her as thanks. She didn't know what particular thanks.

Some days now the thanks came in by ones or twos. Sometimes the thanks came by the dozens.

But she couldn't eat the sandwich because there were people downstairs who needed to eat it more than she did. She sent the sandwich back down to another stranger.

But nobody was a stranger. A prostitute came to wash Jesus's feet. He didn't turn her away.

She was always surprised, but never surprised, that people donated clothes personally to and for her. The Mission had always advertised clothes and food drives and asked for materials for the poor, but frequently strangers brought food and clothes for Eartha.

For decades she'd given such clothes to women and young girls whose size matched hers. These past years, she relied on Grayce and other friends and helpers to get the food and the clothes to the right people. She thought of a thousand things a day, but she couldn't move faster than a hundred.

And that left so much more, every day, to do, and Eartha now looked and moved like a baby bird.

This one winter day, 1971, picked at random, because so many other days would have illustrated the same thing, and almost none of these days were recorded, and almost all this time is lost—

An old man named Simon brought Eartha a chicken breast because she had offered his 97 year-old mother Bertha a chicken breast some 25 years ago, and Simon had never forgotten it.

Simon knew he was dying. He had long wanted to thank Eartha White, but he never knew how to do it.

He'd been so hungry lately, and his young cousin had brought him this chicken. Simon grew basil and rosemary in his sandy small yard. He ate one leg, but gave his neighbors the other leg and wings, and saved the body for the woman who gave his dying mother the body all those years before.

All these life lines and trajectories of giving came together in the middle of the city, and Eartha received Simon's chicken breast and it satisfied her for a moment between the old and fading bright plaster walls of the Mission upstairs.

But there were sirens. And there were always the hungry. And there were always so many people, especially now young people, and she saw them make stupid, desperate decisions that jeopardized their lives and broke Eartha's heart, and to them she would always give the most recent food that had been given her.

There were so many days when the old matriarch barely ate a bite.

She'd not been born for herself, and she had not chosen to be born.

She never saw those who came before her as owing her a life. Instead she saw the privilege of living as predicated on the good she could do other people.

If Guy Stockton didn't deserve Eartha White as a daughter, her life was hers, not his.

What mattered was that Simon of no last name, who remembered Eartha's kindness from decades before, felt the great satisfaction of offering her this gift. A widow's mite.

What mattered was that Eartha could take hope from offering Simon's gift of chicken breast to the strung-out and emaciated boy who called himself John and had just collapsed on the sidewalk outside the Mission.

John might take the chicken breast for granted and forget it or eat it without noticing it. Or John might say it turned his life around.

One Saturday morning, Eartha was surprised to find a little girl crying because she'd frightened her. The girl had told her mother that Eartha was a Gypsy, that she was scared the old woman would steal her.

Eartha, even smaller than she used to be, was smaller than the girl, and her clothes, pulled from piles of donations, were torn and half-rotten. She wore a faux-pearl necklace and a purple hat askew with withered feathers.

*

According to 1971 records, the Mission gave away 9,800 pieces of clothing, distributed 1,000 books, and procured 75 jobs through employment services.

*

On Christmas morning, volunteers at the Mission gave away as many as 300 bags of food to families and individuals who would have had no Christmas dinner otherwise. The annual early afternoon children's Christmas party offered hungry kids toys and fruit and candy and ice cream.

When the night's this dark and January's this cold and wet, there's more smell and touch than color.

You might as well be a dog. There's always sound. Sirens. From a boarded-up Davis Street building that's lived a thousand lives, A.M. radio plays Gil Scott-Heron and friends singing, "We have something to offer you. We have music to offer you."

Midwinter smell of some decaying animal; later winter smell of the sweetness of hard pine aging in old houses. No other sweetness like that particular wood.

No other sweetness like that wood when it ages. No other sweetness like that particular wood aging in houses built a particular year in this particular neighborhood's climate in this particular winter.

If you know that sweet smell, you know this 1970s January on Davis Street in LaVilla.

Gil Scott-Heron and friends in chorus: "Spirits may come into view. We have spirits to offer you."

Last spring, in this particular labyrinth of houses more than a century old, attics and basements and alleys and mysterious walled-up rooms, staircases that ascend into walls where doors once stood, Civil War bullets and pot bongs beneath porches, the smell of spring that so rots Florida incorporates the smell of a dead human body.

Right here. This beautiful line of tall wooden houses full of secrets and rooms and halls.

The Florida spring rots everything. And it grows everything in the rot. Detritivorous. Springtime Florida crawls all over itself like a millipede, a tick, a horsefly, a patch of ringworm.

And a few houses away, an A.M. station playing Gil Scott-Heron and friends singing, "Seasons may change. And feelings may change. But music remains."

Yes.

Music remains.

Grayce Bateman hadn't known, 27 years before, as a new graduate of Walker's Business College and Stenotype Institute, that when she accepted the job as Eartha's personal secretary, she would become Eartha's closest friend and take over leadership of the Mission when Eartha died.

She didn't know she would travel with Eartha to the White House, where Eartha would accept a national lifetime humanitarian award from President Nixon.

She didn't know that when Eartha finally began to weaken in her early '90s, Grayce would push this tiny soft-spoken but magisterial woman's wheelchair to City Hall and the Courthouse and all over the city.

When Grayce hired a nurse to take care of Eartha on weekend nights at home, Eartha considered that nurse's presence an intrusion and sent her away.

The interviewer asks if Eartha had been ill. Hadn't she recently had an operation?

Grayce says, "Yes, she did have an operation, and the reason for the operation was that she fell and broke her hip."

"Recently?" the interviewer asks.

And Grayce says, "That was the cause of her death."

"Oh," says the interviewer, "I don't think the newspapers ever said—"

1974. January winter.

Eartha had fallen. She had fallen down the stairs. She had always refused to use that elevator for anything other than feeding the animals, though others could use it so long as they didn't knock over the food and water bowls.

Grayce came to work one Monday morning earlier than usual. The sun hadn't begun to light the sky.

She turned her key in the door and it creaked on its ancient hinges. The building had known so much life. It was far older than its years. It compounded atmospheres on atmospheres. It was an experienced building.

Grayce came up the wooden steps. The first thing she did when she came into the Mission every morning was visit Eartha's second-floor bedroom. She communed with Eartha there, in the still of the early morning, the only time it was usually quiet on West Ashley. She met with Eartha before dawn as only two old friends, long dedicated to their cause, could do.

But this particular Monday morning, Eartha could barely rise up in her bed. Getting out of bed would have been impossible.

Eartha said her shoulder hurt, her leg felt dead.

Grayce knew she'd broken bones. Maybe a rib. Eartha couldn't stand for Grayce to touch her.

Grayce stood there at the side of Eartha's bed, looking down into her ancient face, and Eartha grabbed her hand, squeezed it weakly, and pulled it to her side.

Both of them knew.

Grayce asked her if she had fallen during the night.

Eartha didn't answer. She didn't need to.

An ambulance came, its lights flashing and sirens blaring into the LaVilla dawn, hardly unusual sights and sounds in 1974.

Grayce rode in the ambulance with Eartha to the hospital. She told the driver she hoped Eartha hadn't broken her hip. X-rays soon showed that's exactly what had happened. By early afternoon, Eartha was in surgery.

Eartha had hurt herself repeatedly through the years, starved herself, broken bones.

In the mid-1960s, a newspaper had reported, "The large number of friends of Miss Eartha M. M. White, founder-president of the Clara White Mission, the Old Folks' Home, Mercy Hospital, various other charitable agencies, and a substantial citizen, welfare, civic and religious leader here for practically all of her lifetime, will regret to learn that she has been confined to her home as a result of injuries suffered in a fall."

But there had been encouraging news. "She is on the mend, improving swiftly, and will soon be released to return to her many busy duties attendant to the agencies she heads."

She'd not been confined entirely to bed—just after Eartha's death, Grayce Bateman would say you couldn't confine her to bed as long as she was conscious—but she "remained indoors still doing what she can for the unfortunates who number so many and who directly benefit through many of the agencies she administers."

1974. The Clara White Mission meant Eartha. It meant all the people she'd sought to help. In her '90s she seemed both fragile and immortal. She was brittle and old, but the Mission was Eartha and the Mission wouldn't die.

The surgeon told Grayce that Eartha was probably too weak and too old to last much longer.

Now instead of visiting Eartha in her second-floor bedroom when she first came to the Mission every morning, Grayce first went to her side in the hospital before going into the office.

Eartha's face seemed ancient. She must have been a thousand years old. Her face was so beautiful, even in unconsciousness. Each line had been earned. Each wrinkle, each pucker. She had lived so much life in that face, the long life of a community in all its pain and activism and celebration and endurance.

Grayce came to her hospital bed every morning, but after surgery, Eartha never regained consciousness.

So Grayce wrote in her 1994 book *Grayce Reminiscences* [sic].

But 20 years earlier, Grayce told Betty Koehler that Eartha had begun to recover in late afternoon the day of her surgery.

"She had gone into recovery, and it would be night, you know, so I told 'em I'd be back the next morning, and there was the night nurse, that night, and she had come out of recovery and they put her in Intensive Care. And. She recognized. Well, she recognized *everybody*. But her body wasn't strong enough anymore."

Which assertion is the truth?

Memory is less reliable than we'd like to believe, and over time, narrative adjusts itself according to its own internal logic.

So many years, Grayce had come to Eartha's bedside at dawn. In that hospital room, how could it be that Eartha wouldn't know Grayce was there?

Even when Eartha was unconscious, Grayce must have known that Eartha knew. Their connection had grown so deep, like the roots of 200 year-old oaks. They connected far beneath language. They connected through the dawn of each day.

"Now, she," asks the interviewer, "it was in the Mission here that she—?"

"She fell downstairs in the hall," Grayce said.

"Miss White was a person that never gave up. She was in a wheelchair, but she tried her best to do things and get up and walk. And this she should *not* have done. But, right at the time she fell, I mean, you can be right in here, and she'll send you downstairs to carry a message, but she may be, you may be thinkin' that she's secure, you know, and then you come back, and she's up, walking down the hall, you know, anything can happen. If she had stayed put, where she *s'posed* to be, she would not have fallen."

"She didn't want to give up to the fact that she was a complete invalid, you know. Her mind was very alert, but her body was very weak."

"And she fell not too long before she broke her hip and fractured her arm. And she came through that with flying colors."

"But as I say, what happened to her happened when somebody's back was turned. And you could watch her every minute, and try to help her up, but she wanted to get up herself, you know."

On Thursday, a nurse called Grayce at the Mission and told her over the phone that Eartha White was dead.

At long last, Eartha's great heart finally failed.

In February 1975, Eartha's goddaughter Vivian Chaves says, "Most of the time, especially after her mother's death, at every holiday, I used to like to cook, and I liked to cook for the family, so every holiday that I cooked, and she was in the city, I would always take her dinner, up until Thanksgiving, was it Thanksgiving?, uh, yes, Thanksgiving of last year. I didn't get to give her Christmas dinner. I kept calling down there, but uh, uh, I didn't get any answer, and that's the time when she was in that wheelchair. So therefore I didn't get to give her Christmas dinner of 1973. That was '73, because she died in January of '74."

Local television news broadcasts announced Eartha's death at 6 that evening. The phone hadn't stopped ringing since just after Grayce had received the tragic call. By 11 o'clock that night, national news bureaus reported Eartha's death.

At about midnight, the congressman came by to tell Grayce how sorry he was that Eartha was gone.

Charles Bennett would serve Florida in the House of Representatives for 44 years. He was the rare politician who remembered your name, no matter who you were, and understood what you felt. On the midnight the white congressman drove into LaVilla to meet Grayce at the Mission, he was just short of halfway through his tenure in the House. He called her "Amazing Grayce."

Eartha had known Bennett long before he ran for office, and in his youth, she told him he had the abilities to do good work if good work was what he wanted to do. He'd sought her out when he was a boy looking for opportunities to volunteer and chances at political activism. In the 1990s, Bennett said he was one of the innumerable souls Eartha had mothered.

*

Sirens cried in the streets outside the Mission.

Here was the tragic paradox. Eartha was the Mission, but Eartha was gone. The Mission lived, so Eartha remained.

But that night, with the old phone ringtones echoing off the walls, Eartha's end was the end of a world.

The world had never been older, but the world had always been old.

LaVilla was the center of the world, and LaVilla had lived untold lifetimes. LaVilla was the oldest city on the planet.

And Eartha had always been the center of love in LaVilla. And everything else had orbited Eartha White.

*

Grayce went home in the middle of the night. She'd begun the day before daylight. She'd begun it with visiting Eartha unconscious. She'd ended it, all by herself, with the enormity of the great living sun-of-the-system that was the Mission. She didn't know who this building was if not Eartha. She didn't know who (not what) everything that Eartha White had done could be without her.

In archives at the Mission, I found Eartha's funeral wishes.

"After all of my just debts have been paid, I direct that the sum of $500 be allowed for my funeral expenses. It is my wishes to have a silent funeral without song or preaching."

Almost 30 years before her death, Eartha told the crowds who'd come to West Ashley for the Mission's rededication that these ceremonies reminded her of the funerals of people she'd loved.

"But tonight, I've got it on them. You will not have to come to my funeral. Because I'm not going to have one," she said mysteriously.

And then she explained. "Oh I don't mind my remains, the old house that I live in, being laid here. You might take a look at it, for after all, I won't be there."

She told her audience what she did *not* want at her funeral. "I don't want no beautiful casket, no. That money could go to make someone happy. Other than just going in the ground. I don't want you to sing a song. I don't want you to pray a prayer."

She told her 1947 audience she didn't want those things "because tonight, you have done these things while I can hear it."

On this old recording, I hear thunderous applause followed by a break in sound, heavy static, then Eartha's voice far distant behind the whooshing noise of the stylus riding over a phonograph warp, as though time is washing everything clean. Whoosh-whoosh. Whoosh-whoosh. Whoosh-whoosh. Whoosh-whoosh.

I'm sitting in the Special Collections room at UNF, enormous headphones covering my ears, and my innumerable failures at this project embarrass me.

It's painfully obvious that I cannot meet her. I cannot know her. Some days it's more obvious than others. I might be sitting at my usual library table, sifting through folders and folders of receipts, lists of the names of people the Mission helped about whom nothing else is known, 1920s meeting minutes for the Citizens Industrial Insurance Company for which Eartha was secretary, patent office letters regarding a tea recipe, her notebook of hairstyling instruction notes from studying "beauty culture" as a teenager in New York just before her opera career.

I want to meet Eartha so badly that her shadow walks into my dreams. I fall asleep with questions for her. I dream that she meets me on a distant periphery between us. I can only see her in silhouette. I can't see anything else.

It's like how I felt the presence of my mother in the hospital room when my first daughter was born. My mother died from ALS—Lou Gehrig's Disease—when I was 12 years old. Sometime after midnight 12 years later, when Emily was on her way into the world, doctors and nurses rushed into the room all at once. I felt small and scared and stupid. I didn't understand what was happening. I kept asking, but the greatest urgency was not to inform me. Within an hour a nurse told me a prolonged contraction had greatly stressed the baby's heart.

Then everything was quiet. A nurse perused paperwork. I was so young, *too* young. My wife had gone into labor a week early. And we'd passed midnight into a new date, which the nurse wrote down in her paperwork. August

24th. That's when I realized that Emily would be born on my mother's birthday.

But I felt Emily coming. And I felt my mother. And even as I wished my daughter and my mother could know each other, even as that impossibility broke my heart, I felt the two of them together with me.

It was the last time I felt my mother's presence, and it was the first time I felt my daughter's.

Eartha's shadow reminds me of that night. Eartha was *not* the child who came to Clara after Clara's 12 children died, and Eartha never had a child. And my mother did not come to me when I needed her after she died. But my mother came to me 12 years later when Emily was born. Eartha sends me her shadow.

Yet this shadow feels so much like my own lost mother that I feel I've failed Eartha White.

I realize the transaction is ludicrous. I cannot offer Eartha myself, and Eartha never knew me. Nor am I black, disenfranchised, terrorized by the Ku Klux Klan in 1920 or dying alone of tuberculosis in 1930.

I don't believe in parapsychology, but in the psychogeographical hauntings of place through history. I don't believe in ghosts, but in the hauntings of absence in our lives, the failures of connections we desperately need to make.

One night I dreamt I was a student in a community-college history class and Ju'Coby Pittman was the professor. I repeatedly showed up for class only to find that the meeting time had once again been changed without my knowledge.

I'm sitting in the Special Collections room, wearing oversized headphones, listening to Eartha's 27-year personal secretary speak into a tape recorder a few months before I was born.

And since Grayce Bateman would direct the Clara White Mission from 1974 to 1985, only retiring after 40 years of service to the Mission, Grayce had been, in Eartha's waning years, more of an assistant director—no, a best friend—no, a long-lived sister—than a personal secretary.

I'm listening to Grayce talking about Eartha's death, one month after Eartha had gone. 1974. I'm listening to Grayce discussing Eartha's death 40 years ago. Four months before I was born.

Surely this is a visitation. If nothing else is ghostly, this is. In 2014, I hear Grayce speak in 1974. I hear her precise wording and cadence. I hear a television in the background. I hear police sirens on nearby streets. And I see Grayce's wrinkled hands and pleated dress and large-rimmed glasses and the kindest eyes and the sweetest smile.

169

It was with humility and diligence that Grayce agreed to the leadership of the Mission. Eartha had shared with Grayce her giving life for nearly 30 years. Grayce had no selfish ambition. She wanted to keep Eartha's lifework going. It was a daunting task. It was devotion.

Despite the rumors that Eartha had amassed a private fortune from her charities over the years, Grayce had to figure out how to get new transportation for the Mission's clothing distribution.

Though dozens and sometimes hundreds of people, desperate for clothing, came to the Mission on a daily basis, Grayce and other Mission workers regularly drove across the sprawling city and its rural hinterlands. They provided clothing for giveaways in Sweetwater, Oceanway, the beaches, Picketville, Mandarin, Orange Park, and Baldwin, and of course they went to the city's inner neighborhoods.

All the Mission had was that ancient station wagon that kept breaking down. A Mission committee had resolved to get a van but didn't know where they might get the funding. A call for donations didn't suffice.

Though Jacksonville once had streetcars, as had most cities and towns in North America, the cars and their tracks had been gone for decades. The city had since limited its public transportation system to buses, and as city politicians assumed only poor people rode buses, routes remained inefficient and the buses themselves were often late or sidelined for slow repairs.

The committee met again to talk about applying for a grant. Someone had raised the windows to let air into the upstairs rooms, and rain pattered persistently against the side of the Mission.

Eartha long had a direct line to the consciences of the city's powerful and wealthy. Most charitable non-profit organizations were becoming savvy to grant-writing practices, applying for special tax exemptions, and illustrating humanitarian good as also, if not primarily, being economically profitable, but Eartha had run the Mission personally and purely. She was more Mohandas Gandhi than Bill Gates.

When Jessie Ball du Pont, wealthy philanthropist and widow of the local banking and real estate magnate Alfred du Pont, died four years before Eartha did, she had entrusted the Jessie Ball du Pont Fund to provide aid to humanitarian organizations.

At her death in 1970, du Pont's estate was valued at $42 million.

In 1984, the du Pont Fund awarded the Clara White Mission $18,000 for the purchase of two vans to deliver food and clothing across the city and its outlying towns and trailer parks and exurbs.

170

The beginning of the soup kitchen that during its existence has fed thousands. The house in the picture is the home of Miss White on First Street

Even as the crack cocaine epidemic spread and crime skyrocketed in LaVilla and East Jacksonville and Oakland and the city's desperate inner neighborhoods, Grayce communed in that old Mission building with her mothering mentor. Eartha had been dead a decade.

So many times, just being in the Mission, Grayce felt Eartha all around her. For so long, the Mission and Eartha had been one and the same, and now that Eartha's body was gone, her building was her body.

But the building was not the Mission any more than Eartha was her body.

Sometimes, hours after the sun went down, 14 hours after Grayce had started her day, she walked down a hallway and ran her fingers lightly along the walls. She touched the wallpaper Eartha had touched and the walls between which Eartha had slept for so many decades.

The building was the headquarters of the Mission, and the Mission was Eartha's heart.

Down on the street outside, traveling nurses in health care vans screened the poor and the homeless for high blood pressure, tuberculosis, hepatitis, dental decay, heart problems, and sexually transmitted diseases.

When you were desperate and came to the Mission for a free meal, volunteer workers asked your name, your address (if you had one), your Social Security Number (if you knew it), the person who referred you (if applicable), and what you needed. The required questions maintained the Mission's credibility with outsiders, though the questioner's gracious heart might be prepared to bypass the prerequisites.

Grayce said she had asked the same questions in 1988 as Clara and her daughter Eartha asked in 1908. They had moved from Pippin Street, where they'd lived together for 21 years, to 233 Eagle Street before it became West 1st, right behind Bethel Baptist.

Since before Eartha could remember, her mother had given her own food and clothes to those more desperate. Eartha always remembered when she was a little girl, and the children of former slaves came to her house every Christmas where they received all the toys the community could gather for them.

1908 was alive and well in 1988. Crack had replaced tuberculosis. The three-story former Globe Theatre had replaced the one-story, two-room Eagle Street house that was fronted by a porch filled with hungry men and women, and in front of the porch grew that single sycamore or maple, skeletal and bleak and determined.

171

A white interviewer assisting UNF historians told Florida Representative Mary Singleton in early 1974, "I think it's so terrible that a woman like this could live in this community and until she reaches an age where her age is so phenomenal, I hadn't, I hadn't honestly heard of her."

Singleton repeatedly told Betty Koehler that a lot of people in the black community suspected Eartha was even older than 97 years. These same people knew secrets about Eartha's biological parents.

One of them said the only way black folks in Jacksonville could have any progress at all was if a rich white man felt guilty enough after raping his black maid to fund his clandestine daughter's charities.

Some of them composed conspiracy theories that were too neatly constructed to be true, though these theories helped them make sense of a brutal and chaotic world.

The interviewer, so sweet and well-intentioned, missed most of what Mary Singleton told her, since Singleton was used to coding such information and Koehler wasn't prepared to read code.

Koehler said White Jacksonville had offered her no information on Eartha. "I've called the Haydon Burns Library and I've called the Jacksonville Historical Society and they have nothing."

Though Singleton told her, "I'm surprised at that," she surely wasn't. Singleton had always known that "black news" came from black news sources like *The Florida Star* and *The Jacksonville Free Press* and the Florida edition of *The Pittsburgh Courier*, with its offices in the Clara White Mission. The city's largest newspaper, *The Florida Times-Union*, had published a separate "black star" section, officially called

"News For and About the Colored People of Jacksonville," though the newspaper's editorial stance, well after the Supreme Court ordered public schools to desegregate, continued to argue for racial segregation.

Singleton told Koehler that numerous reporters had come to her in 1972, asking for historical insights and her perspective on Jacksonville's Sesquicentennial, "and I said, 'Why don't you go and talk to Miss White?' And I don't know that anybody ever pursued it."

Eartha never lost her memory. She seemed to remember everything that had touched her life for the last century. Eartha could tell Mary Singleton all about the councilwoman's great-grandmother and her days as a slave, but now almost all recollection of those times in this place had disappeared.

Politely but pointedly, Mary Singleton told her interviewer, a month after Eartha's death, "Historians really should have visited with her. She could remember everything from the time she was a little girl."

PART EIGHT

Still Her Home

172

I punch a code into a buzzer outside the elevators on the fourth floor of the Ed Ball Building downtown. The voice that answers sounds robotic—monotone and electronic.

"Hi, Mr. McKissick," I say into the intercom. "It's Tim Gilmore."

The voice says, "I'll be right there." Two decades ago, throat cancer irrevocably damaged Richard McKissick's vocal cords. Today he speaks through an electrolarynx he holds against his throat.

Sitting in his office overlooking Hogan Street, I'm surprised at just how sharp McKissick still is. He's close to 90 years old. He wears linen dress pants, spectator shoes, a white shirt and dark silk tie, and a champagne-colored vest.

Though it's sometimes hard to understand what he says through his electronic voicebox, he manages to speak movingly. He's thin and kinetic. He speaks with his hands a lot, and there's something elegant about the way he moves his fingers or his head or his whole upper body in accompaniment with a point he's making.

McKissick's a suave but humble man. "I played my role on Ashley Street," he says. He once managed both the Strand and the Roosevelt Theaters there. "Everybody knew me, and I knew everybody on Ashley Street. And I'll say that my words carried a lot of weight, but I didn't realize it then."

McKissick's father had been a prominent LaVilla businessman, and Richard benefited from the family name. He knew everybody in LaVilla. He knew the Boomerangs and says it's a mistake to call them a gang. They were just a group of young men who liked to hang out together and party. And he knew Eartha.

He keeps telling me I have to try to see it, try to see that neighborhood that no longer exists. "You have to capture that. You have to capture it," he says, and his hands and his jawline tense, and his whole face looks like he's seeing what he saw in LaVilla six decades ago and he's trying to will me to see it with him.

173

"Eartha was a kind of magical person. She was always pretty. Even when she grew old, she was pretty. And she was so humble. She had some wealth, but you wouldn't know it to look at her. Her clothes were always tattered. She didn't eat enough."

Eartha embodied a question Jesus asked in the Sermon on the Mount: "And why take ye thought for raiment?" Jesus told his audience to "consider the lilies of the field, how they grow," without taking care to spin thread for their own clothes.

"Sometimes I'd see her just sit out there in her chair in front of the Mission and meet people, meet people one after the other, and she'd be able to give them some food or give them some clothes.

"I lived right behind the Clara White Mission. The Mission faced Ashley Street, and I lived right behind it in an old residential building that faced Beaver Street. And I'd see her all the time."

I mention the many rumors and hints I've heard. I tell him I've seen Eartha's family Bible in the UNF collection, and that she indicates that her father is Guy Stockton.

He tilts his whole upper body back and looks up past the ceiling. "I've heard that," he says. "And the Stocktons had, uh, some *affinity* for blacks." He pauses.

I'm thinking his statement could be taken several ways, but hints one way, when he says something about black people employed as servants and waiters.

"Apparently it wasn't segregation to have black people do your domestic work in your own home," he says and bounces his palms upward as if to say, "Sorry, but I'm saying it like it is."

And he says black waiters at Deerwood Country Club and the wealthy white clubs in Ponte Vedra, well, they never saw Eartha there.

He's expressing something between irony and the sincerest honesty, which doesn't have a word in the English language.

He mentions Isaiah Hart, the so-called founder of Jacksonville, and descendants of Hart's slaves. The black community knew that group of descendants well in his father's generation, or perhaps his father's father's. And the children of Hart's slaves were very "fair." They were, in fact, as white as any white person.

Twice, in the two hours we talk, McKissick refers to the very fair-skinned descendants of Isaiah Hart's slaves.

I understand that Eartha's true biological parentage will always remain unproveable, but in this interview and others, I hear hints of an old narrative that apparently made its *sotte voce* rounds in the black community long, long ago, that Eartha was descended, through slavery, from another line altogether, in fact, from the founder of the city.

174

Richard McKissick is careful to tell me that he has strong opinions, that if I want to get my project right, I need to be "intelligent, broad-minded, and all-inclusive." Yet while he says I need to get as many perspectives on Eartha as I can, he repeatedly and intermittently notes that not many people are left who can remember her.

He tells me Eartha was able to accomplish so much because she connected so well to the city's Southern aristocracy.

"Her persuasiveness came from her relationships with white folks. I'll say this. Eartha was a politically expedient person." She could push points of righteousness behind her to make particular situations work for her.

I tell him I've heard she was, in her early years, strongly influenced by Booker T. Washington, and my statement makes him wince. He leans back and makes a face like he smells something bad. Then he waves his hand as though to shoo the idea way.

But I can see him thinking, evaluating, analyzing, and he says, "You have to think about what people's backgrounds are, and Booker T. Washington was no W.E.B. Dubois. But," he says and waits for what he's going to say, "Eartha, Eartha was a businesswoman, and she was a real negotiator."

I sense that part of what pains him now is that history oversimplifies the past.

Eartha's pragmatism allowed her to work with wealthy whites as much as it allowed her to live harmoniously with tavern keepers and liquor merchants along LaVilla's Great Black Way. "She was a practical person. She didn't interfere. And everybody in the black community and everybody in white Jacksonville respected her."

So much of black history and therefore American history itself, he says, is configured in its relationship to either slavery or the Civil Rights Movement. You can't understand Eartha White without understanding this.

Because most likely Eartha was born 11 years after the Civil War and the Montgomery Bus Boycott happened when Eartha was 79 years old, the long period of Eartha's greatest strength and efficacy extended between slavery and Civil Rights. Eartha White was a pre-Civil-Rights-Movement civil rights leader.

She achieved her Herculean feats during the period of Jim Crow segregation in the South. She was born too soon, too close to slavery, to be a more integral part of Martin Luther King and Rosa Parks and Stokely Carmichael, or, in other words, to be a larger part of the common American *narrative* of the black rise to freedom and self-determination. But the Civil Rights Movement couldn't have happened without earlier leaders like Eartha White.

"I think," McKissick tells me, "that she had already established her life and all her institutions before Civil Rights, and Civil Rights was the next generation, and they knew her projects and her buildings as background, but they didn't know the woman herself as well."

In fact, by the early 1960s, even sometime in the 1950s, after the Mission's rededication, around the time Richard McKissick moved out of LaVilla, he says, "her image began to dwindle. And because her age slowed her down later on, even though she acted otherwise, Eartha flourished most during the time of segregation, the time everybody tried to forget."

Though he's skeptical about a Stockton being Eartha's father, McKissick still says most black people long believed wealthy whites—and sometimes they said Stocktons, sometimes Daniels or Harts—contributed to whatever wealth she had, even if most of it was tied up in property, even if she wore tattered dresses and blouses while she gave so many clothes away.

McKissick talks to me about how news was disseminated through Ashley Street and LaVilla 60 and 70 years ago. He mentions the *Florida Times-Union* insert called "News For and About Colored People."

The insert circulated before the founding of *The Florida Star* and *The Jacksonville Free-Press*, though *The Pittsburgh Courier* worked its Florida Office from the Mission, and many black people read *The Florida Tattler.*

"But for the most part, you have to understand, a great person like Eartha White, her story attracted all kinds of other stories. There were many rumors with no substantiation, because in the black community, there were almost no real media outlets. It was a closed community, a closed circuit."

In the absence of reliable media outlets, rumor flourished, as did words close in definition but on different scale, like "folklore" and "myth" and "legend" and "story" and sometimes even "history."

175

Richard McKissick emphasized to me how in a closed-circuit community, stories take on their own lives. Eartha White was already such an icon, a quasi-mythological figure, that she seemed to float somewhere in the ether outside the Civil Rights protests and the sit-ins and the race riots, her age, birth, family and provenance all shrouded in mystery.

Folklorists rarely find the sources of folk stories. The stories go back and merge with other stories, and attribution rarely exists. Folklorists sometimes refer to the "FOAF" phenomenon, the "Friend of a Friend," a way people who spread legends often claim they know a story is true because some vague relation of a relation first related it. The FOAF is rarely found.

Almost never are folk stories, folk news, and legends the creations of individual people. Stories balance on their motifs—elements of story that are reused almost infinitely, from story to story—so that folk stories come about as creations of the people and their cultures. And that's precisely how Eartha represented her coming into the world.

And that's how folklorist Michael Bell describes "story circles."

"Members of the community gather to share stories that many have heard before," Bell writes. "No one person knows the entire story: this person contributes a bit here; that person adds a bit there. Sometimes people argue. Each gathering is unique, and no story is every complete. Narrative is emergent during this collective process."

Motifs are like archetypes. Folk motifs include ineradicable bloodstains, graves on which no vegetation grows, hair that turns white after a traumatic event, and prophetic namings of charmed people ordained from before their births for some special purpose on earth.

Folk-truth bears a number of advantages over verifiable truth. The very fact that folk-truths contain elements that seem verifiable but are not, ironically, often strengthens them. The story of Eartha's conception speaks of a former-slave-prophet-preacher who lived more than 100 years, and even if the story of his prophetic visit to Clara White can't be verified, his authoritative presence in the story works to grant the story authority. And because verifiable media didn't exist in black Jacksonville, the art and crafting of story and the use of seemingly universal archetypes and motifs comprises the criteria of a story's credibility.

Stories are ghosts. They perform a paradoxical function for the people about whom they tell. Stories keep people alive long after they're dead, but they seem to shift the locus of control from their protagonists to their tellers.

Yet stories tell themselves and live their own lives. Stories walk amongst the populace, seemingly independent of the characters who inhabit them. Even people in great power can't control story. Story is the child of a whole community's imagination, an art that creates itself among the people and pledges no automatic allegiances.

Like a disease, a story is communicable. Its origins almost never exist. Instead of origins, a story seems to arise from traces, and the traces reinvent themselves with every telling.

Not only are there things no one can know about Eartha White, things it's nobody's business to know, but the community around her sought to fill in those blanks throughout her life.

Perhaps Eartha drew a line between her honor, which the stories other people told could impugn, and the dignity she held at the heart of her own experience of herself, which nobody else could ever touch. She certainly lived as though she did.

I have so wanted to approach her. For some reason, I can more easily approach the sweetness in her face in that late 1890s' photograph than that regal and ancient one from the 1970s. I can imagine falling innocently in love with that young Eartha. That ancient Eartha I can imagine kneeling before as though she were a Bodhisattva. But as soon as I make this distinction I see that Bodhisattva gleaming in the face of the younger Eartha as well. It was always there.

176

The dumbwaiter is still in the wall, and its pull-ropes are still intact. Decades ago, it was plastered over. During renovations in 2003, workers uncovered it, then walled it back up again.

Meg Fisher looks to her longtime friend and colleague, Ju'Coby Pittman, and says, "I remember your phone call your first day here, that night after work. 'Oh my God, Fisher, what have I done?'"

When Ju'Coby applied for the job as the fourth executive director of the Clara White Mission in the early 1990s, the board of directors hadn't wanted to tour her through the Mission. After she accepted the job, she found out why.

It had been eight years since Grayce Bateman had stepped down as director. Between Grayce leaving in 1985 and Ju'Coby taking over in 1993, the Mission's deterioration had accelerated.

"There were years of donated items that were never given to the people," Ju'Coby says. "Just stacks and stacks of stuff."

"Floor to ceiling," Meg says. "You couldn't get off of the elevator on the third floor at all. You couldn't take a step off the elevator. There were holes in the roof. There were rats running through the hallways."

"Yes," Ju'Coby says, her eyes widening, "Rats and bats and anything else."

Though blame seems to fall, though not directly from Ju'Coby and Meg, upon the Mission's third president, LaGretta Everett, who took over from Grayce Bateman in 1985, an article in *The Florida Times-Union* as far back as October 1976 says that since Bateman took over the Mission, "the towering, teetering piles of boxes that lined the corridors have been mostly disposed of, and the multitude of cats that Miss White protected from the catcher, even when she was in a wheelchair, have been dispersed."

LaGretta Everett died in 1997 at age 64. The trail she left behind is hard to find. The year before Grayce took over the Mission, LaGretta became her personal secretary and stayed in that position until Grayce retired.

Ju'Coby Pittman and Meg Fisher are both Jacksonville natives. Meg, a white woman with blond hair and blue eyes, went to high school at Andrew Jackson on the mostly black Northside, and Ju'Coby grew up in the Blodgett Housing Projects.

Meg recalls their early years at the Mission. "All these pigeons would fly down through the roof," she says.

The two women laugh about it now, because they hadn't known what they were getting themselves into, and if they had, they probably would have thought they couldn't handle it.

Meg says, "The Mission was dirty, it was dark, and every room was a different color—purple, pink, green. There were window-unit air conditioners and if you plugged them all in at one time, the power went off."

Ju'Coby points to a glass-fronted bookcase that stretches from floor to ceiling and from wall to wall at the back of her office. Several times when the small staff of the early 1990s would meet to discuss new ideas, the bookcase would rattle. "We would laugh, but it wasn't like a big truck was passing by, or anything like that. It used to be kind of an inside joke, you know—"

"That Eartha didn't want us to do something," Meg says. The two women frequently finish each other's sentences.

"It's kind of funny," Ju'Coby says, "Several employees over the years have claimed to *see* Miss White, and I'd say, I used to tease Meg, and I'd say, 'As long as I don't *see* her, I'm good.'"

Meg says, "There's lots of stories, lots of members of the staff have said they've seen her, but I never saw her."

Four and a half feet tall, Eartha was bigger than the city, and her personality is synonymous with the building itself. Whatever you think of ghost stories, even four decades after her death, in one way or another, the Clara White Mission is still her home.

Almost 20 years ago, Meg opened a desk drawer and found a ledger with board minutes from the 1930s. Another day, Meg was cleaning another room and found several of Eartha's hats.

"She didn't throw anything away," Ju'Coby says.

"Just being here, you get a real sense of this Mission being somebody's home, *Eartha's* home," Meg says. "Still."

There's a tranquil quiet for a moment in these second floor offices shared across time by Eartha White and Grayce Bateman and LaGretta Everett and Ju'Coby Pittman, and then Meg repeats, "Still...still."

Uncanny how quiet the Mission is when the sun goes down and the air turns pale blue and the center of the city goes silent.

All the years behind this moment are present in the building. Its years as a jazz and blues club. Folklorists coming here and recording gospel singers. All the feedings, the tens of thousands of meals. The fire. The brass bands playing the Merry Hearts' Club Christmas dinners. The homeless young mothers. The man with his feet frozen away. The orphans. Atmospheres upon atmospheres.

It's as though I remember her.

With the day waning crepuscular outside, I look up the stairs down which Eartha fell. Perhaps it's impossible not to feel her here. The light dims a certain way on the stairs, as if it knows you.

It knows me. I picture dreams I had when I was five or six years old, dreams I still see—trees, buildings, streets. The uncanniness of memory is your own alienation from what and whom you know. The stairs feel familiar to me.

Something about the twilight in particular places.

The bright light of noon can make certain streets, certain houses wholly antipathetic. Being in those places insults me. Depresses me. Clogs my head until I can't think. Sinks my heart into my feet.

But I am alone on the first floor. And though LaVilla is often quiet now like it's never been quiet since before it was a plantation, I cannot but feel it knows me, even if I wondered all along if I could get close enough to know LaVilla.

But at the foot of the stairs I feel something akin to nostalgia. As though I was here long ago, but have no specific memory of it.

I think about how the Mission's come back around. Glibly, I think maybe her immediate followers needed to fail, the Mission to fall to its nadir, its building full of holes, concentrated with donations never dispensed or disbursed, run through with rats and bats, in order to return to new versions of previous success.

I can't take anything away from Ju'Coby and Meg and their colleagues, because the Clara White Mission almost disappeared with the rest of LaVilla.

Eartha's greatness survives through their own revival of Eartha.

179

Not only did Ju'Coby Pittman and Meg Fisher take the helm while the Mission was in steep decline, but Mayor Ed Austin had decided to eliminate the whole district as part of his "River City Renaissance" plan.

In promotional materials, Austin claimed his redevelopment plan would move Jacksonville past "the threshold to become the 'Next Great American City,'" a promise the city's mayors have made since before Hans Tanzler dubbed it the "Bold New City of the South" in the late '60s.

A February 1993 *Florida Times-Union* editorial linked Austin's and Tanzler's visions and declared, "Time to Be Bold, Again." It exhorted the city to "Get excited, Jacksonville. A new plan is in your future."

In 1993, Austin saw LaVilla as an ugly "front door" to downtown from Interstate 95. And city officials saw no reason the razing of LaVilla shouldn't include the Mission. After all, it had been nearly 20 years since Eartha White died, and she and LaVilla had both passed their primes by then anyway; the City had written the neighborhood off as a crack den and hotbed of prostitution.

Pittman remembers how Frank Nero, then-director of the Downtown Development Authority, told her and Fisher that if they could get enough people interested in LaVilla, the city might be willing to reconsider.

Fisher remembers city council members suggesting paradoxically that if the Mission really wanted to bring the City around to its cause, they might not want to have all those homeless people hanging around.

When a plague of fires spread through LaVilla in 1992, neighborhood residents sardonically called it Nero's Urban Renewal, making an accidental historical pun.

To strengthen the Mission's case against demolition, Joel McEachin of the Jacksonville Historic Preservation Commission worked personally with Ju'Coby and Meg to get the Mission historic designation.

Meanwhile as the United Way prepared to exit its role as the Mission's primary funding source, the Jesse Ball DuPont Fund stepped in. The fund still operates as the bequest of one of the wealthiest residents in Jacksonville's history, once again tying Eartha White to historic white wealth.

In return for the loss of the neighborhood surrounding the Mission, the Mayor's Office promised an enormous recreation center, stimulus money for new downtown housing, and a "greenbelt" between the interstate and downtown. All it delivered was the greenbelt in the form of empty fields where a thriving neighborhood once stood.

I remember seeing Ed Austin in the grocery store in Riverside. He seemed such a kind and grandfatherly comfortable old man.

180

When I first ask Ju'Coby if the City had really wanted to take this building and the Mission down, she responds, "Oh, *did* they!"

"They definitely wanted us gone. They challenged us," Ju'Coby says. "They said if you really want to save this neighborhood, then you need to develop some kind of coalition. They didn't think we could do it, so then it became a threat."

So Ju'Coby and Meg and the new staff developed plans to save their block of West Ashley Street, which had always been, after all, the heart of LaVilla.

"The City looked at us as just a soup kitchen, and they thought, 'We don't need any more homeless programs downtown,'" Ju'Coby says. Of course no one working for the City explained that despite the gauntlets they'd thrown down, the decision to demolish the Mission was a *fait accompli*. "They had already made up their minds."

In 2014, after the last two decades of success stories, it might seem the Mission was fated to remain. But in fact, Eartha's whole enterprise came so close to disappearing with the rest of LaVilla that it's easy to forget how easily what's lost is forgotten.

Against all the conspiracy theorists who believed Eartha secretly harbored great wealth, the new Mission liquidated Eartha's few landholdings. They sold derelict housing property and the former Frolic Theater on West Ashley that Eartha had used as a center for aid to black soldiers.

Now, one of LaVilla's few new developments, LaVilla School of the Arts, a magnet middle school, stands where the Frolic used to be (and where writer Stephen Crane's "common law" wife Cora once owned a brothel).

The Mission leveraged its funding, and in the process, discovered that the majority of homeless services they currently provided were to war veterans. So the Mission became eligible for federal Veteran's Affairs funds, though some local politicians told them then, before President George W. Bush launched wars in Iraq and Afghanistan, that nobody was interested in homeless war veterans.

181

I stand in Eartha's bedroom on the second floor of the Mission. Night falls.

It was here that Grayce held Eartha's hand after Eartha fell down the stairs. It was here that Grayce held Eartha's hand days before she died.

It was here that Eartha had gone to bed, night after night, decade after decade, and it was here that she rose before dawn every day.

It was here she sometimes put a stranger to bed in her stead, someone starving or bleeding or ready to kill himself, someone who needed anything she could offer, after which she would remove herself to other rooms and corners.

In Eartha's bedroom, I feel the whole building as Eartha. The Mission is to this building as Eartha was to her body. But longer lived. Eartha's body lasted only 97 years, unless Eartha's body is this building.

People claim to see Eartha's ghost here because she made this Mission her life. She never left to go home. This place was home. She never separated herself from the people she sought to help.

I look out the window through which she looked thousands of times, though the LaVilla I see so differs from Eartha's LaVilla, though the LaVilla Eartha saw in 1970 so differed from the LaVilla she saw in 1940.

The bedroom is quiet. The bedroom is empty. But this emptiness is not empty. This emptiness is full. As Eartha's life was full. As Eartha obtains in the fullness and the emptiness of these halls and these rooms.

182

In Eartha's bedroom, I remember this sad country gospel song my mother requested at the Southern Baptist church we attended throughout my early childhood, my early "church home" as the people there called it, in the days when she was dying.

The first verse says, "This old house I'm living in is needing repair. / The windows and the shutters are letting in the cold, cold air. / I say to myself, I'm gonna fix it when I can get the time. / But all I've been getting lately is leaving on my mind."

That decrepit house differs violently with the strong house my mother had been for me, and with Eartha as the "storehouse for the people."

I remember what Eartha said in her 1947 rededication speech—"I'm not going to have [a funeral.] Oh I don't mind my remains, the old house that I live in, being laid here. You might take a look at it, for after all, I won't be there."

The second verse continues, "I guess I should be looking for a better place to live, / But I can't seem to get excited about this old world and what it can give. / I couldn't care less if I could buy it all with a solitary dime. / For what good would this old world do me with leaving on my mind?"

These lyrics sound suicidal to me now. I didn't hear them that way when I was 11 years old and lay for hours, every night, against my paralyzed mother's side, inhabiting her sickness as my way of living in the world.

Ironically, in that sickness, I had love and I had a world, I dwelt within an "old house" with the world itself walled safely away outside. If I could have remained forever in that sickened womb, I could have stayed ignorantly and sorrowfully happy. I know that's not true, and I certainly was not happy.

After she died, I used to listen to a cassette tape recording of a small-town Georgia preacher named Wally Bearden singing "Leaving on My Mind."

After both verses, the chorus says, "Lately I've got leavin' on my mind. / Seems that's all I think about most of the time, / How that soon and very soon I'll leave these troubles far behind. / Lately I've got leavin', leavin' on my mind."

I've seen my father, Depression-era son of a farmer, grandson of sharecroppers, cry twice. Once was when he heard me listening to that low-quality cassette recording of "Leavin' on My Mind" two months after my mother died.

I can't remember the other time.

When I stand in Eartha's bedroom, I see the old house has been fixed. Someone had the time. Someone found just what this old world could give. And someone had a dime.

It's just such a goddam shame that someone always has to have a dime.

In Eartha's bedroom, I understand Eartha White as a long life, a grand edifice, stretching back to the birth of Clara and before—Clara who saw her mother sold at auction downtown—and extending forward through Eartha's decline in old age, the near death of the Mission, and its resurgence in the 21st century.

Ju'Coby Pittman tells me, "Anytime we think we have a new idea, a new possibility for the Mission, we end up finding out that somewhere along the way, Miss White had already thought of it."

Eartha White has come to reclaim herself, to come, as Ju'Coby and Meg say, "full circle," returning to the earth to bring forth from the earth. As the earth has always contained the world, the earth has always been a storehouse for the people, and Eartha reclaims her strength in the origin of her name.

Another morning, I'm riding out to Moncrief Springs with Peggy Ezell, who oversees the culinary gardens and farm operations for the Mission, and I ask her what Eartha would think of the current directions toward which the Mission tends. Peggy tells me Ju'Coby Pittman keeps Eartha White alive.

Then Peggy nods her head emphatically and says, "Eartha White is alive again through Ju'Coby Pittman."

I love what Ju'Coby's doing with the Mission, and such a quote might work wonderfully for Ju'Coby should she run for political office, yet I think of Eartha White in a higher capacity than office, like Saint Francis, or Gandhi, or Jane Addams. Or even, bearer of her own standard, Eartha White.

Now I see where I'm supposed to take this search, and I'm almost there.

But it's late at night, and I'm sitting against the truncated column of a blighted river birch near the northeast corner of Jefferson and West Ashley. I'm trying to soak the place into me. I felt Eartha in the Mission, but I want to see what comes to me outside. When it's come, I'll walk to the final place I expect to meet her.

I'm tired. I'm worried I'm burning myself out. I try to slow things down. I close my eyes and listen to my breathing fill my chest, empty my chest, fill my chest. I see stars against the backs of my eyelids. Phosphenes pulse with diamonds and dominoes.

When I open my eyes, it's not the jazz clubs and the Chinese laundry and pool halls and barbershops I see.

I know the streetcars and the taverns are here. I don't feel time as passing. It comes as accumulations of atmospheres. The world gets older and older, even when the earth that contains the world renews itself with every springtime. The world gets ever older, and urban renewal's the most childish idea.

So even though I stand in the Collected Works of LaVilla in the winter of early 2014, tonight I see LaVilla before LaVilla.

I can't see clearly. I see as through a scrim. I find my eyes incapable and stupid. Trees stand skeletal, river birches deciduous, but also evergreens—magnolias and pines.

The hairs on my arms and the back of my neck stand up. My skin crawls, creeps like millipedes, and for a second, I scratch at my chest to get some prickling arthropod out of my shirt. But that's not what's there.

When I calm myself, when I square my shoulders, I know there's nothing to be scared of at all. What comes over me is strange as fear, but its opposite. It's a mysterious peace that spreads through every part of me.

Suffering, terrible suffering, has inhabited the ground of this culinary garden at the side of the Mission, suffering subsumed into something better—a distillation that does not nullify or excuse the cruelty and pain that called this pre-LaVilla LaVilla home. If it did, it could not transmute it.

I think back to my original naïve conception of one vast novel about Ottis Toole and Eartha White, the "Devil's Child" and the "Angel of Mercy," and perhaps I've written that novel after all in *Stalking Ottis Toole* and *In Search of Eartha White*. If someone had brought Ottis Toole as a little boy to Eartha White on Ashley Street, Eartha would have loved him and cared for him.

How bizarre and how silly that these two books now seem my ersatz attempt to parallel William Blake's *Songs of Innocence* and *Songs of Experience*, or, more accurately, his *Marriage of Heaven and Hell*.

I had thought these books were one as The Tree of Knowledge of Good and Evil. Just as Adam and Eve are exiled from the Garden of Eden for eating from that tree, these two books together would cast me far from innocence, but redeem me from its loss. I hope I am not that selfish.

I connect the earlier plantings premised on brutality, the plantation LaVilla had been, to the culinary garden planted as part of Ju'Coby Pittman's visionary synthesis of feeding the poor and re-greening urban Jacksonville. Nobody can say that under Ju'Coby's leadership, the biggest problem with environmentalism in Jacksonville is "the unbearable whiteness of green," that pun on Milan Kundera's *Unbearable Lightness of Being*.

If the garden I see from this midnight river-birch trunk, through my closed eyelids, mystagogically—if I can so wholly and childishly trust where my heart and head now take me, is some landscape through time from 1896, as now seems clear, then this beautiful benevolent face that smiles across a century is that of a young woman whose fiancé's just died. I can't understand the kindness of her smile in the context of all this suffering.

Her face smiles through the winter of deciduous trees, embedded in angelic kindness. This angel's kinky hair stands out from her face like a halo.

"I know you," I say. "I met you once, a long, long time ago."

She calls me a name no one's called me since I was a little boy. She says, "I've always looked after you," and I cry.

But I can't understand why. "And I looked for you for such a long time," I say. "I've looked for you ever since you died."

And when she tells me, "I've always been here," I feel cared for, and loved, and I feel that everyone is loved, and I tell her, "We need you here."

And she says, not just to me, but to everyone who reads this page: "I'm here. I'll always be here. Waiting for you."

Now I see where I'm supposed to take this search. I'm almost there.

He says he doesn't need fame, attention, praise. He wavers between asking me to keep him on deep-background and telling me how much more work I have to do.

Each time we meet, Richard McKissick realizes how much more there is to tell. Each time we meet and walk through LaVilla, he realizes how much is gone and how much will *be* gone when *he*'s gone.

We're standing in front of the Mission, and Richard remembers walking down West Ashley and seeing Eartha sitting out front. He speaks through his electronic voicebox while students nail together wooden garden beds on the sidewalk. I lean in close to Richard to hear him. I sometimes feel like I need to hold him up, grateful that he lets me.

He still moves his upper body rhythmically when he speaks, moves his neck side-to-side to match the feeling in what he says, but he feels thin and frail.

We walk slowly and closely down the sidewalk, our heads angled toward each other, his head to be heard and mine to hear. It's a strangely and comfortably intimate choreography. It surprises me.

Manuel's Tap Room, Lounge and Grill, 622-26 West Ashley St., Jacksonville, Fla., Manuel Rivera, proprietor. Newly opened, it is the most exclusive place of its kind in Jacksonville for drinking, dining and dancing. Open 24 hours a day

Where the culinary garden grows today, Richard remembers Brad's Café. Next to Brad's, on the street level of the Mission building was Ralph Tisdale's Roosevelt Barber Shop. On the other side of Brad's stood wood-frame houses.

The look in his eyes is strange. He looks like he sees what's here now and simultaneously sees 65 years ago. The look in his eyes is fully present and deeply distant.

He remembers the Knights of Pythias Hall, the tallest building from that era's West Ashley, where the biggest jazz and blues names played—Ella Fitzgerald, Cab Calloway, Billie Holiday, Duke Ellington.

Richard points up and down the street, remembers, he says, where two story houses stood, and Lenape's Tavern— whose outer walls were saved from demolition only to remain a shell of a building more than a decade ago.

I don't think I've ever seen the particular cast of eye I see in Richard's eyes right now. Distance is close and proximity is sharp but distant. There's no word for it. I ask him, "How clearly can you see this in your mind's eye? I mean, to me it seems you see it very clearly."

His emotion and surety carry through his electronic voicebox as he tips his head forward and says, "Absolutely."

We've walked back down the block. He points at the southwest corner of West Ashley and Broad, across from the Mission, says that was the Imperial Pharmacy. The Imperial Pharmacy decades later became Perk and Loretta's Soul Lounge.

"Next to that," Richard says, indicating a demarcation on the earth only he can see, just west of his vision of the Imperial Pharmacy, "was a Chinese laundry."

And just west of the Chinese laundry was a bar called Manuel's Taproom. Manuel was Chula Papa Rivera. At the moment, Richard can't recall what was just west of Manuel's, but the other side of this hiatus was Lenape's Bar—"Lenape" pronounced like the New Jersey-area Indian tribe—and the upstairs Wynn Hotel, where Louis Armstrong frequently stayed when he played at the Knights of Pythias. The Richmond Hotel, around the corner on Broad Street, was more stylish, but Armstrong preferred to stay less than a block from where he'd play. Richard points to the northwest corner of Ashley and Jefferson where where he once managed the Strand Theater.

We stop for a second while a fire engine speeds by, its siren screaming through the ghosts of LaVilla. We hold our heads inches apart, prepared to be heard and to hear as soon as we have the chance.

A car stops for the light on Jefferson, and two young men hail Richard through an open window. "Hey, brother!"

Up and down West Ashley and around Broad up to Beaver Street, old men and young men keep stopping him, addressing him with sincere respect or joking with him in ways that show how much they respect him.

One man puts his hand on Richard's shoulder and tells a friend, "This here's the governor." I think of Rodney Hurst calling Richard the "Mayor of Ashley Street." He says, "I told you, you come down here, you gone see the governor. That dude in Tallahassee don't do *nothin'* without checkin' with the *real* governor."

Richard raises his eyebrows, smiles, and doubles over, but we don't hear his laughter because he doesn't hold the electrolarynx up to his throat.

"Richard," I say, "everybody knew you here 60 years ago. Everybody knows you here now."

We've come back to the Mission. Richard points to the other side of the Mission building, what was once the Willie Smith Building, street level, says, "Here was the Hollywood Music Store."

I remember when the Hollywood Music Store was still open in the early 1990s. Joe Higdon opened the store in the 1920s and made it his headquarters for promoting black music and bringing musicians to LaVilla. In the same building were Adolph's Beauty Products and Florida Cut-Price Pharmacy.

And right here on West Ashley, at the street corner just east of the Mission, Richard says, "And right there was, originally, back, during the 19th, the, uh, 20th century, my daddy had a tailor shop in there."

He says, "And on that corner there was a snack bar owned by some Syrians, whom I knew very, very well."

Camilla Thompson, who knew Eartha White for almost 40 years, remembers the place too. "It was called Skaff's. It was a confectionary," she says. "I remember getting out of school at Stanton and going across the street to go in there. They had ice cream and they had these big jars of pickles."

I soon deeply regret not having asked Richard about his father's tailor shop. Walking with him on West Ashley, I feel a little overwhelmed.

It's not just the past coming at me, but the full history of a neighborhood dense and rich at least partly as the ironic result of the injustice of segregation. White Jacksonville confined its black citizens in neighborhoods like LaVilla, and black residents responded by creating the most vibrant, loving, thriving neighborhoods in the city.

And this 88 year-old man, speaking electronically, points to what he sees from decades gone and tries to share it with a young white man. By what right do I receive Richard's memories? When he's gone, they're gone. And my representations of them are but shadows of shadows, recorded by a descendent of the people who oppressed him. I have no right, but Richard shares his memories with me anyway. For the rest of my life, I'll be grateful to him for walking me through them.

He remembers houses side by side across West Ashley from the Stanton School, where novelist and poet and Civil Rights leader James Weldon Johnson was principal.

Richard misses the community in these streets. The black community is now multiply tiered and stretched across the city. And though he says he cannot regret the advancement of black people in American society, he misses when close neighbors lived on these streets and ran their businesses, and when he knew them all, all right here.

He remembers not just when Ashley Street went straight through from the block of Eartha's Mission to the block of the Strand and the Knights of Pythias and the Frolic and the Roosevelt, but when Ashley Street left west from where LaVilla School of the Arts stands today, bearing other two-story wood-frame houses and businesses and lines of shotgun houses past where Interstate 95 knifed across it without feeling or understanding or knowledge in 1960.

187

Newspaper reporters also claimed Ralph Tisdale had borne the title of "Mayor of Ashley Street." He died from heart failure in 2007, 85 years old, in the nursing home Eartha had established on Moncrief Road so many decades ago.

When Hazel Tisdale came at the end of a workday to pick up her husband Ralph from the Roosevelt Barbershop he ran for 55 years at the street level of the Mission building, Eartha, in her 70s and 80s, sometimes climbed into the back of the car, uninvited, and asked Hazel to drive her to some important meeting across town.

Ralph Tisdale gave free haircuts to poor families and destitute people trying to get their lives back together.

Hazel Tisdale remembers when she was a little girl, walking through a wooded area by an old graveyard in the Pine Forest neighborhood where she's lived for almost 90 years. "I saw two white men with a boat and my heart started pounding. I told myself to walk as if I was not afraid, and then when I rounded that corner to run."

When she reached her house, she saw the men stop in the street, looking for her. "They looked everywhere for me. They even looked under the church, but they couldn't find me."

The area that includes Pine Forest still reflects the beginnings of its population. In the land around the Red Bank Plantation house, built in the 1850s, affluent subdivisions emerged, while across St. Augustine Road and Philips Highway, the population is mostly poor and black—as it was prior to the Emancipation Proclamation.

When Ralph Tisdale died, the nursing home had been sold after long decline, but the Mission itself was in full resurgence, regaining strength and vitality more than a century and a half after Clara's birth.

188

I feel dizzy. I feel glib. I feel profoundly moved and incapable of reaching the depths of the lived memory of this neighborhood. Here, at the height of LaVilla's beautiful thriving, was its paradox: the most urban, the healthiest, the most vibrant part of Jacksonville was so by default of segregation. Most of Jacksonville never knew its own rich heart. Most of the city knew nothing of what it missed when it cleared LaVilla away. And when Jacksonville's black people could live and work wherever they wanted, most of them eventually left that once healthy rich heart of the city behind.

And in the 1980s and 1990s, bored middle-class white kids, with little idea Jacksonville was older than them, grew up in split-level ranch-style subdivisions that "slummed" almost as soon as they were built, and these same kids complained that Jacksonville had no culture, no heart. They said Jacksonville was boring.

Richard says, "You have to understand that LaVilla as I remember it was a result of segregation. Black people could not go downtown, to the hotels, they were not allowed by law."

He tells me not to romanticize LaVilla as having existed on its own terms, but he tells me the city and the South itself has not granted LaVilla as he remembers it the proper "cultural respect" and "intellectualization."

The whole time I walk with Richard, my hand often—I realize later—gently touches his shoulder, as much to try to see what he's seeing as to hear what he's saying, sirens blaring in the distance.

In listening to these interviews later, the sirens sound like they're mocking us. LaVilla fell desperately into deep crime in its latter years, but now there's almost nothing here.

Still the sirens provide the background music for these interviews.

189

Long before two black women named Mary Singleton and Sallye Mathis were elected to the City Council in 1967, long before Wilson Armstrong ran for City Council in the 1940s, two black men named George Ross and J. Douglass Wetmore were elected to City Council, from the city's black Ward Six, in 1901.

Since Republicans were the party of Lincoln and Southern Democrats sponsored and supported Jim Crow legislation in retaliation for Emancipation, two black council members meant two Republicans in a segregated ward.

More than 50 years after leaving office in 1907, George Ross declared his opposition to integration. "I, and most members of my race, have no desire to leave our own group, our own people, and mingle with white people in every level of their society."

In walking with Richard McKissick, I try to see what he sees. I try to see the barbershops and theaters and restaurants and law firms and schools in LaVilla and wealthy black neighborhoods like Sugar Hill. They're all decimated, not just by "white flight," but the exodus of black wealth and community in the wake of desegregation.

In speaking of his opposition to integration in the late 1950s, Ross hit the point at which the Supreme Court would pivot. He said, "We do want one thing. We want an equality of opportunity for education."

This statement indicated an equality not yet achieved, but Ross then said, "We have that opportunity in Jacksonville, in fact in all of Florida. Our Negro schools are excellent. I see no reason why Negroes should ever try to integrate the public schools in this city and I certainly hope it never happens here."

Of course the Supreme Court rejected the argument that some students could be kept separate but treated equally and decided that separate inherently means unequal.

A year before Jacksonville's infamous Ax Handle Saturday, which ignited a decade of race riots, Ross said, "I never fail to point out that Jacksonville has been a good place for both Negroes and white people to live, that we have lived in harmony, that we have seen none of the strife that has beset other cities."

What the hell was he talking about? Was this some nonagenarian "Uncle Tom" talk from a man born four years after the Civil War ended? What did he make of Jim Crow? What did he think of the Ku Klux Klan? Was this a last vestige of an accommodationism he found rhetorically necessary as an elected official, albeit in a black district a half century before? Was it senility?

Even Zora Neale Hurston, who claimed she was not of the "sobbing school of Negrohood," said that when she moved from Eatonville in 1904, "Jacksonville made me know that I was a little colored girl. Things were all about the town to point this out to me."

I intend no disrespect to George Ross. My confusion is historically honest. Is this the kind of thinking left over from being successful and black in the early 20th century South, in the years when Eartha first succeeded in so many ventures?

If so, and if Ross was still saying these things by the time Eartha herself was in her early 80s, how much more Progressive was Eartha to have kept the Mission alive, even if brand new Civil Rights activists, 60 years younger, often saw her *modus operandi* as too Booker-T.?

It's obvious why mainstream "white" newspapers would seize upon statements uttered by a former black leader, even from so long before, with which they would agree. It echoes the local white political and civic enthusiasm for the sentiments of Edward Wilmot Blyden, who visited Jacksonville in the late 1800s, espousing ex-slave emigration to Africa.

But the black side of anti-integrationist thinking must be more complicated than the white side.

As late as 1985, in his last book, *The Evidence of Things Not Seen*, his meditation upon the Atlanta Child Murders of 1979 to 1981, that brilliant black intellectual James Baldwin wrote that white Americans couldn't understand that desegregation did not mean integration because they were "quite unable to imagine that there can be anyone, anywhere, who does not wish to be White."

Baldwin says this white conflation of desegregation with integration "smashed every Black institution in this country, with the single exception of the Black church," adding that, "in this, Black people were certainly accomplices."

Baldwin remembers segregated Atlanta thriving with black people all "in hailing distance of each other, and in sight of a church or a poolroom or a bar." But in the early 1980s, he says, none of these black communities (he elsewhere emphasizes the word "community" as against the weaker word "neighborhood") "is what it was" and "the faces there, now, convey a pained and bewildered sense of being abandoned."

Is the great James Baldwin doing what Richard McKissick asks me not to do—romanticizing the thriving urban black community of the past? What Baldwin says about Sweet Auburn in Atlanta is equally attributable to LaVilla.

After desegregation, "the well-to-do Blacks are far from the city's center," and this post-desegregation decimation of the center of the city, Baldwin says, is what Americans describe as progress.

My head swims. I'm a white male 21st-century liberal. I read one of 20th-century America's few "public intellectuals," whom many whites considered radical, loosely paralleling anti-integration sentiments expressed in the 1950s by a black Jacksonville ex-councilman, comments trumpeted by conservative racists as substantiation of their ideas.

LaVilla was dense, full of life, happening, abundant, exuberant, and though its remembrances bring tears to Richard McKissick's eyes, and though its community was denser and richer in most ways than the city's contemporary white community, McKissick says that LaVilla did not exist on its own terms because its concentration was the result of segregation.

190

We walk north on Broad toward Beaver Street, cross to a two-story brick building constructed in 1916, which the Mission is developing into housing for war veterans and students in its Janitorial and Construction Maintenance training program.

Richard keeps reminding me that people lived above their business enterprises all up and down these streets.

As does, even now, Anthony Walton, at the oldest business still operating in LaVilla, Hillman-Pratt, now Hillman-Pratt & Walton Funeral Home, at 525 West Beaver Street, less than a full block from the building where Richard grew up behind the Mission.

The Lawton L. Pratt Funeral Homes, Inc., 525-527 West Beaver St., Jacksonville, the State's oldest funeral establishment. Established in 1900 under meager circumstances, it has grown in facilities and service to measure with any business of its kind in the South. By its courteous, polite, prompt and painstaking service, it has won the title of "The Obliging Undertaker." This building houses and promotes worthwhile civic programs. Its slogan is "The Funeral Home of the Community." A branch is located at 234 South Clara Avenue, Deland, Fla.

The funeral home's been in business since 1900, and the West Beaver Street building was completed a year later. Walton assumed the business a decade ago.

He invites me and Richard inside, shows us large framed photographs of Lawton Pratt, who died in 1956, and whose sister sought to adopt a child from Eartha's adoption services—"I would appreciate it very much if you would get me a boy"—and other LaVilla residents Richard hasn't seen in decades.

We stand in a tiny chapel, original red and gold stained-glass windows, big enough for maybe 20 short pews on either side of the aisle, and the pews too are original.

Richard doubles over. I've seen him do this before while laughing, but this time is different. He takes one of the large framed portraits under the wings of his jacket, takes several steps back from the front of the chapel to the first pew, and his breath blows heavily up from his lungs through his neck, minus electrolarynx. His eyes tear up, and he keeps saying, "Lord have mercy, Lord have mercy, Lord have mercy!"

He remembers two-story wood-frame houses, fronted with balconies, on either side of the funeral home on Beaver Street.

Richard grasps both of Anthony's hands. There's almost nothing left, he says. There's almost nothing left. But this building's still here. And this business is here. Richard tells Anthony he wants to thank him from his own deep memories and his own full heart. He says he wants to thank him on behalf of every black person in Jacksonville and everybody who ever lived in LaVilla.

The longest-lived business in LaVilla is a funeral home. The director has the kindest eyes. Richard keeps asking me to understand, to understand. Then he grabs my hand and says, electronically, "I know you do," but I think he tells *himself* I understand more than he says so to me.

I feel humble and grateful and glib. I feel out-of-place and out-of-time, and I'm both regretful of and thankful for it.

I'm someone who came along too late and wrote something.

Richard and I leave the 113 year-old funeral home and walk into the bright November sunlight of an empty LaVilla.

191

My community college recently put on a performance of Arlene Hutton's play *Letters to Sala*, based on mail secretly saved by a young girl in a Nazi labor camp. In one letter, Sala's sister Raizel implores her to write more, saying, "If you don't write, everything is lost."

How is it I've never heard this sentence before seeing this play?

For just as I remember coming home from school and seeing my mother's typewriter on the kitchen table, and just as I remember waking up and looking at my alarm clock the morning my mother died—I was 12 years old—and later being told her time of death was that very minute I'd looked at my clock, I've always understood that if I did not write, everything was lost.

So I treasure the 23-page book my mother wrote and published in 1981 called *In the Lord I Put My Trust* and the unpublished manuscript she wrote in 1986 called *Death is Swallowed up in Victory*. Both titles are Bible verses.

My mother left the manuscript with my sister Katie with the request that she publish it when Mom died. But Mom's understanding was distorted in her last year of suffering from ALS. She'd become paralyzed from the neck down and paranoid that my father was purposefully mistreating her. He wasn't.

She was angry. Her body was dead weight and she had to ask my father to move her onto her side, or pick up her lifeless leg and rearrange it, or hoist her from the bed, where she spent nearly all her time, to her wheelchair. I remember watching him move her, turn her, lift her. He never meant to hurt her, but inevitably he did.

She was angry. And anger needs a target. Sometimes the most fitting target is the nearest person. For a while, she made me hate my father. She told me he was abusing her. She told me she loved him because a wife had to love her husband, but that she didn't like him. She told me that when he asked her to marry him, he'd promised her the moon and the stars, but she said he never delivered them.

I was so loyal to her. I'd lie in bed next to her while my father shifted her paralyzed body onto its side. When he left the bedroom, she'd tell me I was born for some special reason, that my father didn't feel things deeply enough, that I should never lose my sensitivity. I'd sit in her wheelchair beside her bed and read her the Book of Psalms for an hour or two.

Once, a year or two after she died, my father showed me where he kept his pistol, "just in case" I ever needed to use it. I remember sometimes sneaking into his bedroom when no one was home, pulling open the dresser drawer, picking up the gun and placing the muzzle to my temple. I don't think I'd ever have pulled the trigger.

The last chapter of my mother's first book is called "Happiness at Last." It's about marrying my father. The first chapter of her last book is called "The Diagnosis is Death." The first book was dedicated to her three daughters. The second page of the 1986 manuscript says, "Dedicated to my son, Timothy, who is the bright spot in my life these last days."

Soon after my mother died, my sister Katie dreamt that she answered the phone in her kitchen and our mother was on the other line. She was calling to release her from her promise. "You don't have to publish it," she said.

So she didn't.

I have one of three copies of the manuscript.

"If you don't write, everything is lost."

There are so many mothers in this story.

I bring the loss of my mother to my search for the Mother Teresa of my hometown. Eartha named the Mission for the woman who could not have been more her mother if she'd given birth to her herself.

And though it's pure mythology, Eartha found a self-defining significance in telling the story, year after year, that the prophet / former slave had come to Clara to name her 13th child, the first one to live, after Mother Earth.

192

One April morning when the oaks have stormed Jacksonville with a continuous rain of brown seeds and bright-yellow pollen, when I've seen janitors sweep fallen oak catkins into bursting yellow clouds like mustard gas, I've met Pat Bell on the top floor of the Mission to sort through old files in a back corner of boxes.

I come down to the second floor where Pat's talking to Ju'Coby and a tall thin white man with long wild graying hair. Ju'Coby says something about signing final paperwork and about two old LaVilla houses side-by-side at Jefferson and Monroe.

I know what houses she means. They're tall twin houses with enormous floor plans and two-story corner porches topped by octagonal cupolas. They were built right after the Great Fire of 1901.

So I introduce myself to the tall man and shake his hand. His name is Mills Smith, and his father was City Councilman Mills Smith in the 1950s. He says his father was elected to clean up city corruption, which ensured he made few friends, and "the Machine" squeezed him out of power.

But his father owned some property in LaVilla, and when the City sought to flatten the district in the early 1990s, Mills and his brother fought to hang on to the houses they'd inherited. Even in sagging-wooden deep disrepair, these two houses retain a loveliness that hints at that wonderfully fruitful mycelium the thousands of vanished LaVilla houses and theaters and restaurants and synagogues and churches together formed.

"One day," he says, "I was coming through the neighborhood and I saw this long line of homeless people around the corner from the Mission, waiting to be fed. And I didn't know all the other things the Mission did. But the sun was coming up on the city, and people who needed to be fed were going to be fed, and it just struck me as this beautiful moment, and I mean it was beautiful, and I call it an epiphany."

As I shake his hand this spring 2014 morning, Mills Smith has just donated his family's old Carpenter Gothic houses to the Mission. The houses will be restored and provide shelter for people the Mission helps reclaim their possibilities. His donation saves the houses and saves lives.

Then I hear the Mission's negotiating the purchase of the Hillman-Pratt Funeral Home to convert it to war veterans' and homeless services. There's also talk of the Mission purchasing and renovating the old shell of Lenape's Tavern / Genovar's Hall across West Ashley.

Ju'Coby says she thinks daily about Eartha White. She rolls her eyes and says, "You know what? Sister Eartha White, she's keeping me busy from the grave." She raises her eyebrows and hunches her shoulders and says emphatically, "I just can't keep up with her."

193

Now I'm back at Moncrief Springs, but things are much different than when the kid with the dreadlocks and neck tattoos told me he didn't know who Eartha White was.

Now this piece of earth, so long abandoned, reestablishes its health. Collards and broccoli and cabbages grow in long neat rows that stretch back from Moncrief Road into the sugar cane growing tall against old pines in the distance. A PVC irrigation system threads throughout the winter garden.

The three unattached Corinthian columns stand strong and old, and Eartha's little fieldstone bungalow feels not just present to me now, but sentient.

Walking from the bungalow, past the crops, and over Moncrief Creek, I come to a stand of pines and camphors, on the other side of which is a low building with a wide front porch that workers are converting into a farmers' market.

The former Eartha M. M. White Nursing Home, which became Summer Brook Health Care Center when the Mission sold it, stands somber and deep-red bricked across the street.

The Clara White Mission has transformed Moncrief Springs, and this new direction circles back to Eartha and her ideas.

Crops grow in the fields where the swimming pool and recreation areas once stood, and the Mission has rechristened this land White Harvest Farms. The farmers' market will sell produce grown right here.

The walkover above Moncrief Road will bring kids from Saint Clair Evans Academy elementary school to the farmers' market where they'll have classes in cultivation and grow their own crops in a raised-bed community garden behind the building. Their parents and relatives are invited to help out, and all the produce the children and their families grow will be their own. The neighborhood is one of countless "food deserts" in Jacksonville, poor parts of town whose residents have no access to healthy fresh food.

Eartha's little house will become the historical and cultural museum she'd wanted it to be. It's been empty for the 40 years since she died, since when historians found homeless people breaking in and burning her artifacts in barrels to keep warm.

Standing between rows of mustard greens and stands of sugar cane that front the pines, I feel I'm standing on holy ground. This is Eartha's earth. She's here, "Storehouse for the People." I can feel her, sprouting up green from this ground to feed the children who live in the housing projects up and down Moncrief.

This ground straddles boundaries. It's a winter garden fenced with sugar cane. Its winter greens border 12-foot tall sugar-fibered grasses that grow year-round in South Florida. Thanksgiving's next week, but I'm sweating in North Florida humidity. Everything risen of this ground is green, lush, fecund, abundant, bounteous, gracious, generous, refulgent, benevolent, celebratory.

194

Before driving north from the Mission to Moncrief, I meet Peggy Ezell, assistant director of agriculture at Clara White, at the culinary garden beside the Mission. I've brought my friends Mike Lorr, a sociologist who often writes about urban re-greening, and his wife, Marsely Kehoe, an Art History postdoctoral fellow and lecturer at Columbia University.

We walk through the kitchen area, where volunteers are just finishing the morning's offering of breakfast, and walk past climbing grape tomatoes, rows of garlic, lettuce, cabbage, broccoli, kohlrabi, carrots, mustards, and collards. To one side grows rosemary, sage, chives, parsley, and geranium. Past the spreading ground vines of sweet potato, the sprawling strawberries, and the strange feathery three-year asparagus, are the compost bins where microbial life breaks down death to feed new life.

Peggy Ezell is a soprano vocalist who was voice professor at Jacksonville University for 19 years. After she retired, though she needed to find a different direction for her life, she initially resisted the idea of volunteering at the Mission. The first day she came to West Ashley Street, she knew it was where she should be.

Now the garden, White Harvest Farms at Moncrief Springs, and a partnership with Sysco Foods form the core of the Clara White Mission's Culinary Arts apprenticeship program.

Students in the program work at the garden and the farm, they work in the kitchen in the Mission to serve homeless people lunch each day, and they learn every aspect of preparing food for Clara's at the Cathedral.

Clara's is a "training café" that offers lunch every Friday from 11 a.m. to 1 p.m. in the dining hall at the magnificent St. Johns Episcopal Cathedral downtown, with its gargoyles, grand Celtic crosses, weeping hollies, and statue of St. Fiacre, patron saint of gardeners. Clara's serves between 75 and 200 diners every week.

On the Friday when Mike, Marsely, Peggy, and I meet Ju'Coby at Clara's at the Cathedral, a jazz band plays on stage, and the buffet offers tomato bisque, salads, cornbread stuffing, sugar-glazed ham and turkey with giblet gravy, sweet potatoes, rice pilaf, buttered carrots, zucchini casserole, bread pudding with Bourbon caramel sauce, and sweet potato pie.

Culinary students prepare the food, cook with chefs, wait tables, and maître d'. The café is Friday's culmination of the students' hard workweek. When they complete the program, the Mission helps students find jobs. The program lasts an intensive 20 weeks, and around 70 percent of its graduates have found and maintained skilled restaurant employment.

Peggy says, "We're not just preparing them to get a job flipping burgers. They learn everything from growing the crops to preparing high-end cuisine." Some of them attain further culinary education after completing the Mission's program. Many of them have previously been homeless.

By the end of our meal, Mike, Marsely, and I feel post-prandially comatose. Peggy has been the most gracious host. Ju'Coby seated us herself and asked us what we thought of the farm. She ascends the stage, thanks the jazz band, asks for applause for anybody eating at Clara's for the first time, and introduces a donor who's brought enough canned food to feed hundreds of poor families.

I think about how Eartha lived at the Mission, wore clothes from the donation piles, and ate with the indigent. I wonder when Ju'Coby's going to run for political office, and I hope she does more uncorrupted good there than other politicians. She's kept Eartha alive, and it's hard to imagine anyone doing better than that.

On the way out of the city's grandest cathedral, I buy three stalks of sugarcane as tall as I am. My daughters have never chewed on sugarcane, though certainly some of our long-in-the-tooth old forebears rotted their teeth on it. Tonight I'll cut the stalks at the bands and slice down the centers and we'll gnaw sweetness out of the grassy lignin.

195

From the late 1800s until the early 1970s, the City of Jacksonville disposed of much of its garbage by incinerating it. Peggy remembers black plumes pouring across her childhood skies.

City political leaders had to find some place to dump the ashes once the city's trash was burnt. One of those places was Brown's Dump, just off Moncrief Road at the old city limit prior to 1968 city-county Consolidation.

Within a few years of Eartha purchasing Moncrief Springs where she built the swimming pool and hosted black recreation during segregation, the City of Jacksonville decided that one of the best places to dump its garbage incinerator ash was the boundary of the all-black Moncrief Springs.

Brown's Dump was a 250-acre site that received incinerator ash for less than a decade from the late 1940s until 1953, but the mercury, lead, and other heavy metals and toxins that saturated the soil were dangerous enough to close an elementary school more than half a century later.

In 1955, two years after it shut down the dump, the City built an all-black elementary school atop toxic ash at the northern city limit.

Brown's Dump included ground that stretched from Pearce and West 33rd Streets along the railroad line to Eartha's land and Moncrief Creek. Not only had the spring itself been destroyed, but the ground around it had been layered in several feet of toxic ash.

For years, even as the big gospel bands with their trumpets and French horns and trombones played "When the Saints Go Marching In" and churches baptized crowds of young boys and girls in the swimming pool at Moncrief

Springs, backhoes and large tractors spread burnt trash and mercury, arsenic, lead, and dioxin across acres of ground not far behind them.

In 2001, when city officials admitted to Moncrief residents that attending school at Mary McLeod Bethune Elementary posed significant health risks to their children, parents who'd attended the same school wondered why nobody had mentioned it for half a century.

Then Bethune Elementary, which shared its name with schools all over the South, just as Nathan Bedford Forrest High School once did, ceased operation and sunk under the weight of its abandonment.

Bethune, Eartha's friend, was a Florida educator and Civil Rights leader, while Forrest was the first Grand Dragon of the Ku Klux Klan. Jacksonville's Mary McLeod Bethune closed in 2001, while in 2014, Nathan Bedford Forrest is finally scheduled for a name change.

Now the elementary school is empty and city and state officials have dug up soil beneath houses built where Brown's Dump once stood and replaced the soil with gravel. County health officials offered residents lead testing, but most refused it, whether from a desire not to know, an historically based distrust of authorities, or the fatalism of poor neighborhoods who have no locus-of-control.

196

The transformation of Moncrief Springs into White Harvest Farms illustrates everything miraculous about the earth's constant renewal, and the Concept of Compost illustrates everything miraculous about Eartha White.

Wherever people have farmed, they've understood compost. On a small practical scale, it may mean banana peels and grape stems and coffee grounds and fallen leaves mixed and turned until they achieve a fine, rich, sweet-smelling nutritious soil.

But on a larger scale, all the farming people of the earth, throughout history and prehistory, no matter their religions or faiths, have understand that natural elements reclaim themselves in order to foment new life.

It's the original concept of recycling. The green-arrowed recycling symbol, the lemniscate—the sideways eight that represents infinity, and the ouroboros, the serpent that swallows its tail in cultures across the planet, each work as metaphor for the recycling of death into life.

Walt Whitman wrote about it repeatedly:

"The smallest sprout shows there is really no death, / And if ever there was it led forward life, and does not wait at the end to arrest it, / And ceas'd the moment life appear'd. / All goes onward and outward, nothing collapses, / And to die is different from what any one supposed, and luckier."

And because the crops planted on Eartha's ground at Moncrief Springs produce such rich nutritious harvests today, you have to walk through the smoldering ash dunes shoveled by tractors on nearby land 60 years ago to understand the true reclamation and ouroboric recycling of this land.

In preparation for the farm, the Mission worked with the City of Jacksonville and the Florida Department of Environmental Protection. Although Brown's Dump was located adjacent to Eartha White's land and the present White Harvest Farms, the larger area was designated a "brownfield site," making it eligible for governmental cleanup funding. Contaminated soil was removed and replaced by a depth of several feet of clean soil.

And vegetation always cleans the earth. After all the Mission's and the city's and state's reclamation work, the beans and tomatoes and lettuce continue to perform the greatest miracle, turning every smallest death into nourishment. With the City's nearby incinerated toxins removed and out of reach, the roots of peas and carrots and cucumbers clean the closest depths of compost into nutrition.

This farm is the true story of the earth and Eartha White. She circulates through this soil, forever cleansing, just as the earth is a great and ancient churning cycling storm. The earth is the earthworm, passing everything through its body, and the earth is the resultant sprout and flower.

Everything comes round. Full circle. Storehouse for the people. And the earth is never too exhausted to return to its very own goodness.

197

I'll be grateful to Ju'Coby and to Kevin Carrico, vice president of operations at the Mission, for the rest of my life. They've been gracious enough to let me launch this book in the large dining room in the Clara White Mission in early October 2014.

Whatever Eartha White, at any point in her life, would think of *In Search of Eartha White*, I've learned that she would meet the sincere urgency of my quest with kindness.

Knowing nothing as strange as story, I can hardly believe I'm reading from this book in the same building in which Eartha White lived and died.

Here, in this building, in the Globe Theater, Vaudeville troupes and blues singers performed.

Here, in this building, in the Mission's early years, quilting bees were held and Great Depression Works Progress Administration projects headquartered.

(And barber shops and radio stations and newspaper offices.)

Here, former slaves told folklorists what they remembered of their lives.

Here, the blind were taught to do beadwork and the illiterate to read.

Here, in this very room, tens of thousands of people in need have been fed and clothed.

Here, the Mt. Ararat Male Quartet sang for an elevator fund.

Here, throughout the years, Eartha White brought dozens of stray dogs and cats.

Here, Eartha White was Eartha White, listening to an opera record in the middle of the night.

Here, a fire caught and ravaged the rooms.

Here, Eartha White gave a rededication speech that matched the funeral wishes she typed out, here, on the second floor.

Here, the sirens came.

Here, young men broke all the first-floor windows in the middle of the night in the early 1970s.

Here, infiltrated the rats and the bats and pigeons.

Here, two young women and their dedicated staff staved off a City government out to destroy the vision of Eartha White in the name of urban renewal.

Here, still, beats the moral and ethical heart of Jacksonville, Florida, strong again, as it ever had been.

I so wish I could have met Eartha White. I've tried to meet her every day I've researched and written about her life.

Such a project has failure built into its design, but I've done the best I can do.

I'm left with a surreal and uncanny humility I'm grateful ever to have lived in this body and this mind in this lifetime.

Here, I give Eartha White what little I can return for what she gave of her life.

On the day of the publication of *In Search of Eartha White*, I'll bring the first copy to Moncrief Springs and bury it in the farm.

I'll remember how Eartha chose her clothes from the piles of donations for the poor, and I'll ask what Jesus asked in the Sermon on the Mount—"And why take ye thought for raiment?"

I'll look to the strange blue blooming stars of garlic, and I'll "consider the lilies of the field, how they grow; they toil not, neither do they spin."

Eartha toiled so long. Now these crops resurrect her without undue effort, as the earth has always resurrected itself from the ruins of the world.

After Eartha's sacred ground incorporates my book and my search, the beans and corn and cabbage and eggplant will incorporate that ghost-compost.

And our feasting of that harvest and ingesting the book's remains will become the very smallest symbol for all the good that Eartha White still accomplishes 138 years after she was born.

2.

Brief information about the National Association for the Advancement of White People (NAAWP) in Jacksonville in the 1990s can be found in *The Florida Times-Union*'s "NAAWP's Not Racist, But..." by columnist Tonyaa Weathersbee, published September 19, 1997, and in my own "Marietta: Doublewide Trailer, Thomas Jefferson Elementary, National Hotline for the NAAWP," published at www.jaxpsychogeo.com.

3.

Versions of this naming myth were repeated on at least an annual basis in Eartha's later years. It became a central part of her biography, and the Mission included it in most later biographical material, including programs published for Eartha White's birthday celebrations. A prime example is the souvenir program for the "75th Diamond Birthday Observance of the Useful Life of Eartha Mary Magdalene White," which can be found at the University of North Florida's Eartha White Collection, folder and number W4, 2787.

4. & 5.

See Dan Schafer's "Eartha M. M. White: The Early Years of a Jacksonville Humanitarian," manuscript of May 1976, UNF library's Eartha White Collection, and the obituary of Reverend Henry Harrison, published in *The Florida Metropolis*, September 17, 1917, UNF's Eartha White

Collection, folder and number V1, 0424. Photographs of Harrison: V1, 0425; V1, 0426; V1, 2766, and in Herman "Skip" Mason Jr.'s 1997 book *African-American Life in Jacksonville*, published as part of Arcadia Publishing's

"Images of America" series. The story of the "grand Timucua city" was told by Glenn Emery and published at http://www.jaxhistory.com/Jacksonville%20Story/Timucua,%20Ossachite.htm. Emery's story has been repeated as credible many times, including in Donald Mabry's 2010 book *World's Finest Beach: A Brief History of the Jacksonville Beaches*. When I asked University of Florida archaeologist and anthropologist Jerald Milanich why his 1996 book *The Timucua* made no mention of Ossachite, he said, "There was never a Timucua town called Ossachite; that is a piece of bad historical research by T. Frederick Davis and mentioned in one of his early books; he took the word from a map. It may be a Seminole word."

6.

Eartha's family Bible is kept in the UNF Eartha White Collection. The chronicles of the army pension investigation are best told in Dan Schafer's "Eartha M. M. White: The Early Years of a Jacksonville Humanitarian," manuscript of May 1976, UNF library's Eartha White Collection, and in Carmen Godwin's 2001 University of Florida master's thesis, "'To Serve God and Humanity': Jacksonville's Eartha Mary Magdalene White (1876-1974)." See Carolyn Williams's "Eartha Mary Magdalene White, 1876-1974: The Gentle Community Activist," published in *The Varieties of Women's Experiences: Portraits of Southern Women in the Post-Civil*

War Century, edited by Larry Eugene Rivers and Canter Brown, Jr., and published in 2009. Full pension reports can be found in Widow's Pension Files, Lafayette White, U.S. Army, 34th Regiment, Company D, U.S. Colored Troops, National Archives and Records Administration. The Mary Singleton reference comes from a 1974 audio interview held in UNF's Eartha White Collection. Dan Schafer gave me Eartha's genealogical notes in early February of 2014, with the condition that I give them to UNF's Eartha White Collection when I was through with them.

7.

See Frederick Douglass's *The Narrative of the Life of Frederick Douglass*. Also, Eartha's ticket says "Florida's welcome to the Honorable Frederick Douglass. Reception beginning April 4, 1889. 'This is to certify that the holder of this card has contributed twenty-five cents towards the Douglass reception, beginning April 4th, 1889.'" Eartha also kept a bronze bust of Douglass, which is now housed in the UNF Eartha White Collection. For James Weldon Johnson's reference to Douglass speaking in Jacksonville, see Johnson's 1933 autobiography, *Along this Way*.

8. & 9.

Census years referred to are 1880, 1900, 1920, and 1930. Historical information on the Stockton family comes from the 1909 Florida edition of *Makers of America: An Historical and Biographical Work by an Able Corps of Writers*, Vol. 2., "Published under the Patronage of the Florida Historical

Society, Jacksonville, Florida." Information on the seal placed on the family Bible comes from private correspondence with Dan Schafer.

10.

Audio interviews with Frances Ewell, 1974, are housed in UNF's Eartha White Collection.

11.

Mary Singleton's 1974 audio interview is housed in UNF's Eartha White Collection. The image of Mary Littlejohn comes from *The Crisis*, "Jacksonville Pictorial Number," January 1942, housed in UNF's Eartha White Collection at D1, 0330.

12. through 15.

For the part of Eartha's childhood spent at Fort George Island, see Dan Schafer's "Eartha M. M. White: The Early Years of a Jacksonville Humanitarian," manuscript of May 1976, UNF library's Eartha White Collection, and Carmen Godwin's 2001 University of Florida master's thesis, "'To Serve God and Humanity': Jacksonville's Eartha Mary Magdalene White (1876-1974)." For information on Kingsley and Anna Madgigine Jai Kingsley, see Schafer's 2010 book *Anna Madgigine Jai Kingsley: African Princess, Florida Slave, Plantation Slaveowner* and his 2013 book *Zephaniah Kingsley Jr. and the Atlantic World: Slave Trader, Plantation Owner, Emancipator.* On True Indigo, see Oliver Sacks's 2012 book *Hallucinations.* For earthquake information, see T. Frederick

Davis's 1925 *The History of Jacksonville and Vicinity, 1513-1924*. The photographic image of Eartha White can be found in UNF's Eartha White Collection.

16.

See Larry Eugene Rivers's and Canter Brown's (ed.) 2010 book *The Varieties of Women's Experiences: Portraits of Southern Women in the Post-Civil War Century* and Congressman Charles E. Bennett's 1989 book *Twelve on the River St. Johns*. Schafer quotes come from private correspondence. Nikki Giovanni's

"Nikki Rosa" was published in the 1968 *Black Feeling, Black Talk / Black Judgment*. The *Florida Times-Union*'s "Eartha White: Long Life Spent Helping Others," byline Jessie-Lynne Kerr, appeared on February 8, 1982.

17.

See Dan Schafer's "Eartha M. M. White: The Early Years of a Jacksonville Humanitarian," manuscript of May 1976, UNF library's Eartha White Collection. *The St. Petersburg Times*'s Sunday-supplement *Floridian* magazine article, "Eartha White, Florida's Rich, Black 94-year-old Senior Citizen of the Year," byline Fred Wright, appeared on August 1, 1971. The *Reader's Digest* article, "My Most Unforgettable Character," byline Harold Gibson, appeared in December 1974. I interviewed Camilla Thompson on February 5, 2014. Foundation bank accounts and tax returns from throughout the 1970s and 1980 meeting notations are in the possession of the Clara White Mission. August 26, 1974 board meeting minutes are in the possession of the Mission.

18. & 19.

See Dan Schafer's "Eartha M. M. White: The Early Years of a Jacksonville Humanitarian," manuscript of May 1976, UNF library's Eartha White Collection, and Carmen Godwin's 2001 University of Florida master's thesis, "'To Serve God and Humanity': Jacksonville's Eartha Mary Magdalene White (1876-1974)." The photographic image of Eartha White can be found in UNF's Eartha White Collection.

20.

Grayce Bateman's 1974 audio interview is housed in UNF's Eartha White Collection. *The New York Times* article, "Woman Lives Up to Her Name in Good Works," byline Angela Taylor, appeared on December 4, 1970. This photograph of Eartha, taken between 1970 and 1974, can be found in the State Archives of Florida, *Florida Memory*, at http://floridamemory.com/items/show/35599. *The Michigan Chronicle* article, "Attention, Women's Lib: Some Footsteps to Follow," byline Rita Griffin, appeared on October 17, 1970.

21. through 26.

Letters from James Jordan to Eartha White, dated from January 1895 to March 1896, are housed in UNF's Eartha White Collection, J2, 0508 through 0512, and the letter informing Eartha of Jordan's death is housed at J2, 0513. The photograph of Jordan, from August of 1894, can be found in UNF's Eartha White Collection.

27.

On the fate of Eartha's one-room schoolhouse in Bayard, see *The Florida Times-Union*'s "School's Part of Bayard's Past, in Road's Path," byline Dan Scanlan, published October 23, 2004. For more information on the schoolhouse, see the 1989 Jacksonville Historic Landmarks Commission's *Jacksonville's Architectural Heritage*, revised in 1996. For information on Eartha's school teaching and appointment to teach in Bayard, see Dan Schafer's "Eartha M. M. White: The Early Years of a Jacksonville Humanitarian," manuscript of May 1976, UNF library's Eartha

White Collection, and Carmen Godwin's 2001 University of Florida master's thesis, "'To Serve God and Humanity': Jacksonville's Eartha Mary Magdalene White (1876-1974)."

28.

See Schafer's manuscript and Godwin's thesis, aforementioned. A detailed account of Eartha's rescue of the Afro-American Life Insurance Company's files, and of Dr. J. Milton Waldron's comments, is in the possession of the Clara White Mission. See also Abel Bartley's *Keeping the Faith: Race, Politics, and Social Development in Jacksonville, Florida, 1940-1970*.

29.

The photographic image of Eartha White can be found in UNF's Eartha White Collection. See also *A Pictorial Review of Activities Conducted under Auspices of the Clara White Mission... Jacksonville, Florida* from the early 1930s, housed in UNF's Eartha White Collection, R, 0232.

30.

See Grayce Bateman's 1995 limited publication "Grayce Reminiscences [sic] 40 Years with Clara White Mission Inc. 1945-1985," which can be found in Box 185, Charles E. Bennett Papers, Special and Area Studies Collections, George A. Smathers Libraries, University of Florida.

31.

From *A Pictorial Review of Activities Conducted under Auspices of the Clara White Mission... Jacksonville, Florida* from the early 1930s, housed in UNF's Eartha White Collection, R, 0232.

32.

See Schafer's manuscript and Godwin's thesis, aforementioned. The grape incident is told in a letter E.C. Geiger wrote to Dan Schafer on February 17, 1975. Schafer let me borrow the letter in early February 2014 on condition that I give it to UNF's Eartha White Collection when I was done with it.

33.

Audio interviews with Frances Ewell, 1974, are housed in UNF's Eartha White Collection.

34. & 35.

These letters are housed in UNF's Eartha White Collection, G5, 1750 and G5, 1751.

36.

The Florida Metropolis's "Sister Mary Ann Passed Quietly Away—Will be Missed by Poor of Jacksonville—Entire Life Given to Charity--Death of Angel of Mercy Brings Regrets to Residents of City" was published on January 15, 1914. *The Florida Times-Union*'s "St. Mary's Home Stands as Monument to Beloved Sister Mary Ann" was published on January 30, 1949.

37.

My discussions with Patrician Moman Bell took place from the middle of February to early March, 2014.

See Paul Ortiz's 2005 book *Emancipation Betrayed: The Hidden History of Black Organizing and White Violence in Florida from Reconstruction to the Bloody Election of 1920*.

See Gerda Lerner's "Early Community Work of Black Club Women," published in the *Journal of Negro History*, April 1974, and Iris Carlton-LaNey's "African American Social

Work Pioneers' Response to Need," published in *Social Work: The Journal of the National Association of Social Workers*, July 1999.

The photograph of Margaret Murray Washington, Eartha White, and others in front of the Old Folks' Home can be found at http://digitalcommons.unf.edu/ eartha_images/7/.

Eartha's 1930s' copies of *The Open Door*, published monthly by the Phyllis Wheatley Association, are in the possession of the Clara White Mission.

38.

The anonymous November 15, 1927 letter is housed in UNF's Eartha White Collection, G5, 1805.

39.

The Florida Times-Union's "After 85 Years, Slain Minister's Jacksonville Legacy Lingers—As Adorkaville Fades Away, Some in the City Honors its Dream," byline Steve Patterson, appeared March 7, 2013. Other sites about Kofi and Adorkaville can be found at http://therealstorylauraadorkorkofey.blogspot.com/ and http://www.lauraakofi.org/Jail_and_Court_Case_of_ Princess_Laura_Adorkor_ Koffey.pdf. Garvey's response to Kofi and pertinent *Negro World* references can be found in vol. 10 of *The Marcus Garvey and Universal Negro Improvement Association Papers*, edited by Robert A. Hill, published in 2006. The creed for the Tabernacle African

Universal Church can be found at http://www.taba universalchurch.org/. I also wrote about Kofi and her grave in the Old City Cemetery in my 2012 book *This Kind of City: Ghost Stories and Psychological Landscapes.*

I found Schafer's note, "Garveyite church has paper," on two lose notecards, mostly lists of churches, black businesses, and black fraternal organizations. He offered his explanation to me in private correspondence.

40.

The August 8, 1919 letter from Rev. C.W. White is housed in UNF's Eartha White Collection, A, 0004. The September 12, 1929 letter from W.L. Jones is housed in UNF's Eartha White Collection, A, 0006. The September 27, 1929 letter from Ada Hayward is housed in UNF's Eartha White Collection, A, 0007. The December 7, 1929 letter referring to ads in *The Chicago Defender* is housed at A, 0008. The November 26, 1935 letter from Lusier Nicklack, referring to Mr. Ertha White, is housed at A, 0015.

41.

The August 9, 1929 letter from Emily Norton Stuart is housed in UNF's Eartha White Collection, G5, 1764.

42.

The December 18, 1929 letter from Mirriah McTain is housed in UNF's Eartha White Collection, L5, 1781.

43. & 44.

The July and August 1930 letters from Pearl Thompson are housed in UNF's Eartha White Collection, A, 0011 and 0012. The Humane Society letter of May 5, 1930 is from Mary C. Yarrow, and is housed at G5, 1748. Photographic references are from *A Pictorial Review of Activities Conducted under Auspices of the Clara White Mission... Jacksonville, Florida* from the early 1930s, housed in UNF's Eartha White Collection, R, 0232. The Clarice M. Blue letter is in the possession of the Clara White Mission, as is Eartha's program for the Marian Anderson concert, Franz Rupp at piano, at the Duval County Armory, January 23, 1952. The Children's Home Society letter to Ida Dixon of November 23, 1932 is in the possession of the Clara White Mission.

45.

Letters from Leroy Daniel Singleton are housed in UNF's Eartha White Collection at G5, 1816 through 1819.

46. & 47.

Letters from Ora Williams are housed in UNF's Eartha White Collection at G5, 1789 and 1790.

48.

In early February, 2014, Dan Schafer loaned me numerous materials, including meeting minutes from the "Child Care Division" of the Jacksonville Council of Social Agencies, dated July 20, 1944, under condition that I would donate the materials to UNF's Eartha White Collection when I had finished with them.

Georgia Tann's full story is told in Barbara Bisantz-Raymond's 2008 book, *The Baby Thief: The Untold Story of Georgia Tann, The Baby Seller Who Corrupted Adoption*.

The directions for dictation, deemed middle to late 1940s by archivist Pat Bell and others, are in the possession of the Clara White Mission.

49.

See Schafer's manuscript and Godwin's thesis, aforementioned. See Basil Matthews's 1948 book *Booker T. Washington: Educator and Interracial Interpreter*. See E. Lynne Wright's 2001 book *More than Petticoats: Remarkable Florida Women* and Carolyn Williams's "Eartha Mary Magdalene White, 1876-1974: The Gentle Community Activist," published in *The Varieties of Women's Experiences: Portraits of Southern Women in the Post-Civil War Century*, edited by Larry Eugene Rivers and Canter

Brown, Jr., and published in 2009. See vol. 41 of *The Southern Workman*, published in 1913 by the Hampton Institute. A news release for Eartha's minstrel show, "It Pays to Go

Straight," to be performed at the Knights of Pythias Auditorium for the benefit of the Boys' Improvement Club can be found in UNF's Eartha White Collection at S, 0251. For references to and images of Margaret Murray Washington with Eartha White in Jacksonville, see UNF's Eartha White Collection, Q4, 1164 through 1168. The two-paragraph admonition "Screen the Toys You Get for Little Ones," warning parents about the dangers of children playing with toy guns, is in the possession of the Clara White Mission.

50.

See Schafer's manuscript and Godwin's thesis, aforementioned. All case histories with reference to Eartha White can be found in UNF's Eartha White Collection, K4, 1102 through 1115 and K4, 2006. See Scott Reynolds Nelson's 2008 book *Steel Drivin' Man: John Henry, The Untold Story of an American Legend.* See *The Jacksonville Journal*'s "Mission Sponsors Program for Farm Inmates on 4th, Miss Eartha M. M. White Gives Prisoners Big Day," UNF's Eartha White Collection, no date, no byline, C1, 1045; *The Jacksonville Journal*'s "Duval Prison Farm Inmates Enjoy Fourth; Clara White Mission gives Vaudeville Program for Prisoners," published on July 7, 1933, no byline; *The Jacksonville Journal*'s "Protest Location of Girls School at Raiford," published September 21, 1945, no byline; *The Jacksonville Journal*'s "Prison Farm Abolition Protested," published June 9, 1954, no byline. Willie Elron's letter of July 21, 1930 is housed in UNF's Eartha White Collection, B5, 1652. Henry Devan Johnson's letter of January 16, 1945 is in the possession of the Clara White Mission.

51. & 52.

See Schafer's manuscript and Godwin's thesis, aforementioned. See also Eartha's 1933 booklet *Some Sayings of My Mother*, housed in UNF's Eartha White Collection, I5, 1177, A through F. See the "75th Diamond Birthday Observance of the Useful Life of Eartha Mary Magdalene White," which can be found in UNF's Eartha White Collection, at W4, 2787.

The alcohol and prostitution references can be traced to Eartha's family Bible in UNF's Eartha White Collection and to "A Statement Made by the Civic Round Table of Jacksonville" on prostitution, dated February 6, 1941, in the possession of the Clara White Mission.

See Robert Broward's 1984 book *The Architecture of Henry John Klutho: The Prairie School in Jacksonville*, *The Florida Times-Union*'s "Architect of Old Main Library Wants it Preserved," byline David Bauerlein, published December 21, 2004, the 1989 Jacksonville Historic Landmarks Commission's massive tome called *Jacksonville's Architectural Heritage*, revised in 1996, and T. Frederick Davis's 1925 *The History of Jacksonville and Vicinity, 1513-1924*. Joel McEachin, the City's senior historic planner and one of the creators of *Jacksonville's Architectural Heritage*, helped me make sense of these years and addresses.

The slave auction notice can be seen at http://www.florida memory.com/items/show/212335.

54. through 57.

See Mary Mungen Jameson's invaluable 2010 book, *Remembering Neighborhoods of Jacksonville, Florida: Oakland, Campbell's Addition, East Jacksonville-Fairfield—The African American Influence*. See the booklet Eartha published in 1933 called *Some Sayings of My Mother*, housed in UNF's Eartha White Collection, I5, 1177, A through F. The photographic image of Clara White's funeral cortege can be found in UNF's Eartha White Collection.

58. through 62.

The image of Eartha White with "unidentified man" is housed in UNF's Eartha White Collection, H5, 2673. For musical and Vaudeville references, including those of the Rabbit Foot Company, I'm indebted to Peter Dunbaugh Smith's masterful 2006 Florida State University dissertation *Ashley Street Blues: Racial Uplift and the Commodification of Vernacular Performance in LaVilla, Florida, 1896-1916*.

63.

R.A. Crump's letters of February 7 and May 3, 1922 are housed in UNF's Eartha White Collection, G5, 1774 and 1775.

64. & 65.

The Sammis letters are housed in UNF's Eartha White Collection at E4, 1064 through 1073. Other E4 Sammis documents include property tax receipts, a bill for road pavement, and photographs.

66.

Blind Blake information is based on Drew Kent's liner notes from a JSP Records' 2003 release of a boxed set of *Blind Blake: All the Published Sides*, and private correspondence with former *Florida Times-Union* columnist and author of a forthcoming book about Blind Blake, Sharon Weightman Hoffman.

67.

See Peter Dunbaugh Smith's 2006 Florida State University dissertation *Ashley Street Blues: Racial Uplift and the Commodification of Vernacular Performance in LaVilla, Florida, 1896-1916*. Also, see Lillian Gilkes' wonderful 1960 biography *Cora Crane, A Biography of Mrs. Stephen Crane*.

68.

For LaVilla and its number of square blocks seen as a public nuisance, see Mayor Ed Austin's 35-page booklet *Jacksonville—River City Renaissance—A Vision for the Rebirth of our City*, published in 1993.

69. through 71.

See Peter Dunbaugh Smith's 2006 Florida State University dissertation *Ashley Street Blues: Racial Uplift and the Commodification of Vernacular Performance in LaVilla, Florida,*

1896-1916. On Squire English, see pertinent city directories. On Blyden and Squire English, see Hollis R. Lynch's 1970 book *Edward Wilmot Blyden: Pan-Negro Patriot, 1832-1912.* The photographic images of Squire English and the Vaudeville comedian can be found in UNF's Eartha White Collection. A letter from Jacksonville Mayor John T. Alsop regarding Eartha White and the Silas Green Show, dated January 25, 1929 is housed at UNF's Eartha White Collection at I4, 0423.

Also important in this consideration is the masterful 2000 Spike Lee film *Bamboozled*, about a contemporary televised syndication of minstrelsy, full of blackface Jim Crow racial jokes about black people stealing chickens and watermelon, that turns out to be disturbingly popular. The film can be fittingly paired with Mel Brooks's equally troubling *The Producers*, in which a tax shelter scheme to make a money-losing Broadway musical in praise of Hitler accidentally produces a hit that unearths something unforgivably repulsive hiding beneath American popular culture.

72.

See Schafer's manuscript and Godwin's thesis, aforementioned. Charles Loeb's comments can be found in the June 1933 edition of *The Friend*, housed in UNF's digital

commons at http://digitalcommons.unf.edu/cgi/
viewcontent.cgi?article =1009&context=eartha_materials.
Camilla Thompson interview, conducted February 5, 2014.

73. through 77.

The image of Abraham Lincoln Lewis's Sugar Hill home can
be found in *The Crisis*, "Jacksonville Pictorial Number,"
January 1942, housed in UNF's Eartha White Collection at D1,
0330.

See Schafer's manuscript and Godwin's thesis,
aforementioned. See also Robert Cassanello's 1995 Florida
Atlantic University dissertation *African-American Protest in
Jacksonville, Florida, 1895-1920*, Congressman Charles E.
Bennett's 1989 book *Twelve on the River St. Johns*, and Paul
Ortiz's 2005 book *Emancipation Betrayed: The Hidden History
of Black Organizing and White Violence in Florida from
Reconstruction to the Bloody Election of 1920*. The NAACP
telegram can be found in the Library of Congress—NAACP
Collection, Group 1, Administration File, Subject File,
Discrimination, Voting—Jax, FL 1920. See also Michael J.
Klarman's "The White Primary Rulings: A Case Study in the
Consequences of Supreme Court Decisionmaking," published
in *The Florida State University Law Review* in Fall 2001.

The 1922 image of the Ku Klux Klan comes from *New Georgia
Encyclopedia*'s listing, "Ku Klux Klan in the Twentieth
Century," entry by Shawn Lay, July 7, 2005. The 1935 image
of the Fort Lauderdale, Florida hanging of Rubin Stacy,
courtesy Long Island University, can be found at

http://www.legendsof america.com/photos-
americanhistory/Rubin-Stacy-7-19-1935-Miami-FL-2.jpg.
Stacy was a homeless sharecropper who came to the door of
a white woman named Marion Jones to ask for food. A white
South Florida mob hounded and hung Stacy, without trial, for
having frightened a white woman by begging food.

On poll tax positions, see Paul Ortiz's 2005 book
*Emancipation Betrayed: The Hidden History of Black
Organizing and White Violence in Florida from Reconstruction
to the Bloody Election of 1920.*

July 1922 letters from Mary Talbert about the formation of
the Executive Committee of the Anti-Lynching Crusaders are
housed in UNF's Eartha White Collection at Y2, 0648 and
0649.

Billie Holliday first sang and recorded "Strange Fruit" in
1939. In 1999, *Time* magazine called it the "song of the
century."

79. & 80.

See National Public Radio's "The Sound of 1930s Florida Folk
Life—Blues Songs, Rural Life Focus of Library of Congress
Web Archive," reported by Barrett Golding, on February 28,
2002, http://www.npr.org/programs/atc/
features/2002/feb/ wpa_florida/020228.wpa_florida.html
and http://hearingvoices.com/transcript.php?fID=23.

81.

For the Works Progress Administration's cooperation with the Clara White Mission, see Schafer's manuscript and Godwin's thesis, aforementioned, *A Pictorial Review of Activities Conducted under Auspices of the Clara White Mission... Jacksonville, Florida* from the early 1930s, housed in UNF's Eartha White Collection, R, 0232, and the June 1933 edition of *The Friend*, housed in UNF's digital commons at http://digitalcommons.unf.edu/cgi/viewcontent.cgi?article=1009&context=eartha_materials. The 1936 letter is in the possession of the Clara White Mission.

82.

The Jacksonville Journal's "Hopping John is Latest Love of Jax Citizenry," no byline, was published on November 4, 1932.

83.

See June 1933 edition of *The Friend*, housed in UNF's digital commons at http://digitalcommons.unf.edu/cgi/viewcontent. cgi?article=1009&context=eartha_materials.

84.

See the Works Progress Administration, *Slave Narratives: a Folk History of Slavery in the United States From Interviews with Former Slaves, Florida Narratives.*

85.

See *A Folk History of Slavery in the United States from Interviews with Former Slaves, TYPEWRITTEN RECORDS PREPARED BY THE FEDERAL WRITERS' PROJECT 1936-1938* at http://memory.loc.gov/mss/mesn/030/030.1.txt. Also, "Negro Folk Customs and Folk Lore," Works Progress Administration, Container A591 in "Zora Neale Hurston: Recordings, Manuscripts, Photographs, and Ephemera," housed in the Archive of Folk Culture, Library of Congress. "Interesting Characters" is excerpted from "Negro Folk Customs and Folk Lore," sections on Wilhelmina Kiser and Mollie Peartree, UNF's Eartha White Collection, O3, 0776 and 0777.

86.

Milk Fund documents can be found in UNF's Eartha White Collection, D2, 0624 through 0627b. For historical information on tuberculosis, see Michael Bell's masterful 2011 book *Food for the Dead: On the Trail of New England's Vampires*. See also Marsha Dean Phelts's wonderful 2010 book *An American Beach for African Americans*, and *A Pictorial Review of Activities Conducted under Auspices of the Clara White Mission... Jacksonville, Florida* from the early 1930s, housed in UNF's Eartha White Collection, R, 0232.

Letters from James Jordan to Eartha White, dated from January 1895 to March 1896, are housed in UNF's Eartha White Collection, J2, 0508 through 0512, and the letter informing Eartha of Jordan's death is housed at J2, 0513.

87.

The ghost story Eartha tells can be heard, in her own voice, at http://floridamemory.com/blog/2013/02/21/eartha-m-m-white-tells-a-true-life-ghost-story/.

90. through 94.

Theodore Redding's comments are annotated in Daniel Schafer's notes from interviews, April 28, 1976. See also James Weldon Johnson's 1912 *Autobiography of an Ex-Colored Man* and Nella Larsen's 1929 novel *Passing*. See *Yale Bulletin & Calendar*'s "Director Spike Lee Slams 'Same Old' Black Stereotypes in Today's Films," byline Susan Gonzalez, published on March 2, 2001. See also Johnson's 1933 autobiography *Along this Way.*

See William Wilbanks's 1998 book *Forgotten Heroes: Police Officers Killed in Early Florida, 1840-1925.* See Tera W. Hunter's 1998 book *To 'Joy My Freedom: Southern Black Women's Lives and Labors after the Civil War.* Promissory notes from Eartha White on behalf of Thomas Baxter can be found in UNF's Eartha White Collection at A5, 1361, 1397, and 1398. Tom Baxters and Backsters are listed in LaVilla and Jacksonville census records in 1880 and 1885. The February 1975 Vivian Chavez audio interview is housed in UNF's Eartha White Collection.

95. & 96.

See Abel Bartley's *Keeping the Faith: Race, Politics, and Social Development in Jacksonville, Florida, 1940-1970*, as mentioned in the body of the chapter. See the biography of John E. Mathews, Jr., son of the "White Primary" John Mathews, at http://www.unf.edu/library/specialcollections/manuscripts/john-mathews/ John_Mathews_Biography.aspx. On the "White Primary" bill, see *The St. Petersburg Times*'s "Tom Beasley May Decide White Primary Dispute," byline Stanmore Cawthon, published on November 28, 1946; the Associated Press's "Solons Cool on White Primary," no byline, wired on March 8, 1947. See also Michael J. Klarman's "The White Primary Rulings: A Case Study in the Consequences of Supreme Court Decisionmaking," published in *The Florida State University Law Review* in Fall 2001.

Eartha's letter to Governor Millard Caldwell, Western Union telegram undated, is in the possession of the Clara White Mission. Likewise, the Western Union telegram to the Hon. Dilworth Clarke.

On the Moores' murder, see http://www.nbbd.com/godo/moore/. Fittingly, in conjunction with the myth of Eartha's naming, Langston Hughes wrote a poem called "The Ballad of Harry Moore," which says, "From the earth his voice cries, / No bomb can kill the dream I hold."

I emailed Abel Bartley and asked him if he had any further information about Eartha White's opposition to Wilson Armstrong's candidacy, or if he had recordings or transcripts of his interview with Eric Simpson that he might share. He responded that he had no more information and that his recordings were unavailable.

97.

See Herman "Skip" Mason Jr.'s 1997 book *African-American Life in Jacksonville*, Maura Wolfson-Foster's 2013 book *The Whetstonian*, and *The Florida Times-Union*'s "He Put Mark on Piece of City's History," about the Jefferson Street Pool, byline Mark Woods, published March 10, 2006.

98.

See Maura Wolfson-Foster's 2013 book *The Whetstonian*.

99.

Quotes from Walter Whetstone are from private conversation in the summer of 2013. Quotes from Meg Fisher are from private conversation in the fall of 2013.

The July 25, 1933 letter from J.C. Bradley is housed in UNF's Eartha White Collection at G5, 1770. Two tickets for the April 29, 1948 Mt. Ararat Male Quartet Program to benefit the Clara White Mission are housed in UNF's Eartha White Collection at S, 0247, A & B. Grayce Bateman's remembrance of Eartha at the White House dinner is quoted in *The Florida Times-Union*'s "Mission: Friend Still Feeding Founder's Flock," byline Cynthia Parks, published on October 27, 1976. Lilly White photographs in this chapter come from *A Pictorial Review of Activities Conducted under Auspices of the Clara White Mission... Jacksonville, Florida* from the early 1930s, housed in UNF's Eartha White Collection, R, 0232, and from a separate photograph housed in the collection at H5, 2078. Other photographs of Eartha with various kinds of animals can be found in the collection at H5, 1219; H5, 1223; H5, 1224; H5, 2075; etc.

100. & 101.

Audio interviews with Frances Ewell, 1974, are housed in UNF's Eartha White Collection. See also the important 1946 study, *Jacksonville Looks at Its Negro Community: A Survey of Conditions Affecting the Negro Population in Jacksonville in Duval County, Florida.* Early-1930s communiques entitled "Mission Plans Lectures on City Streets" and "Mission Moves to Reduce Homicides" are in the possession of the Clara White Mission.

102.

In early February 2014, Dan Schafer leant me his copy of the July 11, 1947 meeting minutes for the Council of Social Agencies' Meeting of the Organizing Committee for the Jacksonville Urban League, on condition that I donate the minutes to UNF's Eartha White Collection when I was finished with them.

See the program entitled, "Dedication Ceremonies of the Clara White Mission, Inc., New Building and Launching of Mortgage Liquidation Drive, Sunday, July 13th, through Friday, July 18th, 1947," housed in UNF's digital commons at http://digitalcommons.unf.edu/eartha_materials/30/. Photographs of the rededication are housed in R, 0184 through R, 0190. See also Robert Broward's

1984 book *The Architecture of Henry John Klutho: The Prairie School in Jacksonville*. Bethune's and Randolph's letters were published in the program for the "75th Diamond Birthday Observance of the Useful Life of Eartha Mary Magdalene White," housed in UNF's Eartha White Collection, at W4, 2787. Camilla Thompson interview, conducted February 5, 2014.

The photograph of Eartha White, A. Philip Randolph and others at a Chicago meeting to discuss the March on Washington can be found in UNF's Eartha White Collection at B4, 1983. The letter from A. Philip Randolph to Eartha about writing a "Negro

History of Florida" can be found at J, 0063, A through C. The photograph for an "appreciation tea" given for A. Philip Randolph in Jacksonville on March 3, 1963 is housed at B4, 2676, A and B. On A. Philip Randolph's and Bayard Rustin's involvement in the 1963 March on Washington for Jobs and Freedom, see *Ebony* magazine's "Masses Were March Heroes," byline Lerone Bennett Jr., published November 1963. See also Andrew Edmund Kersten's *A. Philip Randolph: A Life in the Vanguard*, published in 2007.

103.

Eartha's rededicatory speech was recorded on cassette in 1974 from a phonographic recording of the event in 1947. The speech was presumed lost, but UNF Special Collections Librarian Jim Alderman found the recording for me.

104. through 109.

Sidney Entman's 1976 audio interview is housed in UNF's Eartha White Collection.

110. through 114.

Tom Crompton's 1976 interview is housed in UNF's Eartha White Collection. For images of homes from Sugar Hill, see *The Crisis*, "Jacksonville Pictorial Number," January 1942, housed in UNF's Eartha White Collection at D1, 0330. See Maxine Jones's "'Without Compromise or Fear': Florida's African American Female Activists," published in *Florida Historical Quarterly 77* in Spring 1999. See Carolyn Williams's "Eartha Mary Magdalene White, 1876-1974: The Gentle Community Activist," published

in *The Varieties of Women's Experiences: Portraits of Southern Women in the Post-Civil War Century*, edited by Larry Eugene Rivers and Canter Brown, Jr., and published in 2009. Documentation of the 1963 E. J. L'Engle bequest of $5,000.00 payable in monthly installments of $200.00 is in the possession of the Clara White Mission. Likewise, the May 25, 1932 letter from Edward M. L'Engle to Eartha White. Camilla Thompson interview, conducted February 5, 2014. Private correspondence with Jim Alderman. See Schafer's aforementioned manuscript.

115. through 119.

References to Moncrief Springs come from Grayce Bateman's 1995 limited publication "Grayce Reminiscences [sic] 40

Years with Clara White Mission Inc. 1945-1985," which can be found in Box 185, Charles E. Bennett Papers, Special and Area Studies Collections, George A. Smathers Libraries, University of Florida. The earliest mentions of Moncrief Springs I've found come from the Southern poet Sidney Lanier's 1876 book *Florida: Its Scenery, Climate, and History*. *The Florida Times-Union*'s "Legend of Buried Treasure Clings to Moncrief Springs," was published on October 28, 1951. *The Jacksonville Journal*'s "Moncrief Springs, the Splendor Has Vanished," byline Christine Burger, was published on July 20, 1963. The photographs in these chapters come from the latter story. The City of Jacksonville Planning and Development Department's June 2004 "45th and Moncrief Neighborhood Action Plan," which enumerates many of the neighborhood's troubles and underdeveloped characteristics, can be found at http://www.coj.net/ departments/planning-and-development/docs/ community-planning-division/plans-and-studies/45th-and-moncrief-nap.aspx. Camilla Thompson interview, conducted February 5, 2014.

The Associated Press's "Legend Claims Treasure Buried in Jacksonville," no byline, was published in *The Lakeland Ledger* on May 15, 1985. Wesley B. Plott's 1980 book *Antique Bottles Found in Northeast Florida* was Xeroxed and stapled long before the days when independent publishing was acceptable. Wesley B. Plott was "indie" before "indie." For my own writing about Plott's book, his bottle collecting, and his florist and antique glass store The Purple Petunia in Jacksonville's Riverside neighborhood, please see "Riverside Avondale: Purple Petunia Filling Station and Antique Bottle Collection" at http://jax psychogeo .com/west/riverside-avondale-purple-petunia-filling-station-and-antique-bottle-collection/.

120. through 124.

See Grayce Bateman's 1995 limited publication "*Grayce Reminiscences* [sic] 40 Years with Clara White Mission Inc. 1945-1985," which can be found in Box 185, Charles E. Bennett Papers, Special and Area Studies Collections, George A. Smathers Libraries, University of Florida.

125.

Eartha's post cards from London, Paris, and Jerusalem, her letter from Belgium, and documentation of each place she visited in 1955 are in the possession of the Clara White Mission. Information on Eartha's 1955 visits to Egypt and Versailles are housed in UNF's Eartha White Collection at S4, 1947 and S4, 1948. *The Jacksonville Journal*'s "Committee Meets Angel of Mercy at Airport on her Return from Europe," no byline, appeared on September 10, 1955.

126. & 127.

Mary Singleton's 1974 audio interview is housed in UNF's Eartha White Collection. For J.J. Daniel's and Stockton, Whatley, Davin's role in Jacksonville-Duval County Consolidation, see Richard Martin's 1968 book *Consolidation: Jacksonville, Duval County, The Dynamics of Urban Political Reform*. See *The Florida Times-Union*'s "Picture This: Deerwood Deserted," byline Charlie Patton, published on February 21, 2003. See the Deerwood Country Club website at http://www.deerwood homeowners.com. *Forbes* magazine's latest listing of Gate Petroleum is at http://www.forbes.com/lists/2008/21/ privates08_Gate-

Petroleum_8S5S.html. *The St. Petersburg Times*'s Sunday-supplement *Floridian* magazine article, "Eartha White, Florida's Rich, Black 94-year-old Senior Citizen

of the Year," byline Fred Wright, appeared on August 1, 1971. See also Carmen Godwin's 2001 University of Florida master's thesis, "'To Serve God and Humanity': Jacksonville's Eartha Mary Magdalene White (1876-1974)."

129.

Anonymous interview took place in April of 2014.

130.

My private conversation with Ju'Coby Pittman and Meg Fisher took place in the fall of 2013.

131. & 132.

See Grayce Bateman's aforementioned "Grayce Reminiscences [sic] 40 Years with Clara White Mission Inc. 1945-1985."

The Florida Times-Union's "The Happiest Kids in Town (Toy Giveaway)," no byline, was published in December 1976 and is included in Grayce Bateman's aforementioned *Grayce Reminiscences* [sic] 40 Years with Clara White Mission Inc. 1945-1985."

133. through 148.

Information on the Richmond Hotel can be found in numerous publications, including the 1989 Jacksonville Historic Landmarks Commission's *Jacksonville's Architectural Heritage*, revised in 1996, and Peter Dunbaugh Smith's 2006 Florida State University dissertation *Ashley Street Blues: Racial Uplift and the Commodification of Vernacular Performance in LaVilla, Florida, 1896-1916*. My walkthrough of the Richmond Hotel and interview with Terry DeLoach took place in October of 2013.

See Rodney L. Hurst's 2008 *It Was Never About a Hot Dog and a Coke!: A Personal Account of the 1960 Sit-In Demonstrations in Jacksonville, Florida and Ax Handle Saturday*. The (in)famous photograph of Charlie Griffin was published in the September 12, 1960 issue of *Life* magazine. The Halloween 1969 race riot photograph, and the photograph of an elderly Eartha White standing in front of the Clara White Mission and Roosevelt Barber Shop, both originally published in *The Florida Times-Union*, come from the 1999 book *Jacksonville: Images through the 20th Century*, edited by Bill Foley and M. Jack Luedke.

Jet magazine's "What's Behind Jacksonville's Race Violence?—Shocking Police Action Spurs Negro Students to Strike Back," byline Simeon Booker, was published on April 9, 1964. Oprah Winfrey's televised remembrance of Johnnie Mae Chappel, dated June 1, 2008, can be found at http://www.oprah.com/ oprahshow/Remembering-Johnnie-Mae-Chappell. *The Florida Times-Union*'s "Justice to Review Civil Rights Figure's '64 Killing—Woman Slain as Race Riots Swept City," byline Paul Pinkham, appeared on December 4,

2002. *The Florida Times-Union*'s "A Broken Family Comes Together in Quest for Justice—39 Years Ago, Johnnie Mae Chappell Was Gunned Down, and Now...," bylines Paul Pinkham and Alliniece T. Andino, appeared on March 23, 2003. *Folio Weekly*'s "Florida Gov. Silent on Demand for Justice in Chappell Murder," byline Susan Cooper Eastman, appeared on March 10, 2005. *The Orlando Weekly*'s "Beers for a Racist: It's Not Hard to Find the Man behind One of Florida's Most Notorious Race Crimes," based on an original *Folio Weekly* story, byline Susan Cooper Eastman, was published on January 12, 2006. *The Florida Times-Union*'s half-column article, "Trial Opens in Negro's Death Here," no byline, was published near the end of 1964 and buried in the back of the news section.

See Mary Mungen Jameson's invaluable 2010 book, *Remembering Neighborhoods of Jacksonville, Florida: Oakland, Campbell's Addition, East Jacksonville-Fairfield—The African American Influence.*

Vivian Chavez's recollection comes from a 1974 audio interview held in UNF's Eartha White Collection.

See Richard Martin's 1968 book *Consolidation: Jacksonville, Duval County, The Dynamics of Urban Political Reform.*

149.

The Jacksonville Journal's "Grandma Johnson, 100, Going like 60," byline Helen Bates, was published on August 29, 1969. The funeral program for Arrelia Hilman Johnson, October 31,

1970, can be found in UNF's Eartha White Collection at F2, 0488.

150.

See the City of Jacksonville Planning and Development Department's Site File for LaVilla Harts Map Lot 6 Block 109 and *Jacksonville City Directory* for 1980. See also United States Court of Appeals, Fifth Circuit, 588 F.2d 1100 (5th Cir. 1979), United States of America, Plaintiff-Appellee, v. Eddie C. Allen, Rosa Lee White and Andrew Preston Perkins, Defendants-Appellants. No. 77-5786.

151. through 155.

The image of LaVilla's Masonic Temple can be founed in *The Crisis*, "Jacksonville Pictorial Number," January 1942, housed in UNF's Eartha White Collection at D1, 0330.

The Malcolm X *Playboy* interview, conducted by Alex Haley, was published in May 1963. *The Florida Times-Union's* "*National Geographic* Show to Profile Jacksonville Councilwoman as Demon Buster," byline David Bauerlein, appeared on September 27, 2012. See also Kimberly Daniels's 2005 *Delivered to Destiny:*

From Crack Addict to the Military's Fasted Female Sprinter to Pastoring a Diverse and Multicultural Church, Kim's Story of Hope is for Everyone. Far-right-wing and demon-obsessed *Charisma News's* "Why Celebrating Halloween is Dangerous," byline none other than Kimberly Daniels, has been published and republished on Halloween, most recently in 2013. The company that publishes *Charisma News*, Charisma Media, published Kimberly Daniels's *Prayers that Bring Change*, including prayers for gay men and lesbians, in 2009. For Daniels's expressions of gratitude for slavery as captured in youtube videos, see WTLV-TV *First Coast News*'s "Jacksonville City Council Candidate Kimberly Daniels Has Controversial Video Posted to Youtube," byline Lewis Turner, first televised April 22, 2011, at http://www.firstcoastnews.com/ news/ story.aspx?storyid=201599. The October 10, 1970 promissory note by Andrew Perkins is in the possession of the Clara White Mission.

156. & 157.

See the booklet *Clara White Mission: A Description and Statistics of the 1971 Activities of the Mission, and a Financial Statement for the Year Ended Dec. 31, 1971*, housed in UNF's Eartha White Collection at R, 0205.

158.

The Gil Scott-Heron lyrics come from his and Brian Jackson's 1975 album *First Minute of a New Day*.

159. through 164.

Grayce Bateman's 1974 audio interview is housed in UNF's Eartha White Collection. See Grayce Bateman's aforementioned "Grayce Reminiscences [sic] 40 Years with Clara White Mission Inc. 1945-1985." The newspaper clipping, "Miss Eartha White Injured in Mishap," no byline, no date, no publication title, in the possession of the Clara White Mission, names the "Rev. Robert H. Wilson" minister of Bethel Baptist. Wilson served as Bethel's minister from the early 1950s to the later 1960s.

165.

The February 1975 Vivian Chavez audio interview is housed in UNF's Eartha White Collection.

166. & 167.

The best sources are Grayce Bateman's 1974 audio interview, housed in UNF's Eartha White Collection, Grayce Bateman's aforementioned "Grayce Reminiscences [sic] 40 Years with Clara White Mission Inc. 1945-1985," and Charles E. Bennett's 1989 book *Twelve on the River St. Johns*. I found Eartha's typed funeral wishes on the third floor of the Clara White Mission. Eartha's rededicatory speech was recorded on cassette in 1974 from a phonographic recording of the event in 1947. The speech was presumed lost, but UNF Special Collections Librarian Jim Alderman found the recording for me.

169. through 171.

Each of the items mentioned can be referenced at http://www.unf.edu/library/specialcollections/ manuscripts/eartha-white/Eartha_White.aspx. Reference, again, Grayce Bateman's 1974 audio interview, housed in

UNF's Eartha White Collection, and Grayce Bateman's "*Grayce Reminiscences* [sic] 40 Years with Clara White Mission Inc. 1945-1985." *The Jacksonville Journal*'s "Grayce Bateman Will Retire after a Life of Service," byline Bettye Sessions, was published in March of 1985.

172. through 175.

I interviewed Richard McKissick several times, in his office in the Ed Ball Building downtown, on West Ashley Street in front of the Mission, and on foot throughout LaVilla, in the fall of 2013. Photographs of the Strand Theater are available from UNF's Eartha White Collection at H4, 108 a & b. See Michael Bell's masterful 2011 book *Food for the Dead: On the Trail of New England's Vampires*.

176. through 178.

My private conversation with Ju'Coby Pittman and Meg Fisher took place in the fall of 2013. Minimal information on LaGretta Everett can be found in Grayce Bateman's aforementioned "*Grayce Reminiscences* [sic] 40 Years with Clara White Mission Inc. 1945-1985" and in financial records in the possession of the Clara White Mission. See also *The Florida Times-Union*'s "Mission: Friend Still Feeding Founder's Flock," byline Cynthia Parks, published on October 27, 1976.

179.

See Mayor Ed Austin's booklet *Jacksonville—River City Renaissance—A Vision for the Rebirth of our City*, published in 1993. See also Renaissance Partners' and Langton Associates' *A Proposal for LaVilla Redevelopment* to the Jacksonville Downtown Development Authority, published in 1997. *The Florida Times-Union*'s "Bond Issue—Time to Be Bold, Again," staff editorial, appeared on February 7, 1993.

Images of the destruction of LaVilla, first published in *The Florida Times-Union*, come from the 1999 book *Jacksonville: Images through the 20th Century*, edited by Bill Foley and M. Jack Luedke.

180.

My private conversation with Ju'Coby Pittman and Meg Fisher took place in the fall of 2013. Meg Fisher provided me with the artist's rendering of the proposed redevelopment.

181. through the end.

For notes and images on LaVilla businesses, see *The Crisis*, "Jacksonville Pictorial Number," January 1942, housed in UNF's Eartha White Collection at D1, 0330.

I visited Eartha's bedroom on the second floor of the Clara White Mission three times in the fall of 2013. The photographic image comes from "A Self-Guided Tour of the Eartha M.M. White Historical Museum and Resource Center," compiled by Meg Fisher, vice president at the Clara White Mission, no date.

I found Wally Bearden's December 28, 2011 obituary at http://www.tributes. com/show/93017928. The semi-suicidal song "Leavin' on my Mind" was written by Southern Gospel Music Association Hall-of-Famer (yes, there is such a thing) Rusty Goodman, and the sheet music was produced by Canaanland Music in 1978.

Eartha's rededicatory speech was recorded on cassette in 1974 from a phonographic recording of the event in 1947. The speech was presumed lost, but UNF Special Collections Librarian Jim Alderman found the recording for me.

See aforementioned note about my conversation with Ju'Coby Pittman and Meg Fisher. My conversations with Peggy Ezell also took place in the fall of 2013.

See my previous note about interviewing Richard McKissick. See Herman "Skip" Mason Jr.'s 1997 book *African-American Life in Jacksonville*. I interviewed Anthony Walton at Hillman-Pratt & Walton Funeral Home at 525 West Beaver Street in the fall of 2013. The letter Mrs. P. Pratt Brown wrote Eartha in request of adoption, dated March 10, 1944, is in the possession of the Clara White Mission. I interviewed Camilla Thompson on February 5, 2014.

I first interviewed Hazel Tisdale in October 1998. See *The Florida Times-Union*'s "Teachers Will Get Lessons in History, Three Will Study Past of Pine Forest Area," byline Tim

Gilmore, published on October 14, 1998. See also *The Florida Times-Union*'s "Barber Used Skill to Help Others," byline Jessie-Lynne Kerr, published on May 18, 2007.

The leaflet, "A Record, He Who Runs May Lead," containing the appeal, "To My Fellow Citizens of Ward Six," no date, though Ross served from 1901 to 1907, is housed in UNF's Eartha White Collection at D4, 1055 and D4, 1987-1988. See Abel Bartley's *Keeping the Faith: Race, Politics, and Social Development in Jacksonville, Florida, 1940-1970*. The newsclipping headlined "Negro Ex-Councilman Opposed to Integration," no publication name, no byline, no date but by Ross's age apparently published in 1959 or 1960, can be found in UNF's Eartha White Collection at D4, 1056. See Hollis R. Lynch's 1970 book *Edward Wilmot Blyden: Pan-Negro Patriot, 1832-1912*.

James Baldwin's 1985 *The Evidence of Things Not Seen*, certainly not his best, was this brilliant writer's last book, published two years before his death in 1987.

Zora Neale Hurston's "sobbing school" quote comes from her 1928 essay "How It Feels to Be Colored Me," and her quote about Jacksonville comes from her 1942 autobiography *Dust Tracks on a Road*.

Arlene Hutton's *Letters to Sala* was first performed in 2010, first published in the fall of 2013.

My mother's manuscripts and stapled Xeroxed copies—no ISBNs—are, of course, in limited ownership, including my own.

The final image of Eartha White, undated, but clearly from the early 1970s, is in the possession of the Clara White Mission. Kevin Carrico was kind enough to let me borrow and scan it.

Made in the USA
Columbia, SC
27 October 2020